Exploring the First Vision

Edited by
Samuel Alonzo Dodge and Steven C. Harper

RSC

RELIGIOUS STUDIES CENTER
BRIGHAM YOUNG UNIVERSITY

Published by the Religious Studies Center, Brigham Young University, Provo, Utah.
http://rsc.byu.edu

© 2012 by Brigham Young University.
All rights reserved.

Printed in the United States by Sheridan Books, Inc.

Any uses of this material beyond those allowed by the exemptions in US copyright law, such as section 107, "Fair Use," and section 108, "Library Copying," require the written permission of the publisher, Religious Studies Center, 167 HGB, Brigham Young University, Provo, Utah 84602. The views expressed herein are the responsibility of the authors and do not necessarily represent the position of Brigham Young University or the Religious Studies Center.

Cover design by Art Morrill and interior layout by Katie Skovran.

Cover images: *The Desires of My Heart* © Intellectual Reserve, Inc., *If Any of You Lack Wisdom* by Walter Rane, © Intellectual Reserve, Inc., *The First Vision* by Del Parson © 1988 Intellectual Reserve, Inc.

ISBN 978-0-8425-2818-4
US Retail: $25.99

Library of Congress Cataloging-in-Publication Data

Exploring the First Vision / edited by Samuel Alonzo Dodge and Steven C. Harper.

　　　pages cm

Includes bibliographical references and index.

ISBN 978-0-8425-2818-4 (hard cover : alk. paper) 1. Smith, Joseph, 1805–1844—First Vision. 2. Church of Jesus Christ of Latter-day Saints—History—19th century. 3. Mormon Church—History—19th century. 4. Church of Jesus Christ of Latter-day Saints—Doctrines. 5. Mormon Church—Doctrines. 6. New York (State)—Church history—19th century. I. Dodge, Samuel Alonzo, 1984– editor. II. Harper, Steven Craig, 1970– editor.

BX8695.S6E97 2012

289.3'2—dc23

Contents

Acknowledgments
Samuel Alonzo Dodge   vii

Preface: Standing on the Shoulders of Giants
Steven C. Harper   ix

Joseph Smith's First Vision: Insights and Interpretations in Mormon Historiography
Samuel Alonzo Dodge   xi

The Earliest Documented Accounts of Joseph Smith's First Vision
Dean C. Jessee   1

The Appearance of the Father and the Son to Joseph Smith in 1820
James B. Allen and John W. Welch   41

Joseph Smith's Accuracy on the First Vision Setting:
The Pivotal 1818 Palmyra Camp Meeting
Richard Lloyd Anderson 91

Awakenings in the Burned-Over District: New Light
on the Historical Setting of the First Vision
Milton V. Backman Jr. 171

Rev. George Lane—Good "Gifts," Much
"Grace," and Marked "Usefulness"
Larry C. Porter 199

Emergence of a Fundamental: The Expanding
Role of Joseph Smith's First Vision in Mormon
Religious Thought
James B. Allen 227

The First Vision Story Revived
Richard Lyman Bushman 261

The Significance of Joseph Smith's First Vision in
Mormon Thought
James B. Allen 283

Evaluating Three Arguments against Joseph
Smith's First Vision
Steven C. Harper 307

Contributors 325

Acknowledgments

Samuel Alonzo Dodge

Many people known and unknown to me have enabled me to compile this anthology. Susan and Harvey Black provided the mentoring grant that made it possible. Ann and John Lewis generously added to the fund. The Office of Research and Creative Activities, the backbone of a vibrant culture of undergraduate research and creativity at Brigham Young University, provided still more funding and support.

I also thank Ann Madsen and Emily Reynolds, widow and daughter of Truman G. Madsen, respectively, for giving me access to Professor Madsen's papers. Emily Reynolds was especially helpful. While still engrossed with the enormous task of sorting and archiving her father's papers, she spent several hours sitting at my side helping me as I searched through her father's documents.

The staff at the Church History Library in Salt Lake City facilitated my research. Religious Education at BYU, especially the Religious Studies Center, provided support in various ways and means. Professor Steven C. Harper patiently guided me with invaluable insight as I pursued this project. His role as my academic mentor and friend will influence my historical studies for years to come. Thanks also to the Religious Studies Center staff, including Devan Jensen, Brent Nordgren, Jonathon Owen, Art Morrill, Jeff Wade, Nyssa Silvester, Heidi Sutherland, Dana Kendall, and Katie Skovran, for their editing and design work.

Finally and most importantly, I acknowledge the scholars whose pieces comprise this anthology: historians James B. Allen, Richard L. Anderson, Milton V. Backman Jr., Richard L. Bushman, Steven C. Harper, Dean C. Jessee, Larry C. Porter, and John W. Welch. They generously invited me into their lives, allowing me to interview them. Excerpts of these interviews are printed in the shaded sidebars, and some video excerpts are posted on YouTube. These scholars have given permission to republish in this book some of their finest work. Their seminal articles on Joseph Smith's First Vision deserve to be preserved and made widely known to "rising generations" (D&C 69:8).

Preface: Standing on the Shoulders of Giants

Steven C. Harper

Today's scholars of Joseph Smith's First Vision stand on the shoulders of giants. The saying is at least as old as Bernard of Chartres, who reportedly said that medieval professors like himself "see more and farther than our predecessors, not because we have keener vision or greater height, but because we are lifted up and borne aloft on their gigantic stature."[1] Isaac Newton later used the same metaphor to acknowledge, "If I have seen further it is by standing on ye sholders of Giants."[2] This volume reproduces some of the seminal articles that analyze Joseph Smith's First Vision written by the giants who have studied it for half a century. It is a monument to their contributions, composed of their work.

The past of First Vision scholarship is indispensable to the present. Those of us who study the First Vision today depend very much on the works of the scholars that are reprinted in this volume. Moreover, much of the source material on which their articles are based and on which we depend, they discovered and published. We are beginning to explore further because we can see from their shoulders. This volume contains much of their mentoring.

It also serves as a mechanism for ongoing mentoring. It began with a realization that the work of the scholars republished hereafter, though well known to the students of these venerable mentors, is little known to the "rising generations" (D&C 69:8). This volume preserves and recommunicates that work, if only to the promising young historian Samuel Alonzo Dodge, who interviewed eminent First Vision scholars, gathered their seminal articles, and arranged them for publication here with a contextual introduction he composed. Brigham Young University invests its resources in mentoring the rising generations, including by funding and publishing this project. Those funds were generously supplemented by one of my mentors, Susan Easton Black, and her late husband, Harvey Black. Sam and I gratefully dedicate this volume to them. With a profound sense of indebtedness to the scholars whose work is republished on the following pages, we offer this volume as a monument to the work of my mentors and as a mechanism for continuing to communicate their important work to the rising generations.

Notes

1. John of Salisbury, *The Metalogicon* (Berkeley: University of California Press, 1955), 167.

2. H. W. Turnbull, ed., *The Correspondence of Isaac Newton, 1661–1675* (Cambridge: Cambridge University Press, 1959), 1:416.

Joseph Smith's First Vision: Insights and Interpretations in Mormon Historiography

Samuel Alonzo Dodge

The analysis and teaching of history does not occur in a vacuum. Modern perceptions of history are shaped by new scholarly work, and that work grows out of the debate which has already taken place. In short, the scholarship that went before set the stage for the debates of the present. This is particularly evident as one studies the historiography of Joseph Smith's First Vision. For years, the historical discussion of Mormonism's early periods tended to one of two camps: critics who sought to defame Joseph Smith and discredit the religious movement he launched, or Mormon supporters whose efforts to exonerate the Prophet often resulted in excessive glossing of the blemishes found in the Church's origins.[1] The result was scholastic stagnation, the sympathizers condemning the critics as purely prejudicial and the critics dismissing the others as naive. However, towards the middle of the twentieth century, the historical discipline underwent an important development.

Historians came to understand that due to the inherent biases of all humans, it was futile for historians to try and recreate past events exactly how they transpired.[2] Therefore, rather than disregard the work done by opposing scholarship, historians began using the works from differing scholars as catalysts to propel their own work forward and strive for a more accurate depiction of the past. This disciplinary shift impacted Mormon historical studies of the First Vision.[3]

Joseph's claims of seeing God and Christ in western New York first received detailed scrutiny in Fawn Brodie's well-known biography published in 1945. In her book *No Man Knows My History*, Brodie is critical of what she calls Joseph's "pretended revelation."[4] According to Brodie, Joseph was a "mythmaker of prodigious talent" with a "boundless ambition" to rival that of "modern dictators."[5] Brodie carefully employs a disarming prose in order to present Joseph as a charlatan and dismiss his First Vision as merely a contrived effort to bolster his own claims to divine authority in the eyes of his followers.[6] Though some Mormon scholars tried to refute Brodie's work, most notably Hugh Nibley in his tract *No Ma'am, That's Not History*, for years Mrs. Brodie's book served as the "standard reference" for early Mormon studies.[7] Unable to produce any substantial work to counter Brodie, the Mormon community more or less dismissed *No Man Knows My History* as typical anti-Mormon literature.

Twenty-two years after Brodie first published her book, a new challenge to Joseph Smith's First Vision came in a Christian tract published by Wesley Walters in 1967. In his tract *New Light on Mormon Origins from the Palmyra Revival*, Walters challenged Joseph's story in a particularly professional way, as he left the tired "attacks on Joseph's character and the credibility or veracity of his followers" and instead used the historical record itself as a tool to discredit Joseph's claims as a prophet.[8] Walters's argument was simple: thorough research of western New York's historical record had uncovered "a number of difficulties" which seriously undermined the reliability of Joseph's claims.[9]

Walters argued that Joseph's description of an "unusual excitement on the subject of religion" in the spring of 1820 was anachronistic. According to Walters's research, Joseph's claims were suspect because the historical records "show that in 1820 there was no revival in any of the churches in Palmyra and its vicinity."[10] If there were no religious revivals to prompt Joseph to pray, there would have been no vision, and the whole foundation of Mormonism would need to be reconsidered.[11] Walters reasoned that Joseph's references to religious revivals had their origins in the 1823–24 revivals that are documented in Palmyra's records. Newspapers, family journals, and church records all chronicle religious awakening in 1823–24 but are silent for the years leading up to Joseph's vision. According to Walters, the discrepancy in chronology betrayed a concocted story that Joseph "altered and expanded . . . in several steps as occasion required." It was not merely an opinion that Joseph's First Vision was a fabrication. Walters believed that the historical record proved it.[12]

Walters's use of hard historical documentation clearly set it apart from Brodie's earlier indictment of the Prophet. Whereas Brodie recycled familiar criticisms of Joseph's character, albeit in a very polished fashion, Walters's research had uncovered a wealth of new primary material relating to the environment of Mormonism's early New York period and essentially opened up a subject that "Mormon historians had not really talked about before."[13] In the words of Richard Bushman, Walters had "made [Mormon historians] realize that [they] can't assume anything. . . . Walters was an ingenious researcher . . . [and because] a historian cannot disregard evidence . . . in some way or another we had to account for what he had discovered."[14] Walters's argument was something that Mormon scholars had not confronted much before, a criticism of their religion which took the form of historical method. The very substantial nature of Walters's challenge made it impossible for Mormon historians to dismiss it as mere propaganda or anti-Mormon defamation.

Walters's article proved a catalyst which prompted several Mormon scholars to challenge his claims. Shortly after Walters published his article, Truman G. Madsen, then director of the Institute of Mormon Studies at Brigham Young University, wrote to the First Presidency of the Church explaining the need to "collect basic documentary material on the New York period" in order to "dissolve" the Walters case. With the support of the First Presidency, Madsen recruited various historians "selected for their scholarly competence" and began a massive research effort to respond to the stir Walters created.[15] To lead the effort, Madsen decided to send BYU historians Milton Backman, Larry Porter, and Richard Anderson "to research original letters, church records, diaries, and memorabilia in all the country surrounding Palmyra."[16]

In addition to these historians, an entire body of researchers comprising "some forty scholars" scattered throughout the nation was also involved in the enterprise.[17] Throughout 1967–68, this body of researchers, lawyers, and administrators hunted libraries, archives, court records, journals, and church documents in order to "uncover the context, background, and original documents" pertaining to Mormonism's founding.[18] Each of the scholars was in frequent communication with Madsen, updating him on new documents uncovered and potential caches to be explored.[19] Madsen would in turn recommend which avenues should be searched and who would be the best for the job. The results were impressive.[20] As the project grew, Madsen reached out to a number of other professionals including James Allen, Leonard Arrington, Davis Bitton, Richard Bushman,

Bruce C. Hafen, Daniel H. Ludlow, and T. Edgar Lyon to aid in the project.[21] In a period of just a few months the project had grown into what Madsen considered a "revolutionary" production of scholarship which merited the printing of a special issue of *BYU Studies* in the spring of 1969.

In the articles published in that issue, Mormon scholars contended that Walters's use of church records to indicate a lack of religious activity in 1819–20 was erroneous. According to Walters, membership records indicate that "the Presbyterian church in Palmyra certainly experienced no awakening that year" and neither did the Baptists. In the case of the Methodists, "the Mormon Prophet could hardly have picked a poorer year" to place the revivals, for all their congregations throughout Palmyra's circuit show an actual loss of members for 1819–20.[22] However, in his article "Awakenings in the Burned-Over District," Milton Backman showed that despite Walters's assertions, western New York "was in an almost constant state of revivalism" in the early nineteenth century.[23]

Backman discovered evidence that these revivals continued in their regularity up through the years immediately preceding the First Vision. "On June 19, 1818, for example, a [Methodist] camp meeting was held near Palmyra which, according to one report, resulted in twenty baptisms and forty conversions to the Methodist society."[24] Furthermore, Backman demonstrated that in the years 1819–20, the nearby towns of Geneva and Oaks Corners saw conversions numbering eighty and thirty, respectively. In the case of Oaks Corners, this was an increase from the annual conversion rate of five that had been the norm from 1806 to 1819.[25] In essence, Backman was saying that the Palmyra region was not as religiously dead in 1819–20 as Walters thought. Palmyra fit right in with the "tremendous age of revivalism" that characterized much of the nation during the early nineteenth century.[26]

Walters had anticipated this response while writing his original essay and asserted that the towns in which there was religious excitement in 1819–20 were too far away for the adult Joseph to designate as "the place where we lived" while writing his account.[27] However, when comparing Walters's analysis with that of Backman, Richard Bushman pointed out that both historians used Bloomfield, Junius, Palmyra, Geneva, Oaks Corners, and a number of other towns when dating the revivals, Walters in 1824 and Backman in 1819–20. In total, there were "eight [towns] nearby in 1824 and seven in 1819–20" that experienced revivals "and four more distant in 1824 and twelve in 1819–20."[28] Bushman used Backman's evidence to argue that for Walters, the very towns which he considered close enough for Joseph's revivals in 1824 were too far away when revivals happened there in 1819–20.

Demonstrating that revivals occurred when and where Joseph claimed was only one aspect of the Mormon scholars' response to Walters and Brodie. There was also the matter of the publicity of Joseph's vision. Fawn Brodie was unable to find any references to Joseph's vision in local newspapers. According to Brodie, newspapers "which in later years gave him plenty of publicity" would almost certainly have mentioned Joseph's vision. Because the event "passed totally unnoticed in Joseph's hometown," she reasoned that it was an elaboration of a "half remembered dream" catalyzed by revival excitement later on.[29] However, in December of 1967, Richard Anderson wrote to Truman Madsen claiming that although individual religious experiences may not have caught the attention of local papers, he had found several allusions to the First Vision in regional papers.[30] Though most of these allusions were from people who were "more interested in proving [Joseph's] religious views ridiculous than factually describing" events, Anderson argued that they did indicate that several people knew of Joseph's vision early on.[31] These finds encouraged Anderson to look for more "reminiscences of individuals" to corroborate Joseph's claims. In the same letter, Anderson expressed his desire to search for "some kind of transcript . . . [or] allusion to the First Vision" in the New York region.[32]

The result was Anderson's article "Circumstantial Confirmation of the First Vision Through Reminiscences," published in the special spring 1969 issue of *BYU Studies*. In his article, Anderson strove to pick up "traces of the First Vision" either through "what Joseph had told, or what [people] had observed" about him.[33] Two of these sources, Orsamus Turner and Pomeroy Tucker, both tried to slander Joseph by accusing him of "announcing to the community that Methodism wasn't true" after his initial conversion at a camp meeting. Though these two sources sought to expose Smith as a fraud, Anderson argues that Turner and Tucker ironically helped confirm the prominence of Methodist revivalism in the area prior to 1820.[34] Furthermore, Anderson believes that these circumstantial confirmations further discredit Brodie's thesis that Joseph "was a seeker of buried treasure, [and] not the sincere religious investigator that he [described] himself to be."[35] Anderson asserted that Turner and Tucker moved in the same social circles as Joseph and that their recollections of the Prophet being involved in religious seeking should be given more credit than the "community gossip" of his money digging.[36] According to Anderson, Tucker's statement that Joseph could relate a "marvelous absurdity with the utmost apparent gravity" could be "the community response to Joseph's limited narration of his vision."[37] Anderson's article indicates that perhaps Joseph told his story on a number of occasions.

This assertion was further corroborated when Madsen's researchers brought several little-known or unknown contemporary accounts of Joseph's vision to light. As the multiple accounts were closely examined, some naturally raised the question of Joseph's consistency.[38] Both Brodie and Walters alleged previously that the inconsistencies found in the various accounts indicated a "remarkable evolution in detail" that stemmed from Joseph's need to distance himself from rumors of his "money digging" and later to mollify the dissent he faced within the Church.[39] Understanding the import of this accusation, Truman Madsen wrote to Dean Jessee asking for his particular help in researching the different accounts. Because of Jessee's position in the Church historian's office, Madsen felt that Jessee would have more familiarity with and easier access to the documents than other scholars.[40] Jessee published his landmark article "The Early Accounts of Joseph Smith's First Vision" in the spring 1969 issue of *BYU Studies*.

In his article, Jessee asserts that Joseph's "youth . . . , frontier conditions . . . , [and] a lack of academic training" all contributed to the relatively late compilation of the First Vision story.[41] He and other scholars reconciled the variations in Joseph's accounts. James Allen, for example, has observed that the first record of Joseph's First Vision, written in 1832, is riddled with poor grammar and punctuation. Allen asserts that when it is compared with the much more polished 1838 account, it becomes clear that the six intervening years were a time of impressive intellectual and experiential growth.[42] With this in mind, the variations in the account do not necessarily indicate deception, but rather the simple maturing of Joseph throughout his prophetic career. Or as Dean Jessee and Richard Bushman have both pointed out, experience shapes the way in which all people relate events and Joseph's own perceptions of what the First Vision actually meant and what his role would be as God's prophet unfolded only as the years passed.[43] Thus with each recording of the First Vision experience, different facets of the experience are emphasized. In fact, the accounts would be "more peculiar if [Joseph] had related it the same."[44]

The influence of the publications of these Mormon scholars in response to Fawn Brodie and Wesley Walters can be debated. On the one hand, neither Brodie nor Walters ever modified their previous conclusions in light of the research other scholars produced.[45] *No Man Knows My History* is still lauded by some as the foremost biography of Joseph Smith. Wesley Walters is still regarded by some as the final word on the historical accuracy of Joseph Smith's First Vision. Needless to say, the important contributions made by Truman Madsen and the scholars he organized did not settle the debate, and perhaps they were never meant to. Richard Bushman seemingly put it best when he wrote, "Critics of Joseph's story can claim that there was not enough excitement close enough to Palmyra to satisfy them. But again that all depends on how near is near and how big is big. I doubt very much that historical inquiry will ever settle that question to the satisfaction of all."[46]

What is certain is that Mormon historical studies were profoundly affected by Brodie and Walters. Brodie sought to make Mormons stop and "question" the "moving power of Mormonism."[47] Walters sought nothing less than to "force upon Mormon writers a drastic reevaluation" of the origins of their faith.[48] Both were successful, though not in the ways they imagined. Because of the challenges made by Brodie and Walters, Mormon historians have been driven with indefatigable energy "to search for ... early sources" and dig "deeper and deeper into [those] sources."[49] The quality of work produced by Mormon scholars has only continued to improve since Brodie and Walters. In the long run, Mormon scholarship has benefitted from their work.[50]

Scholarly debate and criticism are important elements of the historical discipline because the contest of ideas leads to deeper research and more thorough analysis. This brief introduction illustrates how the historical debate surrounding Joseph Smith's

First Vision took shape. Fawn Brodie and Wesley Walters were central to the formation of subsequent First Vision scholarship because their work proposed the questions that later formed the historical debate. Subsequently, Latter-day Saint scholars responded to the challenges with an increased energy that greatly benefited the study of early Mormonism. This book is intended to introduce a new generation of readers to those responding Latter-day Saint scholars and their contributions to the historical debate. By coupling historical study with faith, readers will be better prepared to face the challenges that an increasingly competitive world presents (see D&C 88:118). As a practicing member of The Church of Jesus Christ of Latter-day Saints, my personal views of Joseph Smith and early Mormonism resonate with the interpretations presented in this book. However, as an aspiring historian, I have also benefited from learning about these scholars' professionalism. They are exemplary historians as well as men of faith. They showed me that it is possible for a historian to excel in the craft and still "hearken unto the counsels of God" (2 Nephi 9:29).

Notes

1. Davis Bitton and Leonard J. Arrington, *Mormons and Their Historians* (Salt Lake City: University of Utah Press, 1988), xii; D. Michael Quinn, "Joseph Smith's Experience of a Methodist 'Camp Meeting' in 1820," *Dialogue: A Journal of Mormon Thought*, Dialogue Paperless: E-paper, no. 3 (December 2006): 1.

2. Charles A. Beard, "Written History as an Act of Faith," *The American Historical Review* 39, no. 2. (January 1934): 219–31, accessed July 9, 2010, http://www.historians.org/info/aha_history/cabeard.htm.

3. See Richard L. Bushman, "The First Vision Revived," *Dialogue* 4, no. 1 (Spring 1969): 90; W. P. Walters, *New Light on*

Mormon Origins from the Palmyra Revival (La Mesa, CA: Utah Christian Tract Society, 1967), 4, 18.

4. Fawn M. Brodie, *No Man Knows My History* (New York: Vintage Books, 1995), 23.

5. Brodie, *No Man Knows My History,* viii, ix.

6. Brodie, *No Man Knows My History*, 25.

7. James Allen and Leonard Arrington, "Mormon Origins in New York: An Introductory Analysis," *BYU Studies* 9, no. 3 (Spring 1969): 262.

8. Bushman, "First Vision Revived," 82.

9. Walters, *New Light on Mormon Origins*, 4.

10. Walters, *New Light on Mormon Origins*, 5.

11. Walters, *New Light on Mormon Origins*, 18.

12. Walters, *New Light on Mormon Origins*, 15.

13. Richard L. Anderson, interview by author, Provo, UT, July 29, 2009.

14. Richard L. Bushman, interview by author, Provo, UT, July 31, 2009.

15. Truman G. Madsen to First Presidency, April 17, 1968, Truman G. Madsen Papers, The Church of Jesus Christ of Latter-day Saints, Salt Lake City.

16. Truman G. Madsen to First Presidency, April 17, 1968, Truman G. Madsen Papers; see Allen and Arrington, "Mormon Origins in New York," 242.

17. Truman G. Madsen to First Presidency, April 17, 1968, Truman G. Madsen Papers.

18. Truman G. Madsen to Fred Williams, February 22, 1968, Truman G. Madsen Papers.

19. Truman G. Madsen to Milton V. Backman Jr., August 26, 1968, Truman G. Madsen Papers.

20. Conversation between Truman G. Madsen and Charles D. Tate Jr., 1967–68, Truman G. Madsen Papers.

21. Truman G. Madsen to Daniel H. Ludlow, November 10, 1967, Truman G. Madsen Papers; Bruce C. Hafen to Truman G. Madsen, March 6, 1968, Truman G. Madsen Papers.

22. Walters, *New Light on Mormon Origins*, 12.

23. Milton V. Backman Jr., "Awakenings in the Burned-Over District: New Light on the Historical Setting of the First Vision," *BYU Studies* 9, no. 3 (Spring 1969): 301.

24. Backman, "Awakenings," 307.

25. Backman, "Awakenings," 311.

26. Milton V. Backman Jr., interview by author, American Fork, UT, August 12, 2009.

27. Walters, *New Light on Mormon Origins*, 12.

28. Bushman, "First Vision Revived," 87.

29. Brodie, *No Man Knows My History*, 23, 25.

30. Richard L. Anderson, interview by author, Provo, UT, July 29, 2009; Richard L. Anderson to Truman G. Madsen, December 12, 1967, Truman G. Madsen Papers.

31. Richard L. Anderson, "Circumstantial Confirmation of the First Vision through Reminiscences," *BYU Studies* 9, no. 3 (Spring 1969): 376, 383–85.

32. Richard L. Anderson to Truman G. Madsen, December 12, 1967, Truman G. Madsen Papers.

33. Richard L. Anderson, interview by author, Provo, UT, July 29, 2009.

34. Richard L. Anderson, interview by author, Provo, UT, July 29, 2009.

35. Anderson, "Circumstantial Confirmation," 385.

36. Anderson, "Circumstantial Confirmation," 376, 385.

37. Anderson, "Circumstantial Confirmation," 385.

38. Richard L. Anderson, interview by author, Provo, UT, July 29, 2009.

39. Brodie, *No Man Knows My History*, 24, 25; Walters, *New Light on Mormon Origins*, 15, 18.

40. Truman G. Madsen to Dean C. Jessee, March 4, 1968, November 4, 1968, Truman G. Madsen Papers.

41. Dean C. Jessee, "The Early Accounts of Joseph Smith's First Vision," *BYU Studies* 9, no. 3 (Spring 1969): 294.

42. James Allen, interview by author, Orem, UT, July 27, 2009.

43. Dean C. Jessee, interview by author, Orem, UT, July 27, 2009; Richard L. Bushman, interview by author, Provo, UT, July 31, 2009.

44. Dean C. Jessee, interview by author, Orem, UT, July 27, 2009.

45. Richard L. Anderson, interview by author, Provo, UT, July 29, 2009.

46. Bushman, "First Vision Revived," 90–91.

47. Brodie, *No Man Knows My History*, ix.

48. Walters, *New Light on Mormon Origins*, 73.

49. Richard L. Bushman, interview by author, Provo, UT, July 31, 2009.

50. See Bushman, "First Vision Revived," 91–92.

In light of his background, it is not surprising that Joseph did not record his experience that spring morning in 1820 after returning from the grove. (Walter Rane, If Any of You Lack Wisdom, © *Intellectual Reserve, Inc.)*

The Earliest Documented Accounts of Joseph Smith's First Vision

Dean C. Jessee

This essay was originally published as "The Early Accounts of Joseph Smith's First Vision" in BYU Studies *9, no. 3 (Spring 1969): 275–95. It was later revised and published in its current form in John W. Welch and Erick B. Carlson, eds.,* Opening the Heavens: Accounts of Divine Manifestations, 1820–1844 *(Provo, UT: BYU Studies; Salt Lake City: Deseret Book, 2005).*

First Vision Accounts in Context

From the beginning of his public ministry, Joseph Smith struggled to record the events of his life. The conditions in which he was raised did not facilitate a literary course—indigent circumstances, which required the labor of the entire Smith family to meet their daily needs, limited Joseph's schooling. He later wrote that he had been "deprived of the bennefit of an education suffice it to say I was mearly instructid in reading writing and the ground rules of Arithmatic which const[it]uted my whole literary acquirements."[1]

In light of his background, it is not surprising that Joseph did not record his experience that spring morning in 1820 after returning from the grove. Years later, still harboring misgivings about his inability to communicate with the pen, he yearned for deliverance from what he called "the little narrow prison . . . of paper pen and ink and a crooked broken scattered and imperfect language."[2] And his writings contain occasional apologies for his lack of writing skill. Even if his literary preparations had been ideal, disruptive forces in his life had an impact upon his record-keeping ventures. Large gaps in his record coincide with periods of unrest and disorder in his life, and many important portions of his life's story were either lost or never recorded.

Another factor that shaped the historiography of the First Vision grew out of the process of developing a record-keeping plan in the early years of the Church. Problems of defining the nature, scope, and format of a historical record limited the resultant archive, as did difficulties in finding and retaining capable clerical help to assist in the creation and care of the records. Following the 1830 revelation that initiated Joseph Smith's record keeping,[3] procedures for creating pertinent records were slow to develop. It took several years marked by false starts before a format was settled on and the enduring work began on Joseph Smith's History of the Church. As evidence of the challenges he faced, by October 29, 1839 (when Joseph left Nauvoo for Washington, DC, to present the Missouri grievances of his people before the federal government), only fifty-nine pages of his history had been written; and six days after his departure, his scribe, James Mulholland, died.[4] After returning to Nauvoo in March 1840, Joseph lamented the passing of his "faithful scribe" and expressed disappointment that an adequate record of his

> **A New Perspective**
> I was just recently in a Church setting where I reviewed those accounts of the vision and a lady came up and said, "My goodness—that's the most marvelous thing I've ever heard." Obviously, she thought it was wonderful to be able to hear details about the First Vision that she wasn't aware of before. (Dean C. Jessee, interview by Samuel Alonzo Dodge, July 27, 2009, Provo, UT)

Washington trip had not been kept: "I depended on Dr. Foster to keep my daily journal during this journey, but he has failed me."[5] Robert B. Thompson, who was appointed general Church clerk on October 3, 1840, continued writing the history where Mulholland left off. Nevertheless, only sixteen pages were added to the manuscript before he too met an untimely death on August 27, 1841.[6]

By the time Willard Richards was appointed general Church clerk and private secretary to the Prophet in December 1841, a mere 157 pages had been written of a history that would eventually number more than 2,000 pages. The History would not be finished during Joseph's lifetime.[7] Shortly before his death, Joseph Smith summarized the problems that had beset his record keeping:

> Since I have been engaged in laying the foundation of the Church of Jesus Christ of Latter Day Saints I have been prevented in various ways from continuing my Journal and the History, in a manner satisfactory to myself, or in justice to the cause. Long imprisonments, vexatious and long continued Law Suits—The treachery of some of my Clerks; the death of others; and the poverty of myself and Brethren from continued plunder and driving, have prevented my handing down to posterity a connected memorandum of events desirable to all lovers of truth.

He added, "I have continued to keep up a Journal in the best manner my circumstances would allow, and dictate for my history from time to time, as I have had opportunity, so that the labors and sufferings of the first Elders and Saints of this last kingdom might not wholly be lost to the world."[8] The historical records of Joseph Smith's life, including those pertaining to the First Vision, are best seen in this context.

First Vision Accounts Produced by the Prophet

The Church records created during these turbulent years include eight documents in which Joseph Smith recorded details of his initial vision experience. Three of these, with minor differences, are duplications of a previous one.

1. Joseph Smith History Account (1832)

The first of these was a six-page autobiographical narrative intended to be a history of his life and "an account of the rise of the Church," but it was abruptly discontinued, evidently when a new plan for the history was conceived. It was most probably written between February and November 1832 on three leaves that were later cut from the ledger book that contained them.[9] This 1832 narrative contains the earliest known account of Joseph's First Vision and the only account in his own handwriting. In the transcription that follows, the bold-faced type indicates the portions of the document written in the Prophet's handwriting. The remainder is in the handwriting of his secretary, Frederick G. Williams. Underlining is reproduced from the original document. Editorial marks include angle brackets < > to indicate above-the-line insertions. Strikeouts are shown by ~~strikeouts~~. Brackets [ ] indicate editorial comments.

> A History of the life of Joseph Smith Jr. an account of his marvilous experience and of all the mighty acts which he doeth in the name of Jesus Ch[r]ist the son of the living God of whom he beareth

record and also an account of the rise of the church of Christ in the eve of time according as the Lord brough<t> forth and established by his hand <firstly> he receiving the testamony from on high seccondly the ministering of Angels thirdly the reception of the holy Priesthood by the ministring of Aangels to adminster the letter of the Gospel—<—the Law and Commandments as they were given unto him—> and the ordinencs, forthly a confirmation and reception of the high Priesthood after the holy order of the son of the living God power and ordinence from on high to preach the Gospel in the administration and demonstration of the spirit **the Kees of the Kingdom of God confered upon him and the continuation of the blessings of God to him &c—I was born in the town of Charon [Sharon] in the <State> of Vermont North America on the twenty third day of December AD 1805 of goodly Parents who spared no pains to instruct<ing> me in <the> christian religion at the age of about ten years my Father Joseph Smith Siegnior moved to Palmyra Ontario [now Wayne] County in the State of New York and being in indigent circumstances were obliged to labour hard for the support of a large Family having nine chilldren and as it required the exertions of all that were able to render any assistance for the support of the Family therefore we were deprived of the bennifit of an education suffice it to say I was mearly instructtid in reading and writing and the ground <rules> of Arithmatic which**

The 1832 History

In 1969 I had not spent enough time with the manuscript of Joseph Smith's 1832 History to see all that was there—for example, the handwriting changes between Frederick G. Williams and Joseph Smith and the fact that Joseph actually wrote part of it himself. Also, there is an insertion in the part of the text written by Joseph Smith stating that the vision occurred in his sixteenth year. Upon closer inspection it is evident that the insertion was written by Frederick G. Williams, a fact that may help explain the discrepancy between this account and others in dating the vision. (Dean C. Jessee, interview by Samuel Alonzo Dodge, July 27, 2009, Provo, UT) constuted my whole literary acquirements. At about the age of twelve years my mind become seriously imprest [p. 1] with regard to the all importent concerns for the wellfare of my immortal Soul which led me to searching the scriptures believeing as I was taught, that they contained the word of God thus applying myself to them and my intimate acquaintance with those of differant denominations led me to marvel excedingly for I discovered that <they did not adorn> instead of adorning their profession by a holy walk and Godly conversation agreeable to what I found contained in that sacred depository this was a grief to my Soul thus from the age of twelve years to fifteen I pondered many things in my heart concerning the sittuation of the world of mankind the contentions and divi[si]ons the wicke[d]ness and abominations and the darkness which pervaded the of the minds of mankind my mind become excedingly distressed for I become convicted of my sins and by searching the scriptures I found that mand <mankind> did not come unto the Lord but that they had apostatised from the true and liveing faith and there was no society or denomination that built upon the gospel of Jesus Christ as recorded in the new testament and I felt to mourn for my own sins and for the sins of the world for I learned in the scriptures that God was the same yesterday to day and forever that he was no respecter to persons for he was God for I looked upon the sun the glorious luminary of the earth and also the moon rolling in their magesty through the heavens and also the stars shining in their courses and the earth also upon which I stood and the beast of the field and the fowls of heaven and the fish of the waters and also man walking forth upon the face of the earth in magesty and in the strength of beauty whose power and intiligence in governing the things which are so exceding great and [p. 2] marvilous even in the likeness of him who created him <them> and when I considired upon these things my heart exclaimed well hath the wise man said the <it is a> fool <that> saith in his heart there is no God my heart exclaimed all all these bear testimony and bespeak an omnipotant and omnipreasant power a being who makith Laws and decreeeth and bindeth all things in their bounds who filleth Eternity who was and is and will be from all Eternity to Eternity and when I, considered all these things and that <that> being seeketh such to worship him as worship him in spirit and in truth therefore I cried unto the Lord for mercy for there was none else to whom I could go and to obtain mercy and the Lord heard my cry in the wilderness and while in <the> attitude of calling upon the Lord <in the 16th year of my age> a piller of fire light above the brightness of the sun at noon day come down from above and rested upon me and I was filled with the spirit of god and the <Lord> opened the heavens upon me and I saw the Lord and he spake unto me saying Joseph <my son> thy sins are forgiven thee. go thy <way> walk in my statutes and keep my commandments behold I am the Lord of glory I was crucifyed for the world that all those who believe on my name may have Eternal life <behold> the world lieth in sin and at this time and none doeth good no not one they have turned asside from the gospel and keep not <my> commandments they draw near to me with their lips while their hearts are far from me and mine anger is kindling against the inhabitants of the earth to visit them acording to th[e]ir ungodliness and to bring to pass that which <hath> been spoken by the mouth of the prophets and Ap[o]stles behold and lo I come quickly as it [is] written of me in the cloud <clothed> in the glory of my Father and my soul was filled with love and for many days I could rejoice with great Joy and the Lord was with me but [I] could find none that would believe the hevnly vision nevertheless I pondered these things in my heart.[10]

2 and 3. Joseph Smith Journal Account (November 9, 1835) and History (1834–1836)

On November 27, 1832, Joseph began keeping a journal, a practice he continued intermittently to the end of his life.

Although the beginning pages were in his own handwriting, much of the journal was dictated to scribes and was eventually written entirely from their own observations. Extensive gaps in the journal must be bridged, so far as possible, by reference to outside sources. Under the date of November 9, 1835, Joseph dictated to his clerk Warren Parrish the visit of a religious eccentric by the name of Robert Matthias who claimed to be Joshua, a Jewish minister. During the ensuing conversation, Joseph Smith related his early vision experience:

> After I had made some remarks concerning the bible I commenced giving him a relation of the circumstances connected with the coming forth of the book of Mormon, as follows—being wrought up in my mind, respecting the subject of religion and looking at the different systems taught the children of men, I knew not who was right or who was wrong and I considered it of the first importance that I should be right, in matters that involve eternal consequ[e]nces; being thus perplexed in mind I retired to the silent grove and bow[e]d down before the Lord, under a realising sense that he had said (if the bible be true) ask and you shall receive knock and it shall be opened seek and you shall find and again, if any man lack wisdom let him ask of God who giveth to all men libarally and upbradeth not; information was what I most desired at this time, and with a fixed determination to obtain it, I called upon the Lord for the first time, in the place above stated or in other words I made a fruitless attempt to p[r]ay, my toung seemed to be swolen in my mouth, so that I could not utter, I heard a noise behind me like some person walking towards me, I strove again to pray, but could not, the noise of walking seemed to draw nearer, I sprung up on my feet, and [p. 23] and looked around, but saw no person or thing that was calculated to produce the noise of walking, I kneeled again my mouth was opened and my toung liberated, and I called on the Lord in mighty prayer, a pillar of fire appeared above my head, it presently rested down upon me head,

and filled me with Joy unspeakable, a personage appeard in the midst of this pillar of flame which was spread all around, and yet nothing consumed, another personage soon appeared like unto the first, he said unto me thy sins are forgiven thee, he testifyed unto me that Jesus Christ is the Son of God; <and I saw many angels in this vision> I was about 14 years old when I received this first communication.[11]

This journal entry soon found its way into another historical document, Joseph Smith's History, 1834–1836. This particular effort to compile materials toward the publication of a history of the Church had commenced in October 1834 when Oliver Cowdery, the editor of the Church's magazine, the *Messenger and Advocate*, began publishing the history in Kirtland, Ohio. The work appeared serially, initially in the form of correspondence between Cowdery and William W. Phelps, and was anticipated to become a "full history of the rise of the church of the Latter Day Saints, and the most interesting parts of its progress, to the present time." It was announced at the outset by the editor that "our brother J. Smith Jr. has offered to assist us. Indeed, there are many items connected with the fore part of this subject that render his labor indispensable. With his labor and with authentic documents now in our possession, we hope to render this a pleasing and agreeable narrative."[12] In the series of eight letters that followed, Cowdery presented various historical events, beginning in the October 1834 issue with an account of the priesthood restoration and concluding in the October 1835 issue with the visit of Joseph Smith to Harmony, Pennsylvania, shortly after receiving the Book of Mormon plates in 1827.

Toward the end of 1835, Frederick G. Williams and Warren Parrish, two of Joseph Smith's clerks, then copied the eight Cowdery-Phelps letters into a large record book that was designated to become "a history" of Joseph's life. Following the transcription of the eight published letters, the format of the anticipated "history" was changed when another clerk, Warren Cowdery, began copying Joseph Smith's journal into the record, commencing with the September 22, 1835, entry. Warren prefaced his addition with this statement: "Here the reader will observe that the narrative assumes a different form. The subject of it becoming daily more and more noted, the writer deemed it proper to give a plain, simple, yet faithful narration of every important item in his every-day-occurrences."[13] There then follows 142 pages of Joseph Smith's journal entries covering the period from September 22, 1835, to January 18, 1836, when the record was abruptly discontinued, evidently as a different approach to organizing the history again became desirable. Except for a few grammatical alterations to the text, including introductory sentences changed from first to third person, the entry included by Warren Cowdery for November 9, 1835, in which Joseph related his 1820 vision experience to Matthias, is a duplication of the Joseph Smith journal entry for the same date (document 2 above); and thus these two accounts are listed together.

> The conversation soon turned upon the subject of Religion, and after the subject of this narrative [Joseph] had made some remarks concerning the bible, he commenced giving him [Matthias] a relation of the circumstances, connected with the coming forth of the Book of Mormon, which were nearly as follows. ["]Being wrought up in my mind respecting the subject of Religion, and looking at the different systems taught the children of men, I knew not who was right or who was wrong, but considered it of the first importance to me that I should be right, in matters of so much moment, matter[s] involving eternal consequences. Being thus perplexed in mind I retired to the silent grove and there bowed down before the Lord, under a realizing sense, (if the bible be true) ask and you shall receive, knock and it shall be opened, seek and you shall find, and again, if any man lack wisdom, let

[him ask] of God who giveth to all men liberally & upbraideth not. Information was what I most desired [p. 120] at this time, and with a fixed determination to obtain it, I called on the Lord for the first time in the place above stated, or in other words, I made a fruitless attempt to pray My tongue seemed to be swoolen in my mouth, so that I could not utter. I heard a noise behind me like some one walking towards me: I strove again to pray, but could not; the noise of walking seemed to draw nearer; I sprang upon my feet and looked round, but saw no person, or thing that was calculated to produce the noise of walking. I kneeled again, my mouth was opened and my tongue loosed; I called on the Lord in mighty prayer. A pillar of fire appeared above my head; which presently rested down upon me, and filled me with unspeakable joy. A personage appeared in the midst of this pillar of flame, which was spread all around and yet nothing consumed. Another personage soon appeared like unto the first: he said unto me thy sins are forgiven thee. He testified also unto me that Jesus Christ is the son of God. I saw many angels in this vision. I was about 14 years old when I received this first communication.["][14]

4 and 5. Joseph Smith Journal Account (November 14, 1835) and History (1834–1836)

On November 14, 1835, five days after the Robert Matthias visit, Joseph Smith related his vision to Erastus Holmes, from Newberry, Clermont County, Ohio, who had called "to make inquiry about the establishment of the church of Latter-day Saints and to be instructed more perfectly in our doctrine." Joseph dictated a summary of his conversation with Holmes that his clerk Warren Parrish recorded in the Prophet's journal.

> I commenced and gave him a brief relation of my experience while in my [p. 36] juvenile years, say from 6 years old up to the time I received the first visitation of Angels which was when I was about 14. years old and also the visitations that I received afterward,

concerning the book of Mormon, and a short account of the rise and progress of the church.[15]

In a fashion similar to the inclusion of the November 9 journal entry explained above, the November 14 entry was also incorporated into the 1834–1836 History as follows:

> He (Smith) commenced and gave him a brief relation of his experience while in his youthful days, say from the age of six years up to the time he received the first visitation of Angels which was when he was about 14 years old. He also gave him an account of the revelations he ~~had~~ afterward received concerning the coming forth of the Book of Mormon, and a succinct account of the rise and progress of the church up to this date.[16]

6. Joseph Smith History Account (1838)

In March 1838, Joseph Smith moved his family and the center of the Church from Kirtland, Ohio, to Far West, Missouri. Only a month later, on April 27, 1838, while engaged in establishing a new gathering place for the Latter-day Saints in Caldwell County, Missouri, he again began writing a history of the Church "from the earliest period of its existance,"[17] this time with the help of his counselor Sidney Rigdon and his secretary George W. Robinson. Only a small segment of the history was written before the project was suspended, no doubt due to the conditions that forced the removal of the Latter-day Saints from the state later that year and resulted in the imprisonment of the Prophet. Not until June 1839, shortly after his arrival in Illinois from his six-month confinement in Missouri, and again only one month after moving his family into a small log house near Commerce (later Nauvoo), Illinois, to begin anew the process of community building, did Joseph Smith turn his attention back to writing the History. Dictating to James Mulholland,[18] Joseph continued the work he had commenced the previous year—a work that some sixty years later would be edited by the Church historian Brigham H. Roberts and published in six volumes as the *History of the Church of Jesus Christ of Latter-day Saints, Period I, History of Joseph Smith, the Prophet, by Himself.* The beginning pages of this history were in time canonized as scripture in the Pearl of Great Price and contain the best-known account of the First Vision.[19]

> Owing to the many reports which have been put in circulation by evil disposed and designing persons in relation to the rise and progress of the Church of <Jesus Christ of> Latter day Saints, all of which have been designed by the authors thereof to militate against its character as a church, and its progress in the world; I have been induced to write this history so as to disabuse the publick mind, and put all enquirers after truth into possession of the facts as they have transpired in relation both to myself and the Church as far as I have such facts in possession.
>
> In this history I will present the various events in relation to this Church in truth and righteousness as they have transpired, or as they at present exist, being now the eighth year since the organization of said Church. I was born in the year of our Lord One thousand Eight hundred and five, on the twenty third day of December, in the town of Sharon, Windsor County, State of Vermont. <see page Note A 131>[20] My father Joseph Smith Senior[21] left the State of Vermont and moved to Palmyra, Ontario, (now Wayne) County, in the State of New York when I was in my tenth year. <or thereabout.>
>
> In about four years after my father's arrival at Palmyra, he moved with his family into Manchester in the same County of Ontario. His family consisting of eleven souls, namely, My Father Joseph Smith, My Mother Lucy Smith whose name previous to her marriage was Mack, daughter of Solomon Mack, My brothers Alvin (who <died Nov. 19th: 1823 in the 25 year of his age.> is now dead) Hyrum, Myself, Samuel—Harrison, William, Don Carloss,

and my Sisters Soph[r]onia, Cathrine and Lucy. Sometime in the second year after our removal to Manchester, there was in the place where we lived an unusual excitement on the subject of religion. It commenced with the Methodists, but soon became general among all the sects in that region of country, indeed the whole district of Country seemed affected by it and great [p. 1] multitudes united themselves to the different religious parties, which created no small stir and division among the people, Some crying, "Lo here" and some Lo there. Some were contending for the Methodist faith, Some for the Presbyterian, and some for the Baptist; for notwithstanding the great love which the converts to these different faiths expressed at the time of their conversion, and the great Zeal manifested by the respective Clergy who were active in getting up and promoting this extraordinary scene of religious feeling in order to have everybody converted as they were pleased to call it, let them join what sect they pleased yet when the Converts began to file off some to one party and some to another, it was seen that the seemingly good feelings of both the Priests and the Converts were ~~mere pretence~~ more pretended than real, for a scene of great confusion and bad feeling ensued; Priest contending against priest, and convert against convert so that all their good feelings one for another (if they ever had any) were entirely lost in a strife of words and a contest about opinions.

I was at this time in my fifteenth year. My Fathers family was<ere> proselyted to the Presbyterian faith and four of them joined that Church, Namely, My Mother Lucy, My Brothers Hyrum, Samuel Harrison, and my Sister Soph[r]onia.

During this time of great excitement my mind was called up to serious reflection and great uneasiness, but though my feelings were deep and often pungent, still I kept myself aloof from all these parties though I attended their several meetings <as often> as occasion would permit. But in process of time my mind became somewhat partial to the Methodist sect, and I felt some desire to be united with them, but so great was the confusion and strife amongst the different denominations that it was impossible for a person young as I was and so unacquainted with men and things to come to any certain conclusion who was right and who was wrong. My mind at different times was greatly excited for the cry and tumult were so great and incessant. The Presbyterians were most decided against the Baptists and Methodists, and used all their powers of either reason or sophistry to prove their errors, or at least to make the people think they were in error. On the other hand the Baptists and Methodists in their turn were equally Zealous in endeavoring to establish their own tenets and disprove all others.

In the midst of this war of words, and tumult of opinions, I often said to myself, what is to be done? Who of all these parties are right? Or are they all wrong together? And if any one of them be right which is it? And how shall I know it?

While I was laboring under the extreme difficulties caused by the contests of these parties of religionists, I was one day reading the Epistle of James, First Chapter and fifth verse which reads, "If any of you lack wisdom, let him ask of God, that giveth to all men liberally and upbraideth not, and it shall be given him." Never did any passage of scripture come with more power to the heart of man [than] this did at this time to mine. It seemed to enter with great force into every feeling of my heart. I reflected on it again and again, knowing that if any person needed wisdom from God, I did, for how to act I did not know and unless I could get more wisdom than I then had would never know, for the teachers of religion of the different sects understood the same [p. 2] passage of Scripture so differently as <to> destroy all confidence in settling the question by an appeal to the Bible. At length I came to the Conclusion that I must either remain in darkness and confusion or else I must do as James directs, that is, Ask of God. I at last came to the determination to ask of God, concluding that if he gave wisdom to them that lacked wisdom, and would give liberally and not upbraid, I might venture.

So, in accordance with this, my determination to ask of God, I retired to the woods to make the attempt. It was on the morning of a beautiful clear day early in the spring of Eightteen hundred and twenty. It was the first time in my life that I had <made> such an attempt, for amidst all <my> anxieties I had never as yet made the attempt to pray vocally.

After I had retired into the place where I had previously designed to go, having looked around me and finding myself alone, I kneeled down and began to offer up the desires of my heart to God, I had scarcely done so, when immediately I was <siezed> upon by some power which entirely overcame me and <had> such astonishing influence over me as to bind my tongue so that I could not speak. Thick darkness gathered around me and it seemed to me for a time as if I were doomed to sudden destruction. But exerting all my powers to call upon God to deliver me out of the power of this enemy which had siezed upon me, and at the very moment when I was ready to sink into despair and abandon myself to destruction, not to an imaginary ruin but to the power of some actual being from the unseen world who had such a marvelous power as I had never before felt in any being. Just at this moment of great alarm I saw a pillar <of> light exactly over my head above the brightness of the sun, which descended ~~gracefully~~ gradually untill it fell upon me. It no sooner appeared than I found myself delivered from the enemy which held me bound. When the light rested upon me I saw two personages (whose brightness and glory defy all description) standing above me in the air. One of <them> spake unto me calling me by name and said (pointing to the other) "This is my beloved Son, Hear him." My object in going to enquire of the Lord was to know which of all the sects was right, that I might know which to join. No sooner therefore did I get possession of myself so as to be able to speak, than I asked the personages who stood above me in the light, which of all the sects was right, (for at this time it had never entered into my heart that all were wrong) and which I should join. I was answered that I must join none of them, for they were all wrong, and the Personage who addressed me said that all their Creeds were an abomination in his sight, that those professors were all Corrupt, that "they draw near to me with their lips but their hearts are far from me, They teach for doctrines the commandments of men, having a form of Godliness but they deny the power thereof." He again forbade me to join with any of them and many other things did he say unto me which I cannot write at this time. When I came to myself again I found myself lying on <my> back looking up into Heaven. <B See Note P 132 {When the light had departed I had no strength, but soon recovering in some degree. I went home.—& as I leaned up to the fire piece. Mother Enquired what the matter was. I replied never mind all is well.— I am well enough off. I then told my mother I have learned for myself that Presbyterianism is not true.—It seems as though the adversary was aware at a very early period of my life that I was destined to prove a disturber & [p. 132] annoyer of his kingdom, or else why should the powers of Darkness combine against me, why the oppression & persecution that arose against me, almost in my infancy?}>[22] Some few days after I had this vision I happened to be in company with one of the Methodist Preachers who was very active in the before mentioned religious excitement and conversing with him on the subject of religion I took occasion to give him an account of the vision which I had had. I was greatly surprised at his behaviour, he treated my communication not only lightly but with great contempt, saying it was all of the Devil, that there was no such thing as visions or revelations in these days, that all such things had ceased with the [p. 3] apostles and that there never would be any more of them. I soon found however that my telling the story had excited a great deal of prejudice against me among professors of religion and was the cause of great persecution which continued to increase and though I was an obscure boy only between fourteen and fifteen years of age <or thereabouts,> and my circumstances in life such as to make a boy of no consequence in the world, yet men of high standing would take notice sufficient~~ly~~ to excite the public mind against me and create a hot persecution, and this was common <among> all the sects: all united to persecute me. It has often caused me ~~in~~ serious reflection both then and since, how very strange it was that an obscure boy of a little over fourteen years of age and one too who was doomed to the necessity of obtaining a scanty maintainance by his daily labor should be thought a character of sufficient importance to attract the attention of the great ones of the most popular sects of the day so as to create in them a spirit of the bitterest persecution and reviling. But strange or not, so it was, and was often cause of great sorrow to myself. However it was nevertheless a fact, that I had had a vision. I have thought since that I felt much like ~~as~~ Paul ~~did~~ when he made his defence before King Aggrippa and related the account of the vision he had when he saw a light and heard a voice, but still there were but few who believed him, some said he was dishonest, others said he was mad, and he was ridiculed and reviled, But all this did not destroy the reality of his vision. He had seen a vision he knew he had, and <all> the persecution under Heaven could not make it otherwise, and though they should persecute him unto death yet he knew and would know to his latest breath that he had both seen a light and heard a voice speaking unto him and all the world could not make him think or believe otherwise. So it was with me, I had actualy seen a light and in the midst of that light I saw two personages, and they did in reality speak <un>to me, or one of them did, And though I was hated and persecuted for saying that I had seen a vision, yet it was true and while they were persecuting me reviling me and speaking all manner of evil against me falsely for so saying, I was led to say in my heart, why persecute <me> for telling the truth? I have actually seen a vision, "and who am I that I can withstand God" or why does the world think to make me deny what I have actually seen, for I had seen a vision, I knew it, and I knew that God knew it, and I could not deny it, neither dare I do it, at least I knew that by so doing <I> would offend God and come under condemnation. I had now got my mind satisfied so far as the sectarian world was concerned, that it was not my duty to join with any of them, but continue as I was untill further directed, ~~for~~ I had found the testimony of James to be true.[23]

7 and 8. Joseph Smith Account for Barstow History (1842) and for Rupp History (1843)

In 1842, John Wentworth, the twenty-six-year-old editor of the Chicago *Democrat*, requested from Joseph Smith a "sketch of the rise, progress, persecution and faith of the Latter-day Saints" for a friend of his, George Barstow, who was writing a history of New Hampshire. Joseph Smith responded to his request and even included a short account of his First Vision with the response. The historical sketch supplied to Wentworth was apparently not used by Barstow, but it was published in the March 1, 1842, issue of the Nauvoo paper *Times and Seasons*, the first published account of the vision in the United States.

> I was born in the town of Sharon Windsor co., Vermont, on the 23d of December, a.d. 1805. When ten years old my parents removed to Palmyra New York, where we resided about four years, and from thence we removed to the town of Manchester.
>
> My father was a farmer and taught me the art of husbandry. When about fourteen years of age I began to reflect upon the importance of being prepared for a future state, and upon enquiring the plan of salvation I found that there was a great clash in religious sentiment; if I went to one society they referred me to one plan, and another to another; each one pointing to his own particular creed as the summum bonum of perfection: considering that all could not be right, and that God could not be the author of so much confusion I determined to investigate the subject more fully, believing that if God had a church it would not be split up into factions, and

that if he taught one society to worship one way, and administer in one set of ordinances, he would not teach another principles which were diametrically opposed. Believing the word of God I had confidence in the declaration of James; "If any man lack wisdom let him ask of God who giveth to all men liberally and upbraideth not and it shall be given him," I retired to a secret place in a grove and began to call upon the Lord, while fervently engaged in supplication my mind was taken away from the objects with which I was surrounded, and I was enwrapped in a [p. 706] heavenly vision and saw two glorious personages who exactly resembled each other in features, and likeness, surrounded with a brilliant light which eclipsed the sun at noon-day. They told me that all religious denominations were believing in incorrect doctrines, and that none of them was acknowledged of God as his church and kingdom. And I was expressly commanded to "go not after them," at the same time receiving a promise that the fulness of the gospel should at some future time be made known unto me.[24]

In 1843, Israel Daniel Rupp, a Pennsylvania historian, planned to publish a work containing the history and doctrine of religious organizations in the United States as written by representatives of each church. In July 1843, Rupp requested from Joseph Smith a chapter on the Mormons. The book containing the Prophet's response was published the following year under the title *An Original History of the Religious Denominations at Present Existing in the United States*. The portion of the chapter dealing with the First Vision was essentially a reprint of the statement sent to John Wentworth the previous year with very slight changes.

When about fourteen years of age, I began to reflect upon the importance of being prepared for a future state; and upon inquiring the place of salvation, I found that there was a great clash in religious sentiment; if I went to one society they referred me to one place, and another to another; each one pointing to his own particular creed as the "summum bonum" of perfection. Considering that all could not be right, and that God could not be the author of so much confusion, I determined to investigate the subject more fully, believing that if God had a church, it would not be split up into factions, and that if he taught one society to worship one way, and administer in one set of ordinances, he would not teach another principles which were diametrically opposed. Believing the word of God, I had confidence in the declaration of James, "If any man lack wisdom let him ask of God, who giveth to all men liberally and upbraideth not, and it shall be given him."

I retired to a secret place in a grove, and began to call upon the [p. 404] Lord. While fervently engaged in supplication, my mind was taken away from the objects with which I was surrounded, and I was enrapt in a heavenly vision, and saw two glorious personages, who exactly resembled each other in features and likeness, surrounded with a brilliant light, which eclipsed the sun at noonday. They told me that all the religious denominations were believing in incorrect doctrines, and that none of them was acknowledged of God as his church and kingdom. And I was expressly commanded to "go not after them," at the same time receiving a promise that the fulness of the gospel should at some future time be made known unto me.[25]

Contemporaneous First Vision Accounts by Others

In addition to the eight accounts of Joseph Smith's vision directly formulated by him, five others were written by witnesses who heard him relate the experience and reported what he said during his lifetime.

1. Orson Pratt Report (1840)

As one of the members of the Quorum of the Twelve Apostles who assisted in introducing Mormonism in the British

Isles in 1840–41, Orson Pratt arrived in Edinburgh, Scotland, in May 1840. To arouse interest in his message, Pratt published in September 1840 a pamphlet titled *A[n] Interesting Account of Several Remarkable Visions, and of the Late Discovery of Ancient American Records* in which he drew from his personal acquaintance with Joseph Smith for details of the Prophet's First Vision. The significance of the Pratt pamphlet is that it was the first time an account of the vision had been published. The Pratt pamphlet shows some evidence that it was used by the Prophet to formulate the letter he sent to John Wentworth in 1842.

> When somewhere about fourteen or fifteen years old, he [Joseph Smith] began seriously to reflect upon the necessity of being prepared for a future state of existence: but how, or in what way, to prepare himself, was a question, as yet, undetermined in his own mind: he perceived that it was a question of infinite importance, and that the salvation of his soul depended upon a correct understanding of the same. He saw, that if he understood not the [p. 3] way, it would be impossible to walk in it, except by chance; and the thought of resting his hopes of eternal life upon chance, or uncertainties, was more than he could endure. If he went to the religious denominations to seek information, each one pointed to its particular tenets, saying—"This is the way, walk ye in it;" while, at the same time, the doctrines of each were, in many respects, in direct opposition to one another. It, also, occurred to his mind, that God was not the author of but one doctrine, and therefore could not acknowledge but one denomination as his church; and that such denomination must be a people, who believe, and teach, that one doctrine, (whatever it may be,) and build upon the same. He then reflected upon the immense number of doctrines, now, in the world, which had given rise to many hundreds of different denominations. The great question to be decided in his mind, was—if any one of these denominations be the Church of Christ, which one is it? Until he could become satisfied, in relation to

this question, he could not rest contented. To trust to the decisions of fallible man, and build his hopes upon the same, without any certainty, and knowledge, of his own, would not satisfy the anxious desires that pervaded his breast. To decide, without any positive and definite evidence, on which he could rely, upon a subject involving the future welfare of his soul, was revolting to his feelings. The only alternative, that seemed to be left him, was to read the Scriptures, and endeavour to follow their directions. He, accordingly, commenced perusing the sacred pages of the Bible, with sincerity, believing the things that he read. His mind soon caught hold of the following passage:—"If any of you lack wisdom, let him ask of God, that giveth to all *men* liberally, and upbraideth not; and it shall be given him."—James i.5. From this promise he learned, that it was the privilege of all men to ask God for wisdom, with the sure and certain expectation of receiving, liberally; without being upbraided for so doing. This was cheering information to him: tidings that gave him great joy. It was like a light shining forth in a dark place, to guide him to the path in which he should walk. He, now, saw that if he inquired of God, there was, not only, a possibility, but a probability; yea, more, a certainty, that he should [p. 4] obtain a knowledge, which, of all the doctrines, was the doctrine of Christ; and, which, of all the churches, was the church of Christ. He, therefore, retired to a secret place, in a grove, but a short distance from his father's house, and knelt down, and began to call upon the Lord. At first, he was severely tempted by the powers of darkness, which endeavoured to overcome him; but he continued to seek for deliverance, until darkness gave way from his mind; and he was enabled to pray, in fervency of the spirit, and in faith. And, while thus pouring out his soul, anxiously desiring an answer from God, he, at length, saw a very bright and glorious light in the heavens above; which, at first, seemed to be at a considerable distance. He continued praying, while the light appeared to be gradually

"It no sooner appeared than I found myself delivered from the enemy which held me bound. When the light rested upon me I saw two Personages, whose brightness and glory defy all description, standing above me in the air. One of them spake unto me, calling me by name and said, pointing to the other—This is My Beloved Son. Hear Him!" (Joseph Smith—History 1:17) (Sacred Grove photo by Brent R. Nordgren)

descending towards him; and, as it drew nearer, it increased in brightness, and magnitude, so that, by the time that it reached the tops of the trees, the whole wilderness, for some distance around, was illuminated in a most glorious and brilliant manner. He expected to have seen the leaves and boughs of the trees consumed, as soon as the light came in contact with them; but, perceiving that it did not produce that effect, he was encouraged with the hopes of being able to endure its presence. It continued descending, slowly, until it rested upon the earth, and he was enveloped in the midst of it. When it first came upon him, it produced a peculiar sensation throughout his whole system; and, immediately, his mind was caught away, from the natural objects with which he was surrounded; and he was enwrapped in a heavenly vision, and saw two glorious personages, who exactly resembled each other in their features or likeness. He was informed, that his sins were forgiven. He was also informed upon the subjects, which had for some time previously agitated his mind, viz.—that all the religious denominations were believing in incorrect doctrines; and, consequently, that none of them was acknowledged of God, as his church and kingdom. And he was expressly commanded, to go not after them; and he received a promise that the true doctrine—the fullness of the gospel, should, at some future time, be made known to him; after which the vision withdrew, leaving his mind in a state of calmness and peace, indescribable.[26]

2. 1842 Orson Hyde Report (1842)

At the 1840 April conference in Nauvoo, Elder Orson Hyde spoke of a prophecy calling him to "a great work" among the Jews, a work that would "prepare the way" for the gathering of that people. He felt the time had come to fulfill that prophecy by visiting the Jews of Europe and the Holy Land, whereupon the conference authorized him to proceed on his mission. After arriving in London, he wrote, with Joseph Smith's sanction, a treatise on the faith, doctrine, and history of the Church. Continuing this journey, he stopped in Germany, where he studied German, then proceeded on to the Middle East, where he dedicated the Holy Land for the return of the Jews. Returning to Germany in 1842, he translated his book into German and published it in Frankfurt before returning to the United States. Written "in something the manner" of Orson Pratt's 1840 pamphlet, Hyde's work was titled *Ein Ruf aus der Wüste*, the first time an account of the First Vision was published in a foreign language.[27]

> When he had reached his fifteenth year, he began to think seriously about the importance of preparing for a future [existence]; but it was very difficult for him to decide how he should go about such an important undertaking. He recognized clearly that it would be impossible for him to walk the proper path without being acquainted with it beforehand; and to base his hopes for eternal life on chance

or blind uncertainty would have been more than he had ever been inclined to do.

He discovered the world of religion working under a flood of errors which by virtue of their contradictory opinions and principles laid the foundation for the rise of such different sects and denominations whose feelings toward each other all too often were poisoned by hate, contention, resentment and anger. He felt that there was only one truth and that those who understood it correctly, all understood it in the same way. Nature had endowed him with a keen critical intellect and so he looked through the lens of reason and common sense and with pity and contempt upon those systems of religion, which were so opposed to each other and yet were all obviously based on the scriptures.

After he had sufficiently convinced himself to his own satisfaction that darkness covered the earth and gross darkness [covered] the nations, the hope of ever finding a sect or denomination that was in possession of unadulterated truth left him.

Consequently he began in an attitude of faith his own investigation of the word of God [feeling that it was] the best way to arrive at a knowledge of the truth. He had not proceeded very far in this laudable endeavor when his eyes fell upon the following verse of St. James [1:5]: "If any of you lack wisdom, let him ask of God, that giveth to all men liberally, and upbraideth not; and it shall be given him." He considered this scripture an authorization for him to solemnly call upon his creator to present his needs before him with the certain expectation of some success. And so he began to pour out to the Lord with fervent determination the earnest desires of his soul. On one occasion, he went to a small grove of trees near his father's home and knelt down before God in solemn prayer. The adversary then made several strenuous efforts to cool his ardent soul. He filled his mind with doubts [p. 15] and brought to mind all manner of inappropriate images to prevent him from obtaining the object of his endeavors; but the overflowing mercy of God came to buoy him up and gave new impetus to his failing strength. However, the dark cloud soon parted and light and peace filled his frightened heart. Once again he called upon the Lord with faith and fervency of spirit.

At this sacred moment, the natural world around him was excluded from his view, so that he would be open to the presentation of heavenly and spiritual things. Two glorious heavenly personages stood before him, resembling each other exactly in features and stature. They told him that his prayers had been answered and that the Lord had decided to grant him a special blessing. He was also told that he should not join any of the religious sects or denominations, because all of them erred in doctrine and none was recognized by God as his church and kingdom. He was further commanded, to wait patiently until some future time, when the true doctrine of Christ and the complete truth of the gospel would be revealed to him. The vision closed and peace and calm filled his mind.[28]

3. Levi Richards Report (1843)

A native of Massachusetts, Levi Richards was the older brother of Willard Richards, Church historian and Joseph Smith's secretary, and a cousin of Brigham Young. Levi was a skilled Thompsonian physician. Shortly after his conversion to Mormonism in 1835, he moved to Kirtland, Ohio. He was present during the difficulties that beset the Church in Ohio and Missouri and assisted in the evacuation of the Saints when they were forced out of Missouri in 1838–39. After resettling with the Church at Nauvoo, Illinois, he continued his medical practice, served as surgeon general of the Nauvoo Legion, and was elected a member of the city council. On Sunday, June 11, 1843, after Joseph Smith had spoken to the Saints gathered near the temple, he announced that George J. Adams would lecture that evening on the Book of Mormon. Levi Richards attended the lecture and reported the following:

> At 6 PM. heard Eld. G J Adams upon the book of Mormon proved from the 24th, 28th & 29 of Isaiah that the everlasting covenant which was set up by Christ & the apostles had been broken . . . —Pres. J. Smith bore testimony to the same—saying that when he was a youth he began to think about these things but could not find out which of all the sects were right—he went into the grove &, enquired of the Lord which of all the sects were right—he received for answer that none of them were right, that they were all wrong, & that the Everlasting covenant was broken—he said he understood the fulness of the Gospel from beginning to end—& could Teach it & also the order of the priesthood in all its ramifications—Earth & hell had opposed him & tryed to destroy him—but they had not done it & they <never would.>[29]

4. David Nye White Report (1843)

A visitor to Nauvoo who heard Joseph Smith speak of his vision was David Nye White, the senior editor of the *Pittsburgh Weekly Gazette*. On August 28, 1843, while traveling through the western frontier of America, White stopped in Illinois to visit the Prophet. Two days later, he wrote his perceptions of the "far-famed kingdom of the 'Latter-day Saints,'" which were published in the September 15 issue of the *Gazette*. Included in the article was his report of what the Prophet told him about his 1820 vision. Joseph said:

> The Lord does reveal himself to me. I know it. He revealed himself first to me when I was about fourteen years old, a mere boy. I will tell you about it. There was a reformation among the different religious denominations in the neighborhood where I lived, and I became serious, and was desirous to know what Church to join. While thinking of this matter, I opened the [New] Testament promiscuously on these words, in James, "Ask of the Lord who giveth to all men liberally and upbraideth not." I just determined I'd ask him. I immediately went out into the woods where my father had

a clearing, and went to the stump where I had stuck my axe when I had quit work, and I kneeled down, and prayed, saying, "O Lord, what Church shall I join?" Directly I saw a light, and then a glorious personage in the light, and then another personage, and the first personage said to the second, "Behold my beloved Son, hear him." I then, addressed this second person, saying, "O Lord, what Church shall I join." He replied, "don't join any of them, they are all corrupt." The vision then vanished, and when I come to myself, I was sprawling on my back; and it was some time before my strength returned. When I went home and told the people that I had a revelation, and that all the churches were corrupt, they persecuted me, and they have persecuted me ever since. They thought to put me down, but they hav'nt succeeded, and they can't do it.[30]

5. *Alexander Neibaur Report (1844)*

Another Latter-day Saint who heard Joseph Smith relate his First Vision experience and recorded what he heard was Alexander Neibaur, a convert originally from Germany. After studying dentistry in his native land, Neibaur moved to England, where he set up his practice in Preston. When Latter-day Saint missionaries arrived in England in 1837, Neibaur was among the first converts to the Church. Four years later, he and his family migrated to Nauvoo, Illinois, where he continued his dental practice and, as a linguist, taught German and Hebrew to Joseph Smith. On May 24, 1844, Neibaur, still struggling to master the English language, recorded in his diary what the Prophet had said that day while Neibaur visited in Joseph's home.

> Br Joseph tolt us the first call he had a Revival meeting his mother & Br & Sist got Religion, he wanted to get Religion too wanted to feel & she shout like the Rest but could feel nothing, opened his Bible f the first Passage that struck him was if any man lack wisdom let him ask of God who giveth to all men liberallity & upbraidat[h]

not went into the Wood to pray kneelt himself down his tongue was closet cleavet to his roof—could utter not a word, felt easier after a while = saw a fire towards heaven came near & nearer saw a personage in the fire light complexion blue eyes a piece of white cloth drawn over his shoulders his right arm bear after a wile a other person came to the side of the first Mr Smith then asked must I join the Methodist Church = No = they are not my People, all have gone astray there is none that doeth good no not one, but this is my Beloved son harken ye him, the fire drew nigher Rested upon the tree enveloped him [page torn] comforted Indeavoured to arise but felt uncomen feeble = got into the house told the Methodist priest, [who] said this was not a age for God to Reveal himself in Vision Revelation has ceased with the New Testament.[31]

Other Likely Contemporaneous First Vision Accounts

Should the foregoing historical sources pertaining to Joseph Smith's First Vision seem sparse in some respects, those gaps are primarily the result of inadequate record keeping of his many conversations and discourses on the subject or related topics. If record keeping in the harsh literary environment of the early years of the Church had commenced at the level of efficiency that it later achieved, no doubt other contemporary reports of the vision would be available. This conclusion is strongly suggested by occasions when Joseph is known to have talked about the experience, but no official report was made.

For example, William Phelps, writing to his wife, Sally, in Missouri in June 1835, noted that "President Smith preached last Sabbath, and I gave him the text: 'This is my belovd Son; hear ye him!' He preached one of the greatest sermons I ever heard—it was about 3 ½ hours long—and unfolded more mysteries than I can write at this time."[32]

A year later, in November 1836, Parley P. Pratt informed the Saints in Canada that one of the most interesting meetings he ever attended had been held recently in the Kirtland Temple:

> One week before word was publicly given that Br. J. Smith Jr. would give a relation of the coming forth of the records and also of the rise of the church and of his experience. Accordingly a vast concourse assembled at an early hour. Every seat was crowded and 4 or 5 hundred People stood up in the Aisles. Br. S[mith] gave the history of these things relating many Particulars of the manner of his first visions &c. the Spirit and Powr of God was upon him in Bearing testimony insomuch that many if not most of the congregation were in tears—as for my self I can say that all the reasonings in uncertainty and all the conclusions drawn from the writings of others ... however great in themselves dwindle into insignificance when compared with the living testimony when your Eyes sea and your Ears hear from the living oracles of God.[33]

Aside from the Pratt letter, there are no known additional reports of this discourse, which gave many details of Joseph's First Vision; the date on which it was given coincides with a large gap in the Prophet's journal.

Subsequent Recollections of First Vision Accounts

After the death of Joseph Smith, other witnesses wrote of occasions on which they had heard him speak about his First Vision. For example, on the "special request of a few particular friends," Mary Isabella Hales Horne recalled the time when she had heard Joseph "relate his first vision when the Father and Son appeared to him: also his receiving the Gold Plates from the Angel Moroni.... While he was relating the circumstances, the Prophet's countenance lighted up, and so wonderful a power accompanied his words that everybody who heard them felt his influence and power."[34]

Similiarly, Joseph Curtis recalled a visit of Joseph Smith to Pontiac, Michigan, in spring 1835, where the Prophet, in a meeting there, "stated the reason" for the doctrines he taught:

> As a revival of some of the sec[t]s was going on some of his fathers family joined in with the revival himself being quite young[.] he feeling an anxiety to be religious his mind some what troubled this scriptures came to his mind which sayes if a man lack wisdon let him ask of god who giveth liberaly and upbradeth not[.] believeing it he went with a determinati[on] to obtain to enquire of the lord himself after some strugle the Lord minifested to him that the different sects were rong also that the Lord had a great work for him to do.[35]

The devoted record keeper Edward Stevenson, while also living in Pontiac, heard Joseph speak to the branch of the Church there:

> A great stir was made in this settlement at so distinguished visitors the meetings held were crowded to see and hear the testamonies given which were very powerful I will here relate my own experience on the ocaision of a meeting in our old log school House The Prophet stood at a table for the pulpit whare he began relateing his vision and before he got through he was in the midst of the congregation with uplifted hand. I do believe that there was not one person presant who did at the time being or who was not convicted of the truth of his vision, of an Angle to him his countanance seemed to me to assume a heavenly whiteness and his voice was so peirseing and forcible for my part it so impressed me as to become indellibly imprinted in my mind.[36]

A secondhand report of Joseph Smith relating his vision, remembered many years later, comes from the pen of the diligent southern Utah diarist Charles Walker. In 1893, he attended a testimony meeting one Sunday at which one of the local elders, John Alger, said that when he was a small boy he heard Joseph Smith "relate his vision of seeing the Father and the Son, That God touched his eyes with his finger and said, 'Joseph this is my beloved Son hear him.' As soon as the Lord had touched his eyes with his finger he immediately saw the Savior." At the close of the meeting Walker and others questioned the speaker:

> He told us at the bottom of the meeting house steps that he was in the House of Father Smith in Kirtland when Joseph made this declaration, and that Joseph while speaking of it put his finger to his right eye, suiting the action with the words so as to illustrate and at the same time impress the occurrence on the minds of those unto whom He was speaking.[37]

Conclusion

The primary historical sources of Joseph Smith's First Vision are best understood in the broad record-keeping setting in which they were created. In 1830, a revelation commanded that records be kept in the Church, and the Prophet entered upon the stage of record keeping without the benefit of a well-defined tradition of doing so. He first farmed out the task to others, but when he saw that their effort did not adequately chronicle his personal experience, he belatedly commenced his autobiography. For years he struggled with a format for his personal history, as indicated by the haphazard nature of his earliest attempts to create a record of his life. Another factor that had an impact upon the historical record was the inability of those who heard Joseph speak to make a verbatim report of what he said.

Furthermore, public knowledge of his religious claims and intentions had been the source of much of the persecution against him and his people, which also affected the writing and dissemination of his history. A little more than a year before his

> ### A Compelling Reality
> In the process of reading through the documents and writings of Joseph Smith over the years, my conviction of the credibility of his story and the nature of his mission has increased immensely. The evidence has built detail upon detail, document upon document, to the point where it has become a compelling reality to me. Once I was able to separate the thoughts Joseph Smith put on paper with his own hand from those written by others for him, there was a whole new light cast upon him. I found that his personal writings—few in number compared to his entire archive—were like a vein of gold threading through a mountain. I saw in them a different spirit; I saw a sensitive, caring man whose prose was born of religious experience. I could well believe his words when he said: "I had actually seen a light, and in the midst of that light I saw two Personages, and they did in reality speak to me," and "God is my friend in him I shall find comfort I have given my life into his hands I am prepared to go at his call. . . . I count not my life dear to me only to do his will." (Dean C. Jessee, interview by Samuel Alonzo Dodge, July 27, 2009, Provo, UT)

death, he told the Saints, "The History is going out by little & little in the papers & cutting its way, so that when it is completed it will not raise a persecution against us."[38] The extraordinary opposition and hardships he faced in his role as religious reformer, and the problems associated with the development of a historical record, had a significant impact upon the timing and nature of the records he produced. This context is the lens through which the collection of the pieces of the historical record of Joseph Smith's First Vision is best seen and appreciated.

Notes

1. Joseph Smith History, 1832, in Joseph Smith Letterbook 1, MS, 1, Joseph Smith Collection, Church History Library, The Church of Jesus Christ of Latter-day Saints, Salt Lake City.

2. Joseph Smith to William Phelps, November 27, 1832, in Joseph Smith Letterbook 1, 4; *The Personal Writings of Joseph*

Smith, ed. and comp. Dean C. Jessee, rev. ed. (Salt Lake City: Deseret Book; Provo, UT: Brigham Young University Press, 2002), 287.

3. The opening words of the revelation presented by Joseph Smith at the organization of the Church on April 6, 1830, were "Behold, there shall be a record kept among you" (D&C 21:1).

4. Joseph Smith Jr., "History of the Church," MS, C-1, 1023, Church History Library; *History of the Church of Jesus Christ of Latter-day Saints*, ed. B. H. Roberts, 2nd ed. rev. (Salt Lake City: Deseret Book, 1971), 4:88–89.

5. Smith, "History," C-1, 1023; *History of the Church*, 4:89.

6. Smith, "History," C-1, 1223; *History of the Church*, 4:89.

7. The manuscript of the History shows that the first fifty-nine pages were written by James Mulholland, that Robert B. Thompson wrote at least part of the next sixteen, and that William W. Phelps had written eighty-two pages before Willard Richards began writing. It was not until after Richards's appointment in December 1841 that any significant progress was made on writing the History. Dean C. Jessee, "The Writing of Joseph Smith's History," *BYU Studies* 11, no. 4 (1971): 429–73.

8. Smith, "History," C-1, 1260. See *History of the Church*, 4:470. Speaking to the newly appointed Twelve in February 1835, Joseph remarked,

> If I now had in my possession every decision which has been had upon important items of doctrine and duties, since the commencement of this work, I would not part with them for any sum of money; but we have neglected to take minutes of such things, thinking perhaps that they would never benefit us afterwards. ... [A]nd now we cannot bear record to the church and to the world of the great and glorious manifestations which have been made to us, with that degree of power and authority we otherwise could, if we now had these things to publish abroad.

"A Record of the Transactions of the Twelve Apostles ... ," MS, 1–2, Church History Library; compare *History of the Church*, 2:198–99.

9. Joseph Smith Letterbook 1, 1; *Personal Writings of Joseph Smith*, 9–10. Evidence for the 1832 date comes from handwriting identification and inspection of the ledger book that contained the severed pages. The handwriting reveals that the document was alternately penned by Joseph and Frederick G. Williams, Joseph's scribe and counselor in the First Presidency. Williams converted to the Church in fall 1830 and immediately left for Missouri. His handwriting in the beginning pages of the Kirtland Revelation Book shows that by February 1832, Williams was writing for Joseph Smith, after returning to Ohio. And according to his own statement, he was officially appointed on July 20 as the Prophet's scribe. F. G. Williams, statement, n.d., MS, Frederick G. Williams Papers, Church History Library. From this, it is evident that the writing of the History could have occurred as early as February 1832.

Nor is it likely that the History was written after November 27, 1832, since on that date the ledger book in which it was written was converted to a letterbook for recording important historical Church documents. The evidence for this is two-fold. First, although they were later cut from the volume, the three leaves containing the History match the cut edges still protruding from the binding of the ledger book. The terminal letters of words that were severed when the pages were removed also match. The cut page stubs immediately precede the November 27, 1832, letter entry, the first item in the letterbook. Second, the page numbering indicates this arrangement. The pages of the History were numbered 1 through 6, and the November 27 letter begins on page 1a. Both the last page of the History and the pages of the letter were written by Frederick Williams. He would not have started numbering the pages containing the letter with "1a" had there not been a preceding page 1.

10. Joseph Smith Letterbook 1, 1–3. For the entire text of this narrative, see *Personal Writings of Joseph Smith*, 9–14.

11. Joseph Smith Journal, 1835–36, MS, 23–24, Church History Library; *Personal Writings of Joseph Smith*, 104–5.

12. *Messenger and Advocate*, October 1834, 13.

13. Joseph Smith, "History, 1834–1836," MS, A-1, 105 (numbering from the back of the book), Church History Library; *The Papers*

of Joseph Smith, ed. Dean C. Jessee (Salt Lake City: Deseret Book, 1989–92), 1:97.

14. Smith, "History, 1834–1836," A-1, 120–22; *Papers of Joseph Smith*, 1:125–27.

15. Joseph Smith Journal, November 14, 1835; *Personal Writings of Joseph Smith*, 112–13.

16. Smith, "History, 1834–1836," A-1, 129; *Papers of Joseph Smith*, 1:136–37.

17. Joseph Smith Journal, 1838, MS, 34, Church History Library; *Papers of Joseph Smith*, 2:233.

18. Smith, "History," C-1, 954. See also *History of the Church*, 3:375.

19. See Joseph Smith—History; *History of the Church*, 1:1–20, 32–33, 39–44; and *Papers of Joseph Smith*, 1:267–86, 288, 290–92. When Joseph began dictating this history to James Mulholland on June 11, 1839, the Prophet's large record book containing the above 1835 History account was turned over and retitled as book "A-1" of the ensuing multivolume history. Dates in the opening pages of the narrative indicate that the Prophet was dictating from a text that had been written the previous year. On page 1, reference is made to the "eighth year since the organization of said Church," and on page 8, "this day, being the Second day of May, One thousand Eight hundred and thirty eight." *History of the Church*, 1:2, 18–19. Joseph Smith's journal for April 27, 1838, in the hand of George W. Robinson, notes that he spent the day "writing a history of th<i>s Church from the earliest perion [period] of its existance up to this date." During the first four days of May, the journal adds, "the First Presidency were engaged in writing church History." Joseph Smith Journal, April 27 and May 1–4, 1838; *Papers of Joseph Smith*, 2:233, 237; *History of the Church*, 3:25–26. The statement on page 8 of the History confirms this was the narrative being written on May 2, 1838.

Further evidence that the beginning pages of the History manuscript volume A-1 were copied in 1839 from the Prophet's dictation beginning with the account written the previous year is that the first fifty-nine pages of the manuscript are in the handwriting of Mulholland, who did not begin writing for Joseph Smith until September 3, 1838; a short time later, he discontinued writing during the Missouri imprisonment of the Prophet (October 1838–March 1839) and did not recommence until April 22, 1839. James Mulholland Journal, MS, Church History Library. Mulholland's journal entry for June 11, 1839, notes that he was "writing &c for Church history." In addition, the Prophet's History for that date states, "I commenced dictating my history for my Clerk—James Mulholland to write," and on June 12 and 13, Joseph's History reads, "I continued to dictate my history." Smith, "History," C-1, 954; *History of the Church*, 3:375–76.

20. This insertion added by Willard Richards in 1842 contains the Prophet's account of his 1813 leg operation. See *Papers of Joseph Smith*, 1:268–69; Lucy Mack Smith, *Biographical Sketches of Joseph Smith, the Prophet, and His Progenitors for Many Generations* (London: S. W. Richards, 1853), 62–66; see also LeRoy S. Wirthlin, "Joseph Smith's Boyhood Operation: An 1813 Surgical Success," *BYU Studies* 21, no. 2 (1981): 131–54.

21. An insertion here to "Addendum, note E, page 2" gives birth dates and places of Joseph Smith's paternal ancestors.

22. This insertion is in the handwriting of Willard Richards on pages 132–33 of the History manuscript. According to Richards's diary, this note was written on December 2, 1842, which explains why it does not appear in the History in the *Times and Seasons* that began publication in March of that year. Willard Richards Diary, December 2, 1842, MS, Church History Library.

23. Smith, "History," A-1, 1–4; *Personal Writings of Joseph Smith*, 226–32.

24. Joseph Smith, "Church History," *Times and Seasons*, March 1, 1842, 706–10, in *Personal Writings of Joseph Smith*, 242. Appended to this account was the statement of belief later canonized as the Articles of Faith.

25. Joseph Smith, "Latter Day Saints," in I. Daniel Rupp, comp., *An Original History of the Religious Denominations at Present Existing in the United States* (Philadelphia: J. Y. Humphreys, 1844), 404–10; *Papers of Joseph Smith*, 1:448–49.

26. Orson Pratt, *Interesting Account of Several Remarkable Visions, and The Late Discovery of Ancient American Records* (Edinburgh: Ballantyne and Hughes, 1840), 3–5; *Papers of Joseph Smith*, 1:389–91.

27. Joseph Smith Letterbook 2, 201–6; Orson Hyde and John E. Page to Joseph Smith, May 1, 1840, in Joseph Smith Letterbook 2, 144–45; Joseph Smith to Orson Hyde and John E. Page, May 14, 1840, in Joseph Smith Letterbook 2, 146–47; Orson Hyde to Joseph Smith, June 15, 1841, *Times and Seasons*, October 1, 1841, 551–55. See also *History of the Church*, 4:105–6, 123–24, 129, 386; and *Papers of Joseph Smith*, 1:402–4.

28. Orson Hyde, *Ein Ruf aus der Wüste, eine Stimme aus dem Schoose der Erde* (A Cry from the Wilderness, a Voice from the Dust of the Earth) (Frankfurt: n.p., 1842), 14–16. The text here is a literal translation from the German by Marvin Folsom, professor emeritus of German, Brigham Young University. The text is also reprinted with a translation in *Papers of Joseph Smith*, 1:402–25.

29. Levi Richards Journal, June 11, 1843, MS, Church History Library. See also *The Words of Joseph Smith: The Contemporary Accounts of the Nauvoo Discourses of the Prophet Joseph*, ed. Andrew F. Ehat and Lyndon W. Cook (Provo, UT: Religious Studies Center, Brigham Young University, 1980), 215.

30. "The Prairies, Nauvoo, Joe Smith, the Temple, the Mormons, &c.," *Pittsburgh Weekly Gazette*, September 15, 1843, 3; *Papers of Joseph Smith*, 1:438–44.

31. Alexander Neibaur Journal, May 24, 1844, MS, Church History Library.

32. William W. Phelps to Sally Phelps, June 2, 1835, MS, Church History Library.

33. Parley P. Pratt to the Elders and Brethren of the Church of Latter-day Saints in Canada, November 27, 1836, MS, Church History Library.

34. *Woman's Exponent*, June 1910, 6.

35. Joseph Curtis Reminiscences and Journal, MS, 5, Church History Library.

36. Edward Stevenson, "The Life and History of Elder Edward

Stevenson," MS, 21, Church History Library. See also Edward Stevenson, *Reminiscences of Joseph the Prophet and the Coming Forth of the Book of Mormon* (Salt Lake City: printed by author, 1893), 4–5; and Edward Stevenson, *Juvenile Instructor*, July 15, 1894, 444–45.

37. Charles Walker, diary, February 2, 1893, published as A. Karl Larsen and Katharine Miles Larsen, eds., *Diary of Charles Lowell Walker* (Logan, UT: Utah State University Press, 1980), 755–56.

38. Willard Richards, report of Joseph Smith discourse, in Joseph Smith Journal, April 19, 1843; *History of the Church*, 5:367.

The Appearance of the Father and the Son to Joseph Smith in 1820

James B. Allen and John W. Welch

An earlier version of this article, "Eight Contemporary Accounts of Joseph Smith's First Vision—What Do We Learn from Them?" was authored by James B. Allen and appeared in the Improvement Era *in April 1970.[1] That article was itself a historical landmark. Invited and published by the Church's official periodical, this piece began the work of teaching Latter-day Saints about the various accounts of the vision. Since that time, the scholars whose work is featured in this book have learned much more about the documentary evidence and the historical context of the First Vision. That research is reflected in this version, prepared by James B. Allen and John W. Welch, the Robert K. Thomas Professor of Law at BYU and editor of BYU Studies. This chapter enhances the version of this material as it appeared in 2005 in* Opening the Heavens: Accounts of Divine Manifestations, 1820–1844.[2]

The Restoration of the gospel of Jesus Christ and the history of The Church of Jesus Christ of Latter-day Saints began when God the Father and his Son Jesus Christ appeared to the youthful Joseph Smith in spring 1820.

> ### The 1970 Article
>
> In 1970, at the request of the editors of the *Improvement Era*, I published the article titled "Eight Contemporary Accounts of Joseph Smith's First Vision—What Do We Learn from Them?" By that time people had become aware of the various different accounts of the vision, and many, including Latter-day Saints as well as some people who were not friendly to the Church, began to raise questions. That 1970 *Improvement Era* article was the first discussion of these accounts to appear in any official Church publication. (Some discussion had appeared earlier in *BYU Studies*, but this was not widely known to Church members.) I was surprised and gratified when I received all kinds of compliments from people I knew as well as some that I did not know. The feedback I received from the editor of the magazine as well as other people indicated that it helped many who had heard about these various accounts but were unable to reconcile them until they saw an article that could put them together in a positive way. (James B. Allen, interview by Samuel Alonzo Dodge, July 27, 2009, Provo, UT)

In the brilliant light of this key event, almost everything else in Church history pales by comparison.

Fortunately, Joseph Smith spoke and wrote on several occasions about this sublime and formative experience now known as the First Vision. In addition to numerous circumstantial and secondary evidences that have expanded and supported our historical knowledge of this all-important event, ten accounts in thirteen documents have come down to modern readers from the hand or voice or time of Joseph Smith himself. Few events so central to the foundations of any of the world's religions are so informatively documented.

What do these ten accounts say? What can we learn from them? Who wrote them, and when and why were they written? Why are they not all the same? Are they historically accurate and credible? How well documented is the historical record concerning the First Vision? This overview gives answers to such questions as it analyzes and synthesizes these various accounts, the texts of which are presented in full in "The Earliest

Documented Accounts of Joseph Smith's First Vision," by Dean C. Jessee.[3]

Serious historical interest in gathering and studying the First Vision accounts began in 1965 when Paul Cheesman, a graduate student at Brigham Young University, presented a gentle surprise to scholars studying Mormonism by including in his master's thesis an account of Joseph Smith's First Vision that was largely unknown at that time.[4] What made the new discovery significant was the fact that most people had supposed that the Manuscript History of Joseph Smith, formally begun in 1838, was the first place where the Prophet had committed his remarkable experience to writing. Cheesman's master's thesis demonstrated that an account of the First Vision had, in fact, been recorded in 1832.

In the wake of that find, historians both inside and outside the Church took new interest in Joseph Smith's testimony. Shortly after the 1832 narrative was discovered, another account from 1835, also predating the 1838 Manuscript History, came to light; it was published in 1966.[5] Three years later, Dean Jessee's article detailing four texts of First Vision accounts (1832, printed versions of the 1835 journal entries, and the 1838 manuscript) appeared in *BYU Studies*.[6] In addition, other scholars in the late 1960s began to examine the setting of the vision, seeking to determine the extent to which the events described by Joseph Smith could be verified by other contemporary sources.[7] Mormon historiography thus entered a new era of documentary research as more historical sources needed to be examined and as many outstanding scholars published insightful results from their research.[8] To promote popular awareness and understanding, open treatments of these multiple accounts appeared in the *Improvement Era* and the *Ensign* in 1970, 1985, and 1996.[9] The wave of interest in these important historical documents continues today, with a tide of

> ### "This Young Man Is Telling the Truth"
>
> The first time I saw the 1832 account of the First Vision was when I was allowed to see a microfilm copy of the manuscript in the Church Historian's Office. I will never forget how I felt when I put my head into that microfilm reader, started rolling the film, and saw Joseph Smith's handwriting. As I read through that first written account of the vision, a powerful spiritual feeling came over me that I don't think I had ever experienced before, and it was not quite like anything I have experienced since. It said to me, "This young man is telling the truth!" It was an absolutely convincing handwritten story. It did not use very good grammar and did not have much punctuation. There were only a few very long sentences. But the power that was in it, including the feelings of a young man trying to express how he felt before he went into the grove to pray, was absolutely profound to me. The honesty and integrity of young Joseph Smith as he wrote of his experience only confirmed more strongly than ever before the testimony I already had of that sacred experience. (James B. Allen, interview by Samuel Alonzo Dodge, July 27, 2009, Provo, UT)

studies raising a number of questions and expressing various opinions on several issues.[10] But as interesting as the perspectives of these commentators may be, long after the scholars' personal conclusions have become obscure, the ten basic accounts will rightfully remain the focus of attention among serious investigators and diligent enquirers.

Understanding the Differences in the Accounts

Whenever new historical information is published, a host of questions demand answers, and the disclosure that Joseph Smith told his story more than once was no exception. Scholars asked whether the Prophet's description of his experience squares with other known historical events, to what degree the various accounts are consistent with each other, and how one might explain the differences.

Several factors undoubtedly affected the nature of each of Joseph Smith's accounts: (1) the timing of his narrations, including his age and recent experiences at the time a particular account was given; (2) the circumstances under which he gave each account, including any special purposes he may have had in mind for each particular audience; (3) the possible literary influences of those who wrote for him as his scribes or who reported his words (namely Levi Richards, David Nye White, and Alexander Neibaur); and (4) the extent to which versions written by others (namely Orson Pratt and Orson Hyde) may have emphasized points that most impressed them personally, thus making each version different.

One would hardly expect to find every account to be precisely alike. Obviously, people answer a simple question such as "What happened at the soccer game?" differently depending on who has asked the question. If a man's teenage son, who happened to be a soccer fanatic, were to ask his father this question, the father would know that the son wanted to know who scored which goals and how many players were red-carded. If the man's wife, who had no interest in soccer, were to ask such a question, however, he might know to tell her who he met on the sidelines and if he had yelled too much. Only after such a question has been asked by a number of people and answered with each inquisitor's interests in mind does a full picture of the event begin to emerge.

So it is with the First Vision accounts. It is fortunate that these reports come from a wide variety of circumstances, for no single account tells the whole story. At the same time, all the details in each of the accounts add significantly to the entire picture. The purpose of the following study is to identify the nature of each of these accounts and to examine the details they each provide in order to explain the differences and accentuate the consistency that exists among them.

Actually, the differences in the accounts may be grossly overemphasized, for the truth is that there is wide and credible agreement in detail among them all. Another impressive fact is that the 1832 version, which was the first to be recorded, is very comprehensive. This early narrative includes the essential elements of the more carefully prepared Manuscript History and contains more additional details than any other source. When all the accounts are combined, only a couple of details call for explanation, as given below.

Joseph Smith's Initial Audiences

One of the first steps in reading and understanding these ten historical accounts is to appreciate the various audiences that Joseph Smith had in mind as he wrote or spoke of this overwhelming experience. Processing the meanings and appreciating the implications of that life-changing event cannot have been a short or simple task for him. The vision served as a guiding star throughout his life, a star on which he often took his bearings, no matter his surroundings or circumstances.

Apparently Joseph Smith did not speak often of the First Vision in his teenage years. As he himself understandably said, he kept most of these things to himself and pondered them in his heart. His first audience was his mother, Lucy Mack Smith. Returning to the family log home shortly after his experience in the Sacred Grove, he told his mother, perhaps among other things, that he had learned "that Presbyterianism is not true" (Joseph Smith—History 1:20), as he noted in an addition to the manuscript of his history in 1842.[11] This was an understandable, yet courageous, thing for a young boy to emphasize to his mother, who had recently converted to Presbyterianism.

How much he told in those early years is unknown. Apparently he was judicious and cautious about telling all.

Indeed, the hostile reactions of clergy and the violent opposition from neighbors would have been enough to deter any boy in his midteens. As Joseph stated in his 1838 account, dictated about eighteen or nineteen years after the following reactions occurred, one Methodist preacher responded "with great contempt" when Joseph gave him "an account of the vision" which he had had (Joseph Smith—History 1:21). Joseph soon found that whenever he told his story, it "excited a great deal of prejudice . . . and was the cause of great persecution, which continued to increase. . . . [I continued] to attract the attention of the great ones of the most popular sects of the day, and in a manner to create in them a spirit of the most bitter persecution and reviling" (vv. 22–23).

Indeed, there is no contemporary evidence (that is, documents from the 1820s) to show that Joseph Smith told his story very widely in 1820; and it is not clear, even from his own accounts, how long he continued to tell it. With the reception he apparently received, it was probably not very long. The lack of evidence is not surprising, however, for even if certain ministers warned people not to believe young Joseph, they were also preoccupied with many other things that to them were more important. Since this was a time when many were claiming spiritual experiences, the claims of a fourteen-year-old boy were hardly something the ministers would record. Nor would such a youth have much likelihood of finding his way into the newspapers or diaries of the time, even though he later said that all the "great ones" were against him. To a young boy, the rejection of such an experience by those whom he respected would have been most frustrating, and he would tend to emphasize this frustration as he told of the experience in later years.

In the hostile environment during the fledgling years of the Restoration, even after the Church was first organized, Joseph apparently did not relate the account of his First Vision very widely, for neither the earliest Latter-day Saint nor regional

> ### COHERENT, CREDIBLE, AND CONSISTENT
> These accounts are coherent, credible, and more consistent than some people have surmised. With the full record in view, one sees that Joseph Smith shared his vision experience with intimate groups, the general public, and newspapermen, and he did so spontaneously at their request. The details supplied by each of these accounts add understanding and enhance the credibility of the Prophet's story, as he addressed the particular interests and needs of various audiences. (John W. Welch, interview by Samuel Alonzo Dodge, July 27, 2009, Provo, UT)

publications of the 1830s carried accounts of it.[12] Although early Church literature included several clear allusions to the First Vision,[13] none of these brief references gave specific details. However, the *Reflector*, a contemporary newspaper published in Palmyra, New York, confirms that at least by 1831, those in the community had heard allusions to Joseph Smith's vision (and an indication of the criticism he continued to receive). On February 14, 1831, the clearly anti-Mormon publisher reported on news of the Mormons in Ohio. Joseph Smith, he said, claimed to have received a "commission from God" to establish a religion, and those who would not submit to his authority "would speedily be destroyed." Further, the publisher reported, Joseph Smith's followers affirmed that he "had seen God frequently and personally."[14] While this report did not refer specifically to the First Vision, it is significant that members of the community had at least heard of the Latter-day Saint belief that God had appeared to their leader and that this belief was used as part of the continuing denunciation of the Church.

Because of the scant evidence of the vision in early publications, one writer prematurely suggested in 1945 that Joseph Smith did not even "make up" the story until 1835 or later.[15] That view clearly may be dismissed, for we now know that the Prophet wrote his first account of this vision in 1832. Beginning at least as early as spring 1835, and continuing until his death in

1844, he felt more confident in openly describing his experience to friends, converts, inquisitive visitors, faithful congregations, the public at large, dignitaries, and publishers.

The Audiences for Joseph Smith's Surviving Accounts

With this background in mind, it becomes all the more evident that each document that preserves a contemporary account of the Prophet's First Vision was directed toward a particular audience. Striving to understand the objective that Joseph Smith had in mind as he communicated with each audience helps today's readers appreciate the particular details uniquely conveyed in each of these statements. Editorial marks include angle brackets < > to indicate insertions made by the author of the document. Strikeouts are shown by ~~strikeouts~~. Brackets [ ] indicate editorial comments. Any underlining is reproduced from the original document.

The 1832 account. This important account was written in the second half of 1832, a time when the Church was very small, still only a few hundred members. It is an intimate, personal statement, preserved in the handwriting of Joseph Smith and composed when he was only twenty-six years old.

Significantly, LDS scholars have noted that the language of this first effort to write the story of the First Vision is somewhat reflective of the revivalistic language of the time.[16] This seems only natural, given Joseph Smith's likely memory of attending revivalistic meetings in his youth and probably hearing intensive revival-type preaching that vividly reminded listeners of their sinful nature. In this context, it is not surprising that the 1832 account should strongly emphasize his private feelings, his mourning for his own sins, his exclamation of awe before God, and the individual forgiveness and personal guidance that he received from the Savior as part of the First Vision experience. Having been commanded repeatedly to "say nothing but repentance unto this generation" (D&C 6:9; 11:9; see also 14:8; 19:21), he strongly emphasized his own experience in seeking and obtaining forgiveness.

Joseph also told how a pillar of light came down upon him, how he was filled with the Spirit of God, how the heavens were opened before him, and how he saw and conversed with the Lord, who said to him in the first person, "I was crucifyed for the world that all those who believe on my name may have Eternal life." Precise identifying details or descriptions of externalities are infrequent amidst the rapture of this very personal account. Indeed, Joseph uniquely introduced the vision here by affirming that God "seeketh such to worship him as worship him in spirit and in truth," echoing the New Testament text that "true worshippers shall worship the Father in spirit and in truth" (John 4:23); and, in direct fulfillment of this personal requirement, Joseph said that, as the pillar of light came to rest upon him, "I was filled with the spirit of God."

It is doubtful that the 1832 manuscript was planned for straight publication, at least not in the unpolished form in which it survives. It seems, rather, to have been an early and fervent effort to express, for the benefit of already faithful members of the Church, the Prophet's youthful religious feelings and the powerful spiritual impact that the First Vision had upon him personally. The Church was hardly over two years old at this time, and Joseph had already acted upon the commandment that the Church should begin keeping such historical records.[17] He was successfully gathering faithful followers such as Sidney Rigdon, Frederick G. Williams, Newel K. Whitney, Brigham Young, Parley P. Pratt, William E. McLellin, and Charles C. Rich. As Joseph Smith sat down to write at this time, he could look back on the amazing publication of the Book of Mormon, the restoration of the priesthood, the successful relocation of the Church from New York to Ohio, and other profound events in the promising rise of the Church. His mind reflected on the truly "marvilous experience" and "mighty acts" that his own remarkable life had already enjoyed, and this early account is a powerful expression of how it all began.

In many but not all respects, the year 1832 was good for Joseph Smith, and the 1832 account reflects the positive prospects of this time. Work on the translation of the Bible was progressing smoothly. Eighteen revelations would be received that year, including the major sections 76, 84, and 88 of the Doctrine and Covenants. Missionary work was successfully going forth as several of the brethren had answered calls to serve. Joseph had survived a painful tarring and feathering in March in Hiram, Ohio, but he had traveled successfully to Missouri, the second center of gathering, and returned at the end of July. In October he would travel to Manhattan; and in November, to Albany, New York, and Boston, Massachusetts. He returned on November 6, the joyous day on which his son Joseph Smith III was born. Sometime between the end of July and November, the Prophet found time to begin writing his history. His pages exude an optimistic tone, making no mention of the dark struggles or persecutions that he had experienced during and after the First Vision.

The 1835 accounts. The entry in Joseph Smith's journal for November 9, 1835, tells how he explained his early experiences to Robert Matthias, a curious visitor in Kirtland, Ohio, who claimed to be a Jewish minister called Joshua. His appearance was "some thing singular." He had a grey beard; was about fifty to fifty-five years old; was slender; wore a green coat, pantaloons, and a black fur hat and frequently shut his eyes "with a scowl" when he spoke. Warren Parrish, the Prophet's scribe, recorded the interview as part of the Prophet's daily record. Parrish was necessarily selective in remembering and choosing the points that he included.

Speaking to a total stranger, Joseph's conversation on this occasion tended to deal with objective details rather than intimate feelings. This account is plain, bold, and to the point. We are told that the Prophet remarked "upon the subject of Religion" and spoke "concerning the Bible" (laying a broad foundation for belief), that he then spoke about "the circumstances connected with the coming forth of the book of Mormon" (apparently not saying much about the specific details), and that he focused on his concern about "matters that involve eternal consequ[e]nces" (formulating his anxiety about salvation in generic terms, with which a person of any religious persuasion, Jewish or Christian or other, could identify). This account only briefly alludes to the contention that had arisen among the Protestant sects, simply indicating that Joseph did not know "who was right or who was wrong." Squabbles between Christian ministers would have been of little interest to a Jew. Instead, Joseph turned directly in this narration to the supernatural opposition that soon impeded his petition: his swollen tongue and the alarming sound like some person walking toward him. A Jewish minister would have related to powers of religious opposition such as these. (Ironically, two days later, Joseph would invite Joshua to leave Kirtland, as his doctrines were of the devil.)

Joseph then went on to say in this 1835 narrative that "a personage appeard" in the midst of the pillar of fire that rested above his head and that "another personage soon appeard like unto the first." He (the second personage?) said, "Thy sins are forgiven," and one of them testified that "Jesus Christ is the Son of God." Terms such as "pillar of fire" (as with Moses and Israel in the wilderness, Exodus 13:21) and "like unto" (see Deuteronomy 18:18) would have resonated with Jewish expectations concerning divine manifestations; and the withholding of any mention of a divine name in connection with the Supreme One, together with the mention of "many angels in this vision," would have comported with Jewish sensitivities. Yet the clear assertion of the presence of two divine beings and the unambiguous testimony that Jesus Christ is the Son of God were bold declarations for the relatively young Church leader (not yet thirty years old) to deliver to a listener whom he thought was Jewish.

Three days after dismissing Joshua, on November 14, Joseph told his story to yet another visitor, Erastus Holmes, who wanted to learn about the establishment of the Church and "to be instructed more perfectly in [its] doctrine." The brief journal entry shows that Joseph spoke openly about "the first visitation of Angels which was when I was about 14. years old," other visitations, the Book of Mormon, and the progress of the Church. These were the subjects about which Erastus had asked. Exactly what Joseph said is not reported, but the reference to the visitation of angels suggests that he most likely told Holmes much the same thing that he told Robert Matthias.

This was an opportune time in the Prophet's life for him to be speaking openly about his experiences. In a change from previous years, people were now coming to him and inquiring about the Church. The Quorum of the Twelve Apostles had been organized in February and had gone together on a mission to New England, returning in September. New revelation was coming forth in the form of the Book of Abraham, which Joseph began translating in July and worked on through the fall. The first edition of the Doctrine and Covenants had been published to the world in October, with twelve witnesses resolutely attesting to its divine inspiration. Joseph was meeting regularly with the School of the Prophets. The Kirtland Temple was nearing completion, its dedication only a few months away. In this context, Joseph spoke confidently about the First Vision throughout the year. He also allowed his personal journal with its account of the vision to be copied into the historical record of the Church.

The 1838–39 account. This account is from Joseph Smith's Manuscript History and is the source for the version of the First Vision published in the *Times and Seasons* in 1842 and later in the Pearl of Great Price.[18] The Prophet began working on this history on April 27, 1838, and his journal records that the First Presidency was engaged in this official work May 1–4. On September 3, James Mulholland began working for Joseph as a scribe, but their efforts were soon interrupted by the onset of the Missouri War, convoluted courtroom appearances, and Joseph's incarceration. After his release, Joseph recommenced work on the history on June 11, 1839, with Mulholland serving again as scribe and taking down the Prophet's testimony verbatim, as would a court reporter.

The pages covering the First Vision were apparently written in April–May 1838 and later copied into Joseph's Manuscript History before the end of 1839.[19] Whenever the writing occurred, it is evident that the Prophet intended this narrative to become the basic source for Church literature and that he had a special purpose in mind that does not seem as clear in the earlier renditions. Long the object of almost merciless public abuse, he now told his story in order to correct erroneous reports "put in circulation by evil disposed and designing persons" and "to disabuse the publick mind, and put all enquirers after truth into possession of the facts." With such a purpose in mind, to set the record straight once and for all, it is likely that Joseph would more carefully consider this account than he had the earlier versions.

Public abuse and persecution continued to plague Joseph Smith during this period of his life. Apostasy and the excommunication of several prominent Church leaders also took place. Serious opposition in Kirtland grew to the point that on

> **To Enhance Our Understanding**
> Some people have asked why it's important to study all the different accounts of the First Vision. Why don't we focus only on the one we have in the Pearl of Great Price and leave it at that? That is all right, of course. It's a wonderful account, and it's the official account we use when we are telling our story to the world. But as historians, if we want to know more about Joseph Smith and his feelings and emotions, if we want to know more about the nature of this young man, if perhaps we want to know some of things that he didn't put into the 1838–39 account but that he told to other people, it's important that we study all the accounts in order to enhance our understanding. (James B. Allen, interview by Samuel Alonzo Dodge, July 27, 2009, Provo, UT)

January 12, 1838, in the dead of winter, the Prophet and a large company of followers left Kirtland for Missouri, arriving at Far West on March 12. By October, troubles had erupted into violence, and in November, Joseph Smith was imprisoned in Liberty Jail. He finally arrived at Quincy, Illinois, on April 22, 1839, and only a few weeks later resumed work on his history where he had left off. In this context, it is no wonder that persecution, contention, competition, religious excitement, bad feelings, strife, contempt, bitterness, hatred, and rejection were recalled so vividly and stated so graphically in this 1838–39 account.

Vindicating the Saints also may have been on the Church leader's mind. If so, a full and detailed account was needed in order to be convincing—one that gave dates (1820), descriptions of the weather ("a beautiful clear day"), the time of day ("morning"), and precise quotations of conversations as well as the words of the Lord. A compelling and persuasive narrative was needed to hold and win the attention of a prejudiced public. Like Paul before Agrippa some twenty-five years after the appearance of the resurrected Lord on the road to Damascus, Joseph Smith testified unshakably of what he had seen some eighteen or nineteen years previous. "'Who am I that I can withstand

God,' or why does the world think to make me deny what I have actually seen?" he asked. By denying, he would "offend God and come under condemnation." But just as God had delivered Joseph from the unseen powers when he seemed "doomed to sudden destruction," God would sustain and deliver his Saints in their darkest hours of despair and affliction.

The 1842 account. The beginning of the year 1842 was the heart of Nauvoo's boom time. Property was selling; buildings were being constructed, immigrants were arriving, the Nauvoo Temple was under construction, a third printing of the Book of Mormon was under way, tithing was being collected, and political and religious difficulties were imperceptibly over the horizon. On February 15, 1842, Joseph became the editor of the *Times and Seasons*, involving him directly in the newspaper business.

An account of the First Vision written by the Prophet in 1842 was tied to the newspaper world in several ways. In the same year that his Manuscript History began to be published in the *Times and Seasons*, he was invited to prepare a brief history of the Church for publication by John Wentworth in the *Chicago Democrat*. The resulting letter containing this account was published in the *Times and Seasons* on March 1, 1842. In 1843, Joseph Smith provided Israel Daniel Rupp, a historian who planned to publish a compendium about religious denominations in the United States, with a history of the Church at Rupp's request. The First Vision account submitted to that publication is nearly identical to the account in the letter sent to Wentworth. Rupp published his work in 1844.

From its inception as part of the Wentworth letter, this account was meant for publication by the non-Mormon press. It has the characteristics that one would expect to find in a public relations statement: it is concise, straightforward, unadorned, informative, and matter-of-fact. Its content is reported in a strong, first-person voice: "I began," "I found," "I went," "I determined," "I had confidence," "I retired," "I was enwrapped," "I was expressly commanded." Of particular interest in the public sphere is the unique element in this account that none of the churches "was acknowledged of God as his church and kingdom." Concluding this brief release was an enticing "promise that the fulness of the gospel should at some future time be made known." The tone of this account of the First Vision is confident and self-assured, in keeping with the concluding prediction of the Wentworth letter that the restored gospel would visit every clime and sound in every ear.

The 1843 Levi Richards report. Levi Richards was a prominent citizen of Nauvoo who attended a lecture on June 11, 1843, and heard Joseph Smith tell about his First Vision. Richards's diary entry for that day contains a very brief summary of the Prophet's experience. Joseph's comments came after the lecture of Elder G. J. Adams, who told how "the everlasting covenant which was set up by Christ & the apostles had been broken." The Prophet then testified that, in the grove, he learned "that the Everlasting covenant was broken" and that he understood "the fulness of the Gospel from beginning to end," including "the order of the priesthood in all its ramifications" (the ordinances of baptism for the dead and the endowment had only recently been introduced). Richards was impressed by the confident testimony that "Earth & hell had opposed him & tryed to destroy him—but they had not done it & they <never would.>" This reference to opposition may have included the forces of evil in the grove as well as many other persecutions.

The 1843 David Nye White report. In summer 1843, David Nye White, the editor of the *Pittsburgh Weekly Gazette*, visited Joseph Smith in Nauvoo. White's report, which included an account of the First Vision as related to him by the Prophet, appeared in the *Gazette* on September 15 and was later reprinted in the *New York Spectator* on September 23. It reads as if Joseph Smith's words have been rephrased and paraphrased, making the account seem a bit odd, although obviously consistent with his authentic first-person narratives.[20]

The 1844 Alexander Neibaur report. An entry in the personal diary of Alexander Neibaur illustrates that the Prophet sometimes told the story to small, rather intimate groups. Born in Germany of Jewish parents, Neibaur was converted to the Church in England, where he practiced dentistry. He immigrated to Nauvoo in 1841, where he set up a dental practice and soon became an intimate friend of the Prophet and also taught German and Hebrew to Joseph and others. On May 24, 1844, Joseph told his sacred experience to Neibaur, who recorded it in his diary in the sincere, unpolished style that one would expect from a humble devotee not used to writing in English. A few unique, intimate details contained in this account, such as the description of God the Father ("light complexion blue eyes a piece of white cloth drawn over his shoulders his right arm bear"), bespeak the intimate setting of this narration by Joseph, in the privacy of his home, to his tutor.

The Audiences of Orson Pratt and Orson Hyde

Two additional accounts of the First Vision published during Joseph Smith's lifetime were prepared by members of the Quorum of the Twelve Apostles for inclusion in missionary pamphlets. As close associates of the Prophet, Orson Pratt and Orson Hyde undoubtedly heard the story directly from him and likely had early access to the official 1838–39 version. Their reports are close to that account in style and content, though both also adapted the basic story in ways that were suitable for and reflected their particular audiences, their interests, and their own literary proclivities.

The 1840 Orson Pratt report. In 1840, Orson Pratt of the Quorum of the Twelve published in Scotland a missionary tract entitled *A[n] Interesting Account of Several Remarkable Visions, and of the Late Discovery of Ancient American Records.* His narrative was similar to Joseph's 1838 account, except that it elaborated upon several details. Whether these were given to him by Joseph or whether he was using literary license is not known, but some of his additions find corroboration in other accounts as well.

As a person interested in science, Orson Pratt featured how Joseph was concerned about leaving matters of eternal consequence to "chance, or uncertainties," how problems "occurred to his mind," how he sought "certainty, and knowledge, of his own," and how the Epistle of James had brought him to see that "there was, not only, a possibility, but a probability; yea, more, a certainty, that he should obtain a knowledge." Pratt's detailed description of the light, its brightness and magnitude, its effect on the surrounding trees and "the whole wilderness, for some distance around," and Joseph's mind being "caught away, from the natural objects with which he was surrounded" provides the kinds of empirical data that a scientist would relish and that Scottish empiricism would appreciate.

The 1842 Orson Hyde report. Another member of the Twelve, Orson Hyde, published a missionary tract in Germany in 1842 entitled *Ein Ruf aus der Wüste, eine Stimme aus dem Schoose der Erde* (A Cry from the Wilderness, a Voice from the Dust of the Earth). This tract contained an account of the vision similar to Orson Pratt's account, much of it, in fact, having been translated directly from the earlier publication. To the rationalistic Germans, Hyde emphasized Joseph Smith's concern about basing his hopes not just on uncertainty but on "blind uncertainty," and Hyde averred that the Prophet had been endowed by nature "with a keen critical intellect and so he looked through the lens of reason and common sense and with pity and contempt" on the various "systems of religion." When the forces of evil beset the prayerful youth, the opposition came in the form of "doubts" and "inappropriate images" that filled his "mind," and in the end, Joseph was promised "the complete truth of the gospel." Germans also being known for their authoritarianism, Hyde added that the scripture gave "an authorization for him to solemnly call upon his creator."

Consolidating the Accounts

Mindful of such factors as why, when, where, and to whom the First Vision accounts were given, we turn to an examination of what these accounts actually say. Latter-day Saints believe that Joseph Smith was telling the truth each time he related his experience and that the scribes recorded his ideas as accurately and suitably as possible. Thus, a study of the combined accounts presents some fascinating new insights into the experience and personal development of the young prophet. Not only do we discover in each account more details about what happened both before and after he entered the Sacred Grove, but we also gain valuable insight into how these events affected him personally and helped him in his spiritual growth. What follows is an attempt to weave these accounts into a composite story of Joseph's sacred experience in order to show their collective value and consistency. In the explanations that follow, these accounts are considered. The 1835 account of the Prophet's comments to Erastus Holmes is not listed or discussed because of its brevity.[21] The 1835 journal entry is listed together with its restatement in a later history in column two, and the 1842 Wentworth letter and its virtually identical 1843 reprint are combined in column five. Then we list the 1838 account in Joseph Smith's Manuscript

Joseph Smith and his parents, brothers, and sisters lived in what is now Manchester Township in western New York. Because of the intense outpouring of religious enthusiasm that characterized this region in the early nineteenth century, it has been dubbed the "Burned-Over District." (Photo of replica of the Joseph Smith Sr. farmhouse by Brent R. Nordgren)

History, which has been excerpted in the Pearl of Great Price. We also list the contemporary secondary accounts. For a table presenting all of these details, see pp. 79–83 below.

Situating the Vision

In 1819, young Joseph Smith and his parents, brothers, and sisters lived in what is now Manchester Township in western New York. This region would later be dubbed the "Burned-Over District" because of the intense outpouring of religious enthusiasm that characterized it in the early nineteenth century.[22] While the 1843 White report simply states that Joseph Smith spoke of "a reformation among the different religious denominations in the neighborhood," and while the Neibaur diary briefly mentions "a Revival meeting," only the

1838 narrative gives any detail about the religious excitement that stirred young Joseph's interest. In this light, the question has arisen as to whether a general religious movement of the proportions described by the Prophet in the 1838 account actually took place around 1820 in his area and, if so, whether his description agrees with the known facts. It has even been argued, for example, that no such movement took place in the town of Palmyra in spring 1820, and that therefore Joseph's account is seriously flawed.[23]

The Prophet's words, however, do not present such a problem. The 1838 account merely says that the excitement began "sometime in the second year after our removal to Manchester," which could mean almost any time in 1819 or 1820. Further, his narrative does not specifically state that such a movement centered or even began in Palmyra. By 1819, the Smith family lived outside the village of Palmyra on a farm that was actually in the township (not village) of Manchester.[24] The phrase "in the place where we lived" could easily refer, in context, not to a specific town but rather to the general area.

In addition, this 1838 account referred to the "whole district of Country" being affected by the awakening, and this can be interpreted very broadly. Professor Milton Backman has demonstrated conclusively that there was considerable religious excitement in the general area of the Burned-Over District of western New York in 1819 and 1820 and that "spiritual quickenings" were particularly intense in 1819, as mentioned in Joseph's 1838 account. Indeed, itinerant preachers, camp meetings, intense spiritual experiences, and conversions were all common in the area, and in 1819–20 some sort of revival activity took place in at least ten towns within a twenty-mile radius of the Smith home.[25] Thus Joseph had ample opportunity to know of and become involved in camp meetings and other religious activities in the vicinity of his home during 1817, 1818, or 1819, and none of the accounts of his vision are inconsistent with these facts.

Whether he actually attended very many of these camp meetings is less clear. His 1838 narrative reports that his mind "at different times was greatly excited" because "the cry and tumult were so great and incessant," but the confusion and strife that troubled him so deeply probably extended into general religious discussions and were not limited to camp meetings as such. The Neibaur diary affirms that "the first call he had [came at (?)] a Revival meeting." Joseph's mother, brother, and sister "got Religion" on that occasion, and Joseph "wanted to feel & sho shout like the Rest but could feel nothing." The observation that general confusion rather than revival meetings alone caused his agitation would explain why most of the First Vision accounts make little mention of revivalist excitement.

Dating the Vision

Joseph Smith reached his fourteenth birthday on December 23, 1819. In the familiar 1838 First Vision account, he said that he was "at this time in my fifteenth year," and the Orson Hyde account uses these same words (meaning Joseph was fourteen years old). A few paragraphs later in the 1838 account, Joseph said, "I was an obscure boy only between fourteen and fifteen years of age <or thereabouts,>"[26] the last two words being inserted in the manuscript above the line, possibly at his direction, but not included when it was published in the *Times and Seasons* in 1842. The words "or thereabouts" should not be taken necessarily to contradict the previous statement of his age when the vision occurred, but, rather, simply as part of a very careful approach to writing history. As edited and then published in 1842, the account reflected what Joseph Smith intended the public to understand.

In three other accounts, Joseph simply said (or was reported to have said) that he was "about fourteen years old" when the First Vision was received, when God first revealed himself to him, "a mere boy" (White 1843; see also November 9 and 14, 1835); and the 1842 Wentworth letter account says that Joseph was "about fourteen years of age" when he began to reflect upon the importance of his soul's future state. These uses of the word "about" remind us that the validity of his experience does not hinge on knowing the precise day, month, or year on which that vision occurred, and in light of this uncertainty, it is interesting to note that the scientifically minded Orson Pratt allowed in 1840 that Joseph Smith was "somewhere about fourteen or fifteen" when his spiritual awakening began.

The account that cannot be squared exactly with his having been fourteen when the First Vision was received is the earliest draft, the 1832 narrative. There, Joseph Smith wrote that "at about the age of twelve years" his mind became concerned "with regard to the all important concerns" of his immortal soul. He then became aggrieved that the various denominations did not "adorn their profession by a holy walk" as required by the Bible, and he pondered in his heart many things concerning the darkness of the world for three years, "from the age of twelve years to fifteen," culminating with the vision in that year, as he says, when he was "in the 16th year of my age" (that is, fifteen years old). Here we learn that Joseph's personal spiritual concerns began earlier (at the age of twelve) than we might otherwise have supposed and that his discontent over the contentions, divisions, wickedness, and abominations around him grew over a period of two to three years. It is understandable that, in preparing his 1832 draft, he might have thought of those intense struggles as having lasted a year longer than they actually had.

After more careful reflection, he would consistently report that the answer came in his fifteenth year.

In sum, this examination leads to the conclusion that the First Vision, in all probability, occurred in spring 1820, when Joseph was fourteen years old. The preponderance of the evidence supports that conclusion.

Joseph Smith's Concerns

Joseph Smith's personal spiritual awakenings began at the age of twelve and grew over a period of about two or three years. Several issues, not just a single problem, concerned and perplexed him.

At first, his thoughts turned inward. He was concerned about the eternal welfare of his own soul, as he had become "convicted of [his] sins" (1832). He became almost overwhelmed with the awesomeness of the eternities (1832), and "he began seriously to reflect upon the necessity of being prepared for a future state of existence: but how, or in what way, to prepare himself, was a question, as yet, undetermined in his own mind: he perceived that it was a question of infinite importance, and that the salvation of his soul depended upon a correct understanding of the same" (Pratt 1840).

With so much religious activity going on around him, young Joseph Smith found himself influenced in many ways as he sought answers. He saw four members of his family join the Presbyterian Church, while his own "mind became somewhat partial toward the Methodist sect" (1838). It would not be inconsistent with any of these accounts to conclude that Joseph then became involved in the religious excitement known to have occurred in his area during summer or fall 1819, while he was thirteen years old. At first he desired but could not find the emotional experience he had witnessed in others, as he told Alexander Neibaur, but he continued his quest.

As Joseph struggled, more questions came to his mind. According to his earliest statement, this led to an intensive searching of the scriptures. For a period of time, he tried to evaluate the different denominations and found that they did not agree with what he saw in the scriptures. He determined that various churches had "apostatised from the true and liveing faith" (1832). He was shocked by the confusion, strife, insincerity, and bad feelings he found among those who professed to be religious. Such apprehensions about the world worked within him for several months. He became concerned with the "wicke[d]ness and abominations" of the world and came to mourn "for the sins of the world" as much as for his own sins (1832).

These concerns caused him to consider joining one of the various denominations. Here, however, as recorded in practically all the accounts,[27] he became disillusioned, especially with the fact that the ministers would contend so bitterly for converts. It became so bad, he wrote in 1838, that "great confusion and bad feeling ensued—priest contending against priest, and convert against convert; so that all their good feelings one for another, if they ever had any, were entirely lost in a strife of words and a contest about opinions" (Joseph Smith—History 1:6).

At this point, the youth became even more confused. He still wanted to join a church. When he finally decided to make it a matter of prayer, he had in mind specifically that he wanted to "know what Church to join" (White 1843). In looking at all the churches, he said, "I knew not who was right or who was wrong, but considered it of the first importance to me that I should be right" (History 1835). This burning question is, in fact, mentioned in all the accounts, excepting only Neibaur's short diary entry.

At the same time, young Joseph began to suspect that perhaps none of the churches were right. The first time he recorded the vision he declared that in searching the scriptures he "found that ~~mand~~ <mankind> did not come unto the Lord but that they had apostatised from the true and liveing faith and there was no society or denomination that built upon the gospel of Jesus Christ as recorded in the new testament" (1832). Later he explained his feelings this way: "I often said to myself, what is to be done? Who of all these parties are right? Or are they all wrong together?" (1838).[28] His youthful mind apparently still clung to the hope that one of the contending sects was "right," but at the same time he could not ignore the disturbing possibility that "the true and liveing faith" no longer existed (1832). Orson Hyde went so far as to write that "the hope of ever finding a sect or denomination that was in possession of unadulterated truth left him."[29]

Amid this war of words and feelings, the Prophet's mind was drawn especially to James 1:5. "If any of you lack wisdom," he read, "let him ask of God, that giveth to all men liberally, and upbraideth not; and it shall be given him." Joseph Smith said:

> Never did any passage of scripture come with more power to the heart of man than this did at this time to mine. It seemed to enter with great force into every feeling of my heart. I reflected on it again and again, knowing that if any person needed wisdom from God, I did....
>
> At length I came to the conclusion that I must either remain in darkness and confusion, or else I must do as James directs, that is, ask of God. (Joseph Smith—History 1:12–13)

The influence of this passage is mentioned explicitly in eight of the accounts, and it probably stands behind the 1832 account's affirmation that God is "no respecter to persons" as well.[30]

Joseph Smith's Quest and Struggle in the Grove

Joseph took this provocative scripture deeply to heart, being convinced by the scriptures of God's power and goodness (1832). Having been emboldened by "the lens of reason and common sense" that told him "that there was only one truth" (Hyde 1842), he did not want to rely on chance but to decide in the light of "positive and definite evidence" (Pratt 1840). The youthful Joseph decided then, for the first time in his life, to pray vocally about the matter (1835, 1838). After months of struggle, he finally knew the course he must follow, and sometime in spring 1820 he went "immediately" to a familiar spot in the woods near his home to make the attempt (White 1843).

After months of struggle, Joseph Smith finally knew the course he must follow, and sometime in spring 1820 he went "immediately" to a familiar spot in the woods near his home to make the attempt (White 1843). (Sacred Grove photo by Brent R. Nordgren)

The months of anguish had resulted in obvious spiritual maturity, and he had at least three serious and related questions on his mind as he bowed in fervent prayer: (1) he was concerned for his own salvation and sought forgiveness of his sins (1832); (2) he was concerned for the welfare of mankind in general, for, he said, "I felt to mourn for my own sins and for the sins of the world" (1832); and (3) he wanted to know which, if any, of the churches was right, and which he should join.

No one knows how long young Joseph remained in the grove, but it is clear that before the object of his prayer was accomplished he had a long, desperate, and perhaps almost fatal struggle with the forces of evil from the unseen world. His first effort to pray was fruitless, for, he said, "immediately I was <siezed> upon by some power which entirely overcame me and <had> such astonishing influence over me as to bind my tongue so that I could not speak" (1838). He later told his friends that his tongue seemed swollen in his mouth, so much so that he could not utter a word (1835, 1844).

As he struggled to pray, several strange things happened. Unwanted and distracting thoughts ran through his mind: "The adversary then made several strenuous efforts to cool his ardent soul. He filled his mind with doubts and brought to mind all manner of inappropriate images to prevent him from obtaining the object of his endeavors" (Hyde 1842).

At one point, Joseph said, "I heard a noise behind me like some one walking towards me: I strove again to pray, but could not; the noise of walking seemed to draw nearer; I sprang upon my feet and looked round, but saw no person, or thing that was calculated to produce the noise of walking" (History 1835).

During the struggle, "thick darkness" (1838) or a "dark cloud" (Hyde 1842) seemed to gather around him. He was "severely tempted by the powers of darkness" (Pratt 1840), and he felt that he was "doomed to sudden destruction" and must abandon himself "to the power of some actual being from the unseen world" (1838). It was more of a struggle, more of an agony, than readers may stop to think about. This experience left a deep, indelible impression on Joseph Smith.

What Joseph Smith Saw

Despite this alarm, Joseph was able to gather enough inner strength to continue his fervent supplication and to call upon God for deliverance. It was then that he saw overhead "a piller of ~~fire~~ light" (1832). Every account, except for Richards, mentions "light," two calling it "fire." Three accounts use the word "pillar" (1832, 1835, 1838), and three state that it shone "above the brightness of the sun" (1832, 1838; see also Wentworth Letter 1842). Pratt simply called it "glorious."

It seemed to begin far away, in the heavens (1840), gradually descending (1838, 1840, 1844) above his head (1835, 1838), even increasing in brightness so that "by the time that it reached the tops of the trees, the whole wilderness, for some distance around, was illuminated in a most glorious and brilliant manner. He expected to have seen the leaves and boughs of the trees consumed, as soon as the light came in contact with them. . . . It continued descending, slowly, until it rested upon the earth, and he was enveloped in the midst of it" (1840).

The light first rested upon the trees (1840, 1844); then it seemed that flames spread all around, but nothing was consumed (1835). When the light "rested upon the earth" (1840), it rested upon Joseph, surrounding or enveloping him in light, as five accounts state (1832, 1835, 1838, 1840, 1844).

As soon as the light had come to rest, Joseph felt himself freed from his spiritual enemy, and as the light rested upon him, he was "filled with the spirit of god and the <Lord> opened the heavens upon me" (1832). As Elder Pratt described later, "When it first came upon him, it produced a peculiar sensation throughout his whole system; and, immediately, his mind was caught away, from the natural objects with which he was surrounded; and he was enwrapped in a heavenly vision" (1840), and Elder Hyde explained that the natural world was excluded so that he would be open to heavenly things (Hyde 1842). Joseph Smith simply described it as a "heavenly vision" (Wentworth Letter 1842).

According to three of the First Vision accounts, Joseph saw within the light a single personage, who was soon joined by a second personage. They seemed to stand above him in the air, and their own "brightness and glory" defied all description (1838). There is no doubt that the Prophet intended to convey the message that they were the Father and the Son. (© Gary L. Kapp, The Heavens Were Opened)

According to three of the First Vision accounts, Joseph then saw within the light a single personage, who was soon joined by a second personage (1835, White 1843, 1844). Four of the accounts (1838, 1840, Wentworth Letter 1842, Hyde 1842) simply report that Joseph beheld two personages, without saying whether they both appeared at the same time or one and then the other. Four accounts make the additional point that the two beings were like each other or "exactly resembled each other in features, and likeness" (Wentworth Letter 1842; see also 1835, 1840, Hyde 1842). They seemed to stand above him in the air, and their own "brightness and glory" defied all description (1838). There is no doubt that the Prophet intended to convey the message that they were the Father and the Son.

Because the 1832 account does not explicitly say that two beings were present in the vision, some people have wondered, did Joseph Smith see two personages or one? Did he alter his story as time went on?[31] With a little explanation, these questions can be answered. First, it is clear that the consensus of the First Vision accounts is that two personages appeared. While the brief 1843 Richards report leaves out many details, including any specific mention of God's appearance, all of the other accounts besides the 1832 speak clearly of two divine beings. Second, the remaining account, the 1832 narrative, actually suggests that the vision progressed in two stages: first, Joseph "was filled with the spirit of god and the <Lord> opened the heavens upon me," and second, he "saw the Lord and he spake unto me." The second stage clearly refers to Jesus Christ, who identifies himself as the one who was crucified. Though not explicitly stated, the initial mention of the Spirit of God and the Lord may have reference to the presence of God the Father and his opening of this vision, since it is clear in all the other accounts that the vision was opened by God, who then introduced his Son.[32] To be sure, the main point of emphasis, especially in the official 1838 account, was that "I had actualy seen a light and in the midst of that light I saw two personages, and they did in reality speak <un>to me, or one of them did." Finally, remembering that the 1832 manuscript was an unpolished effort to record the spiritual impact of the vision on him, and that the main content of the heavenly message was delivered by the Son, it is understandable that the Prophet simply emphasized the Lord in the 1832 account. Thus, nothing precludes the possibility that two beings were present.

The various versions of the event do not contradict each other regarding the number of personages, even though they emphasize different ideas and details. Similarly, in two of his accounts, Joseph mentions that he saw "Angels" or "many angels in this vision" (November 9 and 14, 1835), a point that does not contradict but rather supplements the other accounts and confirms that multiple beings were involved.

What Joseph Smith Heard

The messages and information received by Joseph as the vision progressed were all that a person with his concerns could ask for and more. As he listened, he was told several things. Exactly how many things were said we do not know, but the cumulative information from all these accounts presents a clear and consistent collection that could have taken several minutes to deliver.

First in importance, Joseph received an unmistakable knowledge of the reality of Christ, as one of the two personages pointed to the other and said, "This is my beloved Son, Hear him" (1838; see also White 1843 and 1844). Later in the vision, the Savior himself declared, "Behold I am the Lord of glory I was crucifyed for the world that all those who believe on my name may have Eternal life" (1832). From this, Joseph learned that eternal life was possible for all who truly believe on the name of Jesus Christ.

Second, he learned that the Father and the Son knew him personally, for one of them (seemingly the Son) called him intimately by name, "Joseph <my son>," and told him, "Thy sins are forgiven thee" (1832; see also November 9, 1835). Thus purified and filled with the Spirit of God, Joseph Smith was able to stand in the presence of God and behold his glory.

Third, young Joseph was encouraged to go his way and to keep the commandments.

Fourth, undoubtedly astonished at all that was happening, Joseph gained possession of himself and asked the main questions that were on his mind: "which of all the sects was right" and which he should join (1838). Neibaur recalled that Joseph asked, "Must I join the Methodist Church[?]" In response, he was informed that he should join none of them, for all were wrong and none was doing good.

Fifth, he learned something more about the current state of Christianity as the Lord confirmed Joseph's personal conclusion, reached through study of the scriptures, about the Great Apostasy, namely that all churches had gone astray. Even before going into the grove, he understood that the gospel had been preached originally in truth and purity, but that the world had strayed from it. The 1832 account adds to that understanding with these words spoken by the Lord: "The world lieth in sin and at this time and none doeth good no not one they have turned asside from the gospel and keep not <my> commandments they draw near to me with their lips while their hearts are far from me." Levi Richards (1843) reported Joseph Smith as saying he was told "that none of them were right, that they were all wrong, & that the Everlasting covenant was broken." Alexander Neibaur emphasized this same point: "They are not my People, all have gone astray there is none that doeth good no not one, but this is my Beloved son harken ye him."

Sixth, he was instructed that the causes and manifestations of the Apostasy were to be found in sin, corruption, and the teaching of false doctrine. Joseph was told "that all the religious denominations were believing in incorrect doctrines; and, consequently, that none of them was acknowledged of God, as his church and kingdom" (1840), and he was expressly commanded a second time not to join with them (1838). The speaking personage pointedly warned young Joseph that the churches "were all wrong, and . . . all their Creeds were an abomination in his sight," explaining further that some professors of religion "were all Corrupt, that 'they draw near to me with their lips but their hearts are far from me, They teach for doctrines the commandments of men, having a form of Godliness but they deny the power thereof'" (1838). While the 1838 account is the only one that mentions the "Creeds" explicitly, most of the accounts contain equally unambiguous words to the effect that the churches of his day had "erred in doctrine" (Hyde 1842). The word "abomination" also appears exclusively in the 1838 account as one of the words used by the Savior.[33] This biblical term has a range of meanings, all pointing to any impure practices that take people away from God.[34]

Seventh, the Prophet learned that God was not the author of the confusion and contention in the lives of those who professed to be followers of Christ. It was one thing for people to disagree in civility and kindness while pondering various inscrutable mysteries of divine truth; it was another thing for chaos and conflict to reign. At the age of twelve, Joseph was pierced to the soul by "the contentions and divi[si]ons the wicke[d]ness and abominations and the darkness which pervaded the of the minds of mankind" (1832). In the 1835 history, he similarly spoke of "being wrought up in my mind respecting the subject of Religion, and looking at the different systems taught the children of men." Being torn by the "tumult . . . so great

> **FOUNDATIONAL DOCUMENTS**
> The value of these documents is immeasurable. In the history of world religions, no other body of foundational documentation rivals it for its immediacy and size. Think, for example, how few documents have survived from the time of Mohammed. And what would New Testament scholars give for a single letter from Mary about the raising of Lazarus? Or a diary entry by someone who was present when Jesus was baptized by John in the Jordan River? Or a brief report from Peter to the Twelve about what he had just seen and heard on the Mount of Transfiguration? In the case of Joseph Smith and the key events of the Restoration, we enjoy, by comparison, an overwhelming abundance. (John W. Welch, interview by Samuel Alonzo Dodge, July 27, 2009, Provo, UT)

and incessant" as various professors of religion "used all their powers of either reason or sophistry to prove their errors, or at least to make the people think they were in error" (1838), Joseph turned to the Lord for mercy and help.

Eighth, he learned that God was not pleased with the situation in the world. In fact, the Lord said, "Mine anger is kindling against the inhabitants of the earth" (1832).

Ninth, Joseph learned that the Second Coming of the Lord was close at hand. "And lo I come quickly as it [is] written of me in the cloud <clothed> in the glory of my Father" (1832).

Finally, Joseph received a promise that "the fulness of the gospel should at some future time be made known unto me" (Wentworth Letter 1842). Elder Hyde stated, "He was further commanded, to wait patiently until some future time, when the true doctrine of Christ and the complete truth of the gospel would be revealed to him" (Hyde 1842). This promise of further revelation would seem to indicate Joseph Smith's initial calling as a prophet of God.

In addition, Joseph was told "many other things" that he was unable to write (1838).

Aftermath of the Vision

According to scripture, it is impossible for any person to behold Deity with natural eyes (see John 1:18; D&C 67:10–13; Moses 1:2). Joseph Smith made it clear that this profound experience transcended his physical senses (Wentworth Letter 1842; see also Pratt 1840, Hyde 1842) and that it had an exhausting effect upon him. "When I came to myself again," he wrote in 1838, "I found myself lying on <my> back looking up into Heaven," and he told Alexander Neibaur that he endeavored to rise but felt uncommonly feeble.

The effect of this vision on the mind of the youthful prophet was great. After all his earlier confusion, he now felt comforted, and his mind was left "in a state of calmness and peace, indescribable" (Pratt 1840; see also Hyde 1842). Joseph said in his earliest account, "My soul was filled with love and for many days I could rejoice with great Joy and the Lord was with me" (1832). Having been commanded to be patient, he pondered these things in his heart, and he felt that the Lord was with him (1832).

This early account best expresses the tender feelings that must have overwhelmed young Joseph. It is little wonder that he should wish to tell his experience to friends and acquaintances, and one can sense his profound disappointment when, as he stated in the same account, he "could find none that would believe the hevnly vision" (1832). Later he described in detail the immediate unfriendly reception he received upon telling of the vision. He was particularly disappointed at the surprising reaction of a Methodist preacher who "treated my communication not only lightly but with great contempt, saying it was all of the Devil, that there was no such thing as visions or revelations in these days, that all such things had ceased with the apostles and that there never would be any more of them" (1838).

It seemed to young Joseph that he was being attacked from all sides:

> I soon found however that my telling the story had excited a great deal of prejudice against me among professors of religion and was the cause of great persecution which continued to increase and though I was an obscure boy only between fourteen and fifteen years of age <or thereabouts,> and my circumstances in life such as to make a boy of no consequence in the world, yet men of high standing would take notice sufficient~~ly~~ to excite the public mind against me and create a hot persecution, and this was common <among> all the sects: all united to persecute me. (1838)

Conclusion

This chapter does not presume, of course, to provide all the details of what happened at the time of Joseph Smith's First Vision. Joseph himself testified that "many other things did he say unto me, which I cannot write at this time" (Joseph Smith—History 1:20). Nor does this discussion presume to answer all the questions that may be raised about the meaning and implications of the vision. It has simply demonstrated that the account was repeated several times and on several different occasions, even by the Prophet, and that although each narrative emphasizes different ideas and events, none is incompatible with other accounts. There is, in fact, striking consistency throughout the narratives; they combine impressively to give a consistent and coherent picture. A high percentage of the elements shown in the table sporadically appear in multiple accounts, showing a high degree of independent, cumulative corroboration among these accounts.

We offer this information in hopes that it will correct misinformation that has been put in circulation about the authorship, variations, historicity, publications, awareness, and reception of

Joseph Smith's First Vision. Despite the impossibility of providing all the details and answering all conceivable questions,[35] we believe that the documentary evidence amply shows that the First Vision can in truth become meaningful in a personal way when one seeks, as Joseph Smith sought, to reach God through earnest and sincere supplication, seeking to worship him in spirit, righteousness, and truth.

The Various Elements of Joseph Smith's
First Vision, as Recorded or Clearly Implied
in the Contemporary Accounts

	1832 Smith	1835 Smith	1838 Smith	1840 Pratt	1842 and 1843 Smith	1842 Hyde	1843 Richards	1843 White	1844 Neibaur
Situating the Vision									
Joseph's age 14 or about 14		•	•	•	•	•		•	
Joseph's age 15 or about 15	•			•					
Religious excitement of the period			•					•	•
Wanted to get religion									•
Joseph's concern for his soul (or future state)	•	•		•	•	•			
His quest for forgiveness of sin	•								
Joseph's concern for mankind in general	•								
Confusion or strife among denominations	•	•	•	•	•	•			
Insincerity and bad feelings among religionists			•		•				

	1832 Smith	1835 Smith	1838 Smith	1840 Pratt	1842 and 1843 Smith	1842 Hyde	1843 Richards	1843 White	1844 Neibaur
No church built or set up as in New Testament	•						•		
His quest to know which church (if any) was right	•	•	•	•	•	•	•	•	
Convinced of God's goodness and greatness	•					•			
Reason told him there was only one truth				•	•	•			
All could not be right, God not author of confusion					•				
Not to rely on chance but positive evidence				•		•			
His searching the scriptures, James 1:5	*	•	•	•	•	•		•	•
He prayed	•		•				•	•	•
He prayed mightily or fervently		•		•	•	•			
Cried for mercy	•								
Called on God for the first time			•	•					
Realized no church was built on scriptural gospel	•					•			
Wanted to know which church was right		•	•	•	•		•	•	
Heard footsteps		•							
Inability to speak, tongue swollen or bound		•	•						•

	1832 Smith	1835 Smith	1838 Smith	1840 Pratt	1842 and 1843 Smith	1842 Hyde	1843 Richards	1843 White	1844 Neibaur
Beset by doubts and strange images						•			
Tempted or beset by dark powers			•	•					
Thick darkness or cloud			•			•			
Exerted all powers			•						
Prayed again		•	•	•		•			
Felt easier									•
What Joseph Saw and Heard									
Appearance of light or pillar of light	•		•	•	•			•	
Appearance of fire or pillar of fire		•							•
Light brighter than the sun	•		•		•				
Above his head		•	•						
Light descended from above	•		•	•					•
Gradually			•	•					•
Flame rested on trees				•					•
Light rested on Joseph	•	•	•	•					•
Light all around		•		•	•				
First one personage in pillar, then another	†	•						•	•
Two personages			•	•	•	•			
Exactly like each other		•		•	•	•			

	1832 Smith	1835 Smith	1838 Smith	1840 Pratt	1842 and 1843 Smith	1842 Hyde	1843 Richards	1843 White	1844 Neibaur
Glory defies description			•	•	•	•		•	
Appearance of many angels		•							
Joseph asks which church to join or which is right			•					•	•
Father introduced or testified of the Son		•	•					•	•
Joseph called by name	•		•						
Your prayers are answered, special blessing to be given						•			
Thy sins are forgiven	•	•		•					
Go thy way, keep the commandments	•								
Jesus described himself	•								
Join no church			•			•		•	
Do not join Methodists									•
All wrong, none right	•		•						•
None do good	•								•
All in sin, gone astray, broken everlasting covenant	•						•		•
Certain professors were corrupt			•						
Creeds are an abomination			•						
All churches teach false doctrine				•	•	•			
Draw near with lips only	•		•						

	1832 Smith	1835 Smith	1838 Smith	1840 Pratt	1842 and 1843 Smith	1842 Hyde	1843 Richards	1843 White	1844 Neibaur
Form of godliness but deny the power thereof			•						
Forbidden again to join any church			•	•					
None acknowledged as his church, kingdom, people				•	•	•			•
Lord angry, comes quickly	•								
Gospel fullness promised				•	•	•			
THE AFTERMATH									
Lying on his back			•						
Uncommonly feeble									•
Joseph filled with love	•								
Joseph filled with joy	•	•							
Joseph filled with calmness, comfort, peace					•		•		•
Pondered in heart	•								
Lord was with Joseph	•								
Tried to get others to believe the story	•		•					•	•
Many tried to oppose Joseph unsuccessfully			•				•	•	

* Includes the phrase "no respecter of persons," a principle reflected in James 1:5.
† Possibly implied; see discussion on pp. 72–73 above.

Notes

1. James B. Allen, "Eight Contemporary Accounts of Joseph Smith's First Vision—What Do We Learn from Them?," *Improvement Era*, April 1970, 4–13.

2. John W. Welch and Erick B. Carlson, eds., *Opening the Heavens: Accounts of Divine Manifestations, 1820–1844* (Provo, UT: BYU Studies; Salt Lake City: Deseret Book, 2005).

3. Dean C. Jessee, "The Earliest Documented Accounts of Joseph Smith's First Vision," in *Opening the Heavens*, 1–33.

4. Paul R. Cheesman, "An Analysis of the Accounts Relating to Joseph Smith's Early Visions" (master's thesis, Brigham Young University, 1965), appendix D, 126–32.

5. This document, located by Dean Jessee in the Church Archives, The Church of Jesus Christ of Latter-day Saints, Salt Lake City, was first printed in James B. Allen, "The Significance of Joseph Smith's 'First Vision' in Mormon Thought," *Dialogue: A Journal of Mormon Thought* 1, no. 3 (Autumn 1966): 40–41.

6. Dean C. Jessee, "The Early Accounts of Joseph Smith's First Vision," *BYU Studies* 9, no. 3 (1969): 275–94.

7. For example, Wesley P. Walters, "New Light on Mormon Origins from Palmyra (N.Y.) Revival," *Bulletin of the Evangelical Theological Society* 10 (Fall 1967): 227–44; Milton V. Backman Jr., "Awakenings in the Burned-Over District: New Light on the Historical Setting of the First Vision," *BYU Studies* 9, no. 3 (Spring 1969): 301–20; Wesley P. Walters, "New Light on Mormon Origins from the Palmyra Revival," *Dialogue* 4, no. 1 (Spring 1969): 60–81; Richard L. Bushman, "The First Vision Story Revived," *Dialogue* 4, no. 1 (Spring 1969): 82–93.

8. One of the most significant publications of that era was the spring 1969 issue of *BYU Studies*, in which Mormon writers presented the results of research on "Mormon Origins in New York."

9. James B. Allen, "Eight Contemporary Accounts of Joseph Smith's First Vision—What Do We Learn from Them?," *Improvement Era*, April 1970, 4–13; Milton V. Backman Jr., "Joseph Smith's Recitals of the First Vision," *Ensign*, January 1985, 8–17; Richard L.

Anderson, "Joseph Smith's Testimony of the First Vision," *Ensign*, April 1996, 10–21.

10. See, for example, the studies discussed in Dean C. Jessee, "Sources for the Study of Joseph Smith," in *Mormon Americana*, ed. David J. Whittaker (Provo, UT: BYU Studies, 1995), 7–28; Grant H. Palmer, *An Insider's View of Mormon Origins* (Salt Lake City: Signature Books, 2002), 235–58, reviewed by Davis Bitton, "The Charge of a Man with a Broken Lance (but Look What He Doesn't Tell Us)," Steven C. Harper, "Trustworthy History?," Mark Ashurst-McGee, "A One-Sided View of Mormon Origins," and Louis Midgley, "Prying into Palmer," in *FARMS Review* 15, no. 2 (2003): 257–410, and by James B. Allen in *BYU Studies* 43, no. 2 (2004): 175–89. For dozens of other publications about the First Vision, consult the bibliography by James B. Allen, Ronald W. Walker, and David J. Whittaker, *Studies in Mormon History, 1830–1997* (Urbana: University of Illinois Press, 2000), "Smith, Joseph, Jr., First Vision," 933.

11. Backman, "Awakenings in the Burned-Over District," 312–13.

12. Allen, "Significance of Joseph Smith's 'First Vision,'" 30–32.

13. As early as June 1830, a revelation alluded to the remission of sins that probably occurred during the First Vision: "For, after that it truly was manifested unto this first elder, that he had received a remission of his sins, he was entangled again in the vanities of the world." Book of Commandments (Independence, MO: W. W. Phelps, 1833), 24:6, also published in "Revelations. The Articles and Covenants of the Church of Christ," *Evening and the Morning Star*, June 1832, 1, and Doctrine and Covenants 20:5. There are some slight variations in the latter references, including the dating of the revelation as April instead of June. This revelation, known as the Articles and Covenants of the Church, was widely used as the foundational document in the organization of the Church. In 1831, another early revelation read, "Wherefore, I the Lord, knowing the calamity which should come upon the inhabitants of the earth, called upon my servant Joseph, and spake unto him from heaven,

and gave him commandments." Book of Commandments 1:4, also published in Doctrine and Covenants 1:17.

14. *Palmyra (NY) Reflector*, February 14, 1831, 102. Joseph's own testimony on this subject is corroborated by his mother's testimony, as well as by accounts of those in the community who knew him as a young man. Richard L. Anderson's incisive article in the spring 1969 issue of *BYU Studies* carefully analyzes some of these writers, including Mother Smith, and presents convincing verification for Joseph's claims with regard to what was happening both before and after his experience in the Sacred Grove. See Richard Lloyd Anderson, "Circumstantial Confirmation of the First Vision through Reminiscences," *BYU Studies* 9, no. 3 (Spring 1969): 373–404.

15. Fawn M. Brodie, *No Man Knows My History: The Life of Joseph Smith, the Mormon Prophet* (New York: Knopf, 1945), 25.

16. Neal E. Lambert and Richard H. Cracroft, "Literary Form and Historical Understanding: Joseph Smith's First Vision," *Journal of Mormon History* 7 (1980): 31–42; Richard L. Bushman, "The Visionary World of Joseph Smith," *BYU Studies* 37, no. 1 (1997–98): 183–204.

17. In April 1830, a revelation (D&C 21) required that a record be kept in the Church. In March 1831, John Whitmer was appointed to keep a history (see D&C 47:1; 69:2–3).

18. There were a few minor changes between the original Manuscript History and the publication in the *Times and Seasons*. There have been a few additional changes in the account found in the Pearl of Great Price. The reason for these changes is not always clear, although in some cases it was probably simply a matter of improving grammatical style. In any case, the essential details and meaning of the account have not been changed, and the changes are not significant enough to discuss in the text above.

19. Dean C. Jessee, Mark Ashurst-McGee, Richard L. Jensen, eds., *The Joseph Smith Papers: Journals, Volume 1, 1832–1839* (Salt Lake City: Church Historian's Press, 2008), 260–61, and Dean C. Jessee, *Personal Writings of Joseph Smith*, 226.

20. In James Allen's original 1970 article on the First Vision, Allen indicated that this report had been published in the *New*

York Spectator on September 23, 1843. Allen, "Eight Contemporary Accounts," 6. This is correct, but Allen did not realize at the time that it had appeared first in White's own newspaper, as indicated above, on September 15.

21. This account is reproduced in Jessee, "Earliest Documented Accounts of Joseph Smith's First Vision," 10–11.

22. For a full account of the period, see Whitney R. Cross, "The Prophet," in *The Burned-Over District: The Social and Intellectual History of Enthusiastic Religion in Western New York, 1800–1850* (Ithaca, NY: Cornell University Press, 1950), 138–50.

23. See both Walters articles referenced above.

24. Actually, Professor Milton Backman has found that this area was called Farmington township when the Smiths moved there, but the name was changed to Manchester township a few years later. Horatio Gates Spafford, *A Gazetteer of the State of New-York* (Albany, NY: B. D. Packard, 1824), 302–3; and Hamilton Child, *Gazetteer and Business Directory of Ontario County, N.Y., for 1867–8* (Syracuse, NY: printed by author, 1867), 49; quoted in Backman, "Awakenings in the Burned-Over District," 303n5.

25. Backman, "Awakenings in the Burned-Over District," 312–13.

26. The words "or thereabouts" were not included in the *Times and Seasons* account, April 1, 1842, 748, nor are they in the 1981 Pearl of Great Price. It is significant, however, that the Prophet should add them to his manuscript as he was preparing it.

27. The exception is Neibaur, and this account clearly implies the same thing.

28. By way of comparison, Joseph wrote in the 1842 Wentworth Letter, "I determined to investigate the subject more fully, believing that if God had a church it would not be split up into factions," and Orson Pratt wrote, "The great question to be decided in his mind, was—if any one of these denominations be the Church of Christ, which one is it?" The common point in all these accounts is the possibility that none of the churches could be correct.

29. At this point, an interesting problem occurs with respect to the 1838 account. After telling of his asking the heavenly

visitors which of all the sects was right, Joseph added, in parenthesis, "(for at this time it had never entered into my heart that all were wrong)." While this seems somewhat inconsistent, it may actually reflect the real confusion of the fourteen-year-old Joseph, who did not want to believe, deep in his heart, that there was no "true" church, even though his mind already asked the obvious questions: "Who of all these parties are right? Or are they all wrong together?" (1838). The confusion within the account, then, might reflect the actual experience of a young man who had thought the unthinkable and yet had not let it sink into his soul (or heart) because it was not what he wanted to believe. Certainly the deep, personal emotions described in nearly all the accounts could lead to a desire to join some church, and hence Joseph's hesitancy to believe that all were wrong. Compare "History of Joseph Smith," *Times and Seasons*, April 1, 1842, 748, and Joseph Smith—History 1:18. The words in parentheses were published in the *Times and Seasons* as well as in all editions of the Pearl of Great Price down to 1902. In the 1902 edition, the words were deleted and remained so until the 1981 printing, which reintroduced the phrase into the text.

30. We do not know what guided or prompted Joseph, but fortuitously he came to this passage in James.

31. For the best treatment of Joseph Smith's concept of God, showing that the assumption is overstated that the Prophet's ideas about God, the Godhead, and divine embodiment migrated over time, see David L. Paulsen, "The Doctrine of Divine Embodiment: Restoration, Judeo-Christian, and Philosophical Perspectives," *BYU Studies* 35, no. 4 (1995–96): 6–94.

32. As Joseph wrote this line in the 1832 manuscript, he originally wrote "with the spirit of god and *the* opened the heavens" (emphasis added). Perhaps he had intended to write "and he opened the heavens." Later, Joseph inserted the word "Lord," the simplest correction of the error, although one that created an ambiguity. But if David could use the word "Lord" in Psalm 110:1, "The Lord said unto my Lord," to refer first to the Father and then to the Son (see Mark 12:36), so could Joseph.

33. This word also appears in the 1832 account but in the context of Joseph having determined through his own searching of the scriptures and observation of the situation around him that "abominations" and "darkness... pervaded the ~~of the~~ minds of mankind."

34. The term *abomination*, of course, is offensive and jarring to our friends of other faiths. And indeed, it was a very strong word in the vocabulary of Joseph Smith's America. Webster's 1828 *Dictionary of the American Language* defines "abomination" as "1. extreme hatred; detestation. 2. The object of detestation, ... 3. Hence, defilement, pollution, in a physical sense, or evil doctrines and practices, which are moral defilements." Nevertheless, an "abomination" in the biblical sense can include anything that takes a person away from God or his righteousness. The Bible uses the word *abomination* in connection with a wide range of sin or transgression, including idolatry (Deuteronomy 27:15), sexual transgression (Leviticus 18:22; 20:13), human sacrifice (Deuteronomy 12:31), eating ritually unclean animals (Leviticus 11:10–12; Deuteronomy 14:3–8), witchcraft and divination (Deuteronomy 18:9–14), and dishonest business dealings (Deuteronomy 25:13–16). Proverbs 6:16–19 gives a list of seven things, some more serious than others, that are counted as an abomination unto God: "A proud look, a lying tongue, and hands that shed innocent blood, an heart that deviseth wicked imaginations, feet that be swift in running to mischief, a false witness that speaketh lies, and he that soweth discord among brethren." Thus, seeing the creeds as an abomination may be understood in a number of ways, mainly as a shorthand way of referring to the very problems that they had caused, as identified in the First Vision accounts, namely turning people aside from the gospel, teaching incorrect doctrines of men, professing errors and corruptions, and inciting tumult.

35. For further discussions of these and other questions, see Allen, review of Palmer, *Insider's View of Mormon Origins*, 175–89.

The Sacred Grove in Manchester, New York, where Joseph Smith received the First Vision after years of searching for the true church of God. (Photo by George Edward Anderson, August 13, 1907, Anderson Collections, Church History Library)

Joseph Smith's Accuracy on the First Vision Setting: The Pivotal 1818 Palmyra Camp Meeting

Richard Lloyd Anderson

Wesley P. Walters led a charge against Joseph Smith's First Vision in 1967, essentially claiming that the founding prophet described fictitious local revivals preceding the First Vision; therefore, the First Vision was fiction.[1] Joseph Smith reported a personal vision of the Father and his Son Jesus early in the spring of 1820, leaving several accounts about "an unusual excitement" (Joseph Smith—History 1:5)[2] that generated his extended search for the true church.[3] Walters and similar scholars gathered useful data but aimed at the wrong target. This article shows that religious conditions claimed by Joseph Smith must be examined in the years before 1820, for he said his First Vision was preceded by two years of intense investigation. Also, camp meetings are better understood now as they relate to earliest Mormonism, and Michael Quinn recently stressed that the 1818 Palmyra camp meeting discussed here contradicts Walters's theory.[4]

> ### Records of the First Vision
> I've heard some criticize the Church because the Church has not publicized the First Vision records. That is an uninformed statement. The person that maintains that we have not offered the information about the First Vision is simply unaware of what's been done.
>
> The documents and the archives are open, and they're a testimony to the honesty of the Church, which I think is a projection of the honesty of Joseph Smith, who told what he remembered and told it sincerely. People who want to claim contradictions can do so, but the testimony of a sincere, honest man is going to shine through because the statement that he knew he had seen a vision is powerful. When I first read the account of the First Vision, I was Joseph Smith's age at the time he received it, only fourteen, and I knew he was telling me the truth.
>
> I'm willing to be led where the documents lead me. That's what a historian does. If the documents say it, you have to account for it. You have to fit your story into what you're told happened by eyewitnesses. And every time I go to the documents, I find verification for Joseph Smith's story of the First Vision. And so I can speak as a person who's been there, who's looked at the material. In that sense I may be of value to other Latter-day Saints who say, "I trust this historian because he went to the sources." And I can tell you that nothing in the sources has ever shaken my testimony of the divine origin of Mormonism. They have only confirmed it. (Richard Lloyd Anderson, interview by Samuel Alonzo Dodge, July 27, 2009, Provo, UT)

More must be said, however, on how closely this meeting fits into Joseph Smith's pre-1820 chronology. And more can be learned about the large attendance at this 1818 meeting by using other upstate meeting comparisons rather than using random examples from any North American region. At least, the successful Palmyra gathering of 1818 was a contributing cause to the religious confusion that Joseph Smith described in several First Vision accounts. At most, this is probably the "unusual excitement" that "commenced with the Methodists" in and about Palmyra, New York, in the summer of 1818, when Joseph said his serious investigations began (v. 5). This is because Joseph's description best fits a Methodist camp meeting, which took place at Palmyra in

1818 but is otherwise not documented in this location near the beginning of Joseph's investigations of the area churches. Really understanding the impact of this 1818 camp meeting requires a flood of details, which are summarized in the "Conclusions" section, near the end of this article. This is also a useful preview, and the reader who scans these conclusions first will have a road map of Joseph Smith's quest before the First Vision.

Several Brigham Young University scholars responded to the Walters theory in 1969.[5] My 1969 article featured what two Palmyra printers' apprentices remembered about Joseph Smith's teen years.[6] They pictured him as a virtual Methodist convert, a role which he acknowledged (see v. 8). This article adds many recollections from the circuit riders of western New York that recreate the world of the 1818 Palmyra camp meeting, which certainly meets the usage test of "revival," meaning a series of meetings bringing enhanced conviction or an unusual number of conversions. Thus Joseph Smith's basic background of the First Vision is provable, meaning that historical sources beyond Joseph verify the local Methodist activities that Joseph said took place when he was a young seeker. Furthermore, Palmyra recollections and those of Joseph connect him to a known Palmyra Methodist camp meeting that correlates with his own descriptions of beginning to investigate his neighborhood churches.

Joseph's Seeking before 1820

Joseph Smith commented on religious conflicts as they affected him. His real story line was subjective, driven by outer events that raised the inner question of God's reaction to conflicting, confusing churches. His small world was torn open by a sizable Methodist event in 1818, and every gathering afterward attended, and many personal discussions, reopened this internal conflict. Thus Walters chose an irrelevant method for testing

Joseph Smith by locating large revivals, for we know that the unresolved question of which church was right followed the boy through dozens of large and small meetings after 1818, which are well understood because evangelical church worship is so well described in ministers' manuals, diaries, and memoirs. Walters referred to small revivals in Palmyra in 1816–17 and broader conversions there in 1824–25, but he assumed that silence of sources proved a lack of religious vitality in this area in the years 1819–21.[7] Walters arbitrarily isolated 1820, saying that Joseph Smith "claims that he was stirred by an 1820 revival to make his inquiry in the grove near his home."[8] However, this incorrectly interprets Joseph's 1838 history and ignores Joseph's 1832 account, which specifically defines the time of his juvenile experiences. In 1838, Joseph placed his First Vision in early spring 1820 (see v. 14), preceded by an investigation "at length" (v. 13).[9] The peak of his confusion came "in [his] fifteenth year" (v. 7), which began on his fourteenth birthday, December 23, 1819. Yet Joseph placed the Methodist "unusual excitement" long before that (v. 5). Strangely, Walters was aware that in 1832 Joseph placed his seeking as very early, for Walters quoted Joseph's words about carefully examining churches "from age twelve to fifteen."[10] Thus Joseph actively searched for true religion from late December 1817 into the early part of 1820, at the end of which he turned fifteen. The above dates blend as reasonable approximations, though Joseph Smith clearly singles out the complete years of 1818 and 1819 as his time of exploration, with divine resolution in early 1820.

Do "Great Multitudes" Refer to a Local Revival?

Besides misdating Joseph's searching, Walters insisted that conversions could qualify as a "revival" only if there were many and if they were sustained over some time. However,

Joseph Smith sometimes used "revival" or "reformation" of the pre–First Vision scene in Palmyra, though "unusual excitement" was used in his major history, and he probably intended the above terms as synonyms (v. 5). Walters claimed to prove "the absence of any revival in the Palmyra area in 1820."[11] However, that is a puzzling statement in the light of two articles in the *Palmyra Register* on June 23 and July 5, 1820, reporting the sad death of James Couser, victim of "an epileptic fit" after returning drunk "from a camp-meeting which was held in this vicinity." The second article was predictable damage control, explaining to "neighbors who belong to the Society of Methodists" that the original story did not claim that Couser bought liquor "within the enclosure of their place of worship . . . but at the grog shops that were established at, or near if you please, their camp-ground." So the meeting in question was more than a normal Sunday gathering; it was an open-air special occasion for proclaiming Christian forgiveness to expected crowds, since shops were set up, indicating a public attraction normally lasting several days. Walters and Marquardt dismissed this event as only a Methodist camp meeting, not a revival; but in usage then and now, a successful protracted meeting is also a revival.[12]

My worn tenth edition of *Merriam-Webster's Collegiate Dictionary* defines *revival* as "a period of renewed religious interest," which seems to be the Walters-Marquardt understanding; but the above dictionary also considers a revival as "an often highly emotional evangelistic meeting or series of meetings," which defines the Methodist camp meetings of Joseph's youth. Such meetings were among those that nearly converted him, as he said: "In process of time my mind became somewhat partial to the Methodist sect" (v. 8). The Smiths migrated to Palmyra Village in the winter of 1816–17, but (as Mother Smith writes) in two years they had moved two miles south to their large farm, barely over the line into Manchester Township, though their self-built log house was built (perhaps purposely) on the adjoining property, still a few yards within Palmyra Township. Joseph Smith said that this was "the place where we lived" when "an unusual excitement" began with the Methodists (vv. 3, 5).[13] After an unstated time, Joseph began his fifteenth year (December 23, 1819) as the "great excitement" continued and Joseph was still shopping "their several meetings" with his gnawing question of "who was right and who was wrong" (v. 8). But Joseph's canonized account includes bits of history of his feelings, of his locality, and of the broader Finger Lakes area. As stated, the major theme is Joseph's inner agony, with accompanying religious conflict in the region. Yet interfaith conflict expanded in broader rings around Palmyra. Doctrinal quarrels "became general among all the sects in that region of country," until the "whole district of country" was characterized by "great multitudes" choosing among the major evangelical churches (vv. 5–6). Walters and Marquardt claimed such phrases were not true of 1820 Palmyra but were justified only by the 1824–25 increases in the Palmyra area, which added a hundred Baptists, a hundred Presbyterians, and two hundred Methodists to the main Protestant groups.[14] According to these authors, such statistics prove that Joseph merged memories of two eras, necessarily including the 1824–25 Christian conversions in Palmyra to reach larger convert numbers. However, four hundred converts, mostly from two townships, hardly measure up to Joseph's language of "great multitudes" in "the whole district of country." When early circuit ministers use such language of camp meetings, they are more often describing thousands of listeners, not just a few hundred. So the greater area of a "district" greatly increases the converts and members within it.

As before stated, the Walters theory picked 1820 (the wrong year for Joseph Smith's investigations), claimed zero growth then among mainline evangelicals in the Palmyra area, and then speculated that Joseph must have merged memories of 1820 and 1824–25 for Palmyra, when newspapers showed four hundred converts in the area, which loosely could be "great multitudes" joining Palmyra area churches (v. 5). Yet a close reading establishes two contexts: (1) "unusual excitement" in the "place where we lived," expanding to (2) "great multitudes" joining churches in "the whole district of country." Seasoned Mormon historians, including Backman, Bushman, and Hill, faulted the Walters school for essentially rearranging Joseph Smith's words. The Walters group repositioned Joseph's "great multitudes" into Joseph's previous, smaller category, "the place where we lived" (Palmyra vicinity), whereas Joseph had added a new category ("whole district of country") before using the large quantitative adjectives above. In early western New York Methodist sources, "multitudes" attending camp meetings are generally equated with the low thousands, and such numbers exceed the population of Palmyra Village in 1820. In fact, the reiterations of this theory sound less than confident.

The argument was that Joseph must have included four hundred converts made in the Palmyra area in 1824–25, or he could not have used "great multitudes." So the conclusion was made that broad terms like "multitudes" were "scarcely overstatements" for local growth measured for the year before late 1825. Nevertheless, "multitudes" is not equivalent to four hundred converts[15] but is a huge overstatement, not appropriate unless the larger "multitudes" fit into the larger "district" or "region." Yet Joseph's expansive statements about the pre-1820 Palmyra revival make good sense as describing spreading revivals, with fervor breaking out in a locality and broadening throughout a larger territory, a frequent pattern of expression in earlier western New York revival literature. The expansive adjectives of larger convert numbers match Joseph's broader "district" and "region," where conversions were spreading before the First Vision.

Methodist District Growth in Joseph's Youth

As indicated throughout this article, two Palmyra apprentice printers knew Joseph and identified him as temporarily but deeply involved in Methodism. In addition, Joseph himself said that he attended the "several meetings" of the mainline groups, but "in process of time [his] mind became somewhat partial to the Methodist sect, and [he] felt some desire to be united with them" (v. 8). Of course, Joseph also credited the Methodists for igniting his soul and society until the burning questions were extinguished by deity in the forest vision (see v. 5). And afterward he confided his experience to "one of the Methodist preachers, who was very active in the before mentioned religious excitement" (v. 21). The above apprentices later spoke of Joseph's joining the Methodist "probationary class" at Palmyra (Tucker) and even functioning as "a passable exhorter in evening meetings" (Turner).[16] Methodists kept statistics at most levels, and Joseph would be aware of trends. In going to meetings during 1818–19, young Joseph would normally walk two miles to Palmyra, one of ten Methodist preaching stations in the Ontario Circuit, which in turn was grouped with ten other circuits to make the Genesee District. In a rough 1818 comparison, the Methodist circuit surrounding the Smith farm would be about the size of a county, and the large Genesee District would be equivalent to several counties. Since early Methodist church records are missing at Palmyra, Walters looked at the published Genesee Conference records for 1818 and 1819, when the Genesee District still included the Ontario Circuit, where Palmyra Village and environs were located. During the year before the summer of 1819, membership in the Ontario Circuit fell from 703 to 677, a loss of 26 individuals. Yet those flat figures are suspect.

Every other circuit in the Genesee District gained in 1819, with the total Genesee District increasing in membership more than any other district in the Genesee Conference (western New York, and adjacent sections of Canada and Pennsylvania). In 1819, the population of the Genesee District grew from 4,888 to 6,068, an increase of 1,180 Methodist members in the circuits adjoining Ontario Circuit, where Palmyra was central. This was a 24 percent increase in one year in the Methodist Ontario District, which included northwest New York, in the area from Ithaca and Cayuga Lake west to Buffalo.[17] Joseph Smith was in the eye of an upstate Methodist hurricane and expressed that by expansive adjectives ("the whole district of country") and of conversions ("great multitudes"). Non-Methodist growth was less spectacular and measured in more compact districts around Palmyra. In 1819 the Baptists added 310, and the Presbyterians added 276.[18] However, Backman added Presbyterian membership figures in areas roughly the size of the Methodist Genesee Conference in western New York and found that in 1818 and 1819 there were about 1,500 new Presbyterians each year.[19] As the attached chart indicates, Methodist increases in 1819 almost doubled those numbers. Judged by his large-number adjectives, Joseph's 1838 history creates two geographical levels in explaining local as against regional religious conflict, his tighter home area as against expansion throughout a broader "district," possibly intended as the technical Methodist term. The accompanying chart is compiled from the national report, which gave component numbers in the mid-1819 Genesee Conference (western New York and adjacent parts of Canada and Pennsylvania). It features the Genesee District within that conference, and the Genesee District contained the Ontario Circuit (including Palmyra and the Smith farm) and ten other circuits. In his published history, Joseph introduced his pre-1820 investigations with only two peripheral sentences on district increases (see v. 5), part of an extraordinary national expansion in this period: "Between 1770 and 1820 American Methodists achieved a virtual miracle of growth, rising from fewer than 1,000 members to more than 250,000.... This growth stunned the older denominations."[20]

Methodists in Western New York and Nearby Areas, 1817–19[21]

	1817	1818	1819
US and adjacent Canada total (11 North American conferences)	224,853	229,627	240,924
Genesee Conference total (western NY to eastern borders somewhat west of the Hudson River)	17,935	21,046	23,913
District totals within the Genesee Conference			
Oneida District	3,440	4,180	4,580
Chenango District	4,091	4,594	5,161
Genesee District	4,531	4,881	6,068
Susquehanna District	2,760	2,660	2,872
Upper Canada District	1,226	1,995	2,466
Lower Canada District	1,881	2,736	2,766
Circuit totals within the Genesee District			
Eden Circuit	158	246	321
New Amsterdam Circuit[22]	264		
Caledonia Circuit	425	594	623

Bloomfield Circuit	450	616	695
Ontario Circuit (roughly present western Wayne County)	900	703	677
Lyons Circuit	740	594	673
Seneca Circuit	640	693	1,010
Crooked Lake Circuit	333	416	656
Newtown Circuit	224	388	487
Ridgeway Circuit	133	246	331
Clarence Circuit	264	263	350
Canandaigua Circuit		122	200
Buffalo and Black Rock			45

Joseph worried about quarrels among believers, even among his family. As Methodist "unusual excitement" broke out, there was similar conflict in his home and even in travel to church. Both parents had been seekers, but Mother Smith and three siblings settled on Presbyterianism in New York, as Joseph explains (see v. 7). This denomination inherited Calvinism as held by New England Congregationalists on both sides of the family. Yet Joseph Smith took another way after Palmyra's "unusual excitement."[23] In his history, Joseph essentially said he was first shaken by a local Methodist revival, after which he developed some degree of affiliation with them. Joseph's 1844 Hebrew tutor paraphrased Joseph's memories of how an early revival opened the spiritual dilemma, which was still unresolved until the First Vision: "The first call he had a Revival meeting his mother & Br & Sist got Religion, he wanted to get Religion too wanted to feel & shout like the Rest but could feel nothing."[24] The year before, journalist David Nye interviewed Joseph Smith, who then used a synonym for a "revival" before his First Vision: "There was a reformation among the different religious denominations in the neighborhood where I lived, and I became serious, and was desirous to know what Church to join."[25] Among the insights of Neibaur's 1844 account is Joseph's cautious preference for Methodism right up to the beginning of the divine dialogue in the forest: "Mr Smith then asked must I join the Methodist Church." These were either the first words of Joseph's direct query or Neibaur's understanding that this question was in Joseph's heart as the vision opened.[26]

Joseph's Methodist Meetings: Quarterly Conferences

Joseph's religious experiences in 1818 and 1819 can be partially reconstructed once his Methodist participation is known. He received exhortation in local class meetings, by periodic visits of assigned circuit riders, and by his probable attendance at some quarterly meetings, then a standard institution in his area. Scholars now stress the impact of this developed organization, with the camp meeting as a recruiting resource but not necessarily the main proselyting tool. At this period the Methodist investigator was drawn into "a well-defined system of social activities, class meetings, love feasts, quarterly meetings, and camp meetings."[27] Charles Giles (1783–1867) and George Peck (1797–1876) had well-known careers as circuit and district leaders in the Genesee Conference. Their detailed memoirs describe camp meetings and quarterly meetings alternately as outstanding events that brought a steady stream of converts. Quarterly meetings combined church business with worship, bringing together teachers, lay leaders, settled ministers, circuit riders, and the presiding elder of the district. This circuit conference ordinarily had a Saturday-Sunday format, with members and seekers gathering on Saturday "from the surrounding communities and countryside to hear preaching, sing favorite hymns, and fellowship in a festive atmosphere."[28] Charles Giles graduated from circuit preacher to presiding elder of the Oneida District from 1814 to 1817 and also 1822 to 1825, also presiding over the Chenango District in the interval of 1818–21. These districts were comparable to the Genesee District, which included Palmyra and present western Wayne County. As presiding elder, Giles directed quarterly conferences and described their robust pattern:

> In those days our quarterly meetings were noted seasons, which excited general interest. The circuits were large, containing some hundreds of communicants, divided into distinct societies, including many class-leaders, stewards, exhorters, and local preachers. These official members, when they met at these meetings, formed a large quarterly conference, where all the important business connected with the circuit was brought up and obtained conference action. The members of the church, coming from all directions, and from various distances, bringing some of their unconverted friends and neighbours with them to gain blessings and benefits there, added much to the importance and interest of these occasions. . . . Indeed, quarterly meetings then were accounted great seasons, not only by our own church, but by many others in community: they were made the theme of conversation long beforehand, and all necessary preparations were made to attend them. Preachers and members, from neighboring circuits, frequently attended. . . . [C]onversions were common occurrences at these meetings. In the love-feasts tidings were brought in from all parts of the circuit.[29]

In review, Joseph's 1832 handwritten history says he actively searched for the true church "from the age of twelve years to fifteen," that is, from late 1817 to late 1820; but in his official history, Joseph dated the First Vision "early in the spring of eighteen hundred and twenty" (v. 14), thus subtracting most of that year from active investigation.[30] During that 1818–19 period in the Ontario Circuit, only one camp meeting is known that is relevant to Joseph's religious searching. However, in that period, up to eight quarterly meetings were held in the circuit, sometimes accompanied by camp meetings. Borders of the Ontario Circuit roughly fit the western two-thirds of present Wayne County, a twenty-mile square, with Lyons Circuit on the east and Canandaigua Circuit on the south. The quarterly assemblies were often held at larger villages, so as a business center, Palmyra probably hosted a couple of these circuit gatherings during Joseph's two years of church shopping before 1820. He recalled resisting membership but "attended their several meetings as often as occasion would permit" (v. 8). This comes close to saying that Joseph attended Methodist conferences, for Lucy Mack Smith pictures her family as respectful of the Sabbath, suggesting that Joseph could easily attend worship in Palmyra or even in other locations on the Lord's Day. Joseph's society was inquisitive and mobile. Area gatherings attracted believers and near-believers from a dozen-mile radius, and Giles mentions riding roads with double rows of wagons on their way to camp meetings. A quarterly meeting was held periodically at Palmyra and might have been the "unusual excitement" that provoked the juvenile Joseph to seek a church, except that the Palmyra printing apprentices say the meeting of that description was a camp meeting (Turner) or its synonym, a protracted meeting (Tucker).[31]

Aurora Seager Journal, Palmyra, June 1818

A premium source on Joseph Smith's pre-vision life is a journal record of an 1818 Methodist camp meeting near Palmyra, which Joseph certainly knew about and very likely attended. It is discussed here after upstate Methodist expansion because the account is understood by contemporary comparison. This 1818 entry includes raw statistics, recorded in the journal of Aurora Seager, a newly ordained circuit rider who died a year and a half after outlining this Palmyra meeting in his daily record. This remarkable resource was mentioned early by Milton V. Backman Jr. and revisited recently by other scholars.[32] Aurora Seager was born in Connecticut in 1795, and his journal and correspondence furnish a nineteenth-century "pilgrim's progress," moving from teenage introspection to his premature death as a traveling preacher at the end of 1819.

Two principal biographies incorporated Aurora's personal writings,[33] which tell how he started an academic program with classical languages at fifteen, then started teaching two years later at the request of his father, who in 1812 moved his large family to the ten-mile square township of Phelps in western New York, which contained "the flourishing little *Village of Vienna*," later incorporated as the village of Phelps.[34] Young Aurora was industrious and reflective, continuing as a teacher until his Methodist conversion at twenty-two altered his thinking and lifestyle. Like Joseph Smith and others of the period, he later wrote about adolescent doubts and the power of prayer. More concerned with knowing the Savior than with doctrine, Aurora joined the Methodists because he felt their Christlike love. The young man was first licensed as an exhorter and later became a preacher, respected by senior ministers for his sincerity and humility. Aurora wrote that his "inability and unfitness for the work caused me to weep and pray for the promised blessing" of Christ's companionship in his ministry (see Matthew 28:20).[35]

Many young ministers in this environment had battled darkness and rejoiced in victory. After keenly feeling human weakness and isolation, a converted Aurora assured others that the

Savior beckoned all to enter his joyful path. After conversion in early 1817, Aurora temporarily returned to the former residence in Connecticut, comforted a dying married sister, and began his short missionary career. That spring he reported speaking at eight large meetings near Hartford, which generated great interest, though he was in the Calvinist homeland: "A considerable revival took place there, and numbers, especially of the youth, were brought to the knowledge of the truth."[36] In the next year, Aurora changed location but not his preaching pattern, as he spoke at a camp meeting at Palmyra, New York, where twelve-year-old Joseph Smith likely heard Aurora and others like him declare that God had answered their prayers.

Leaving a request for transfer from his eastern New York circuit, Aurora returned to Phelps Township on May 19, 1818, and attended the quarterly conference of this New York circuit the next weekend there. The presiding elder preached on the first day, and typical Sabbath preaching was given the next day by several, including Aurora.[37] He had requested assignment at the 1818 annual Genesee Conference scheduled for Lansing (near Ithaca) in mid-July.[38] In the meantime, his presiding elder asked Aurora to work near his home, and he assisted at nearby Palmyra in the Ontario Circuit as his first assignment, which appears under journal dates of June 19–23, 1818: "On the 19th [Friday] I attended a camp-meeting at Palmyra. The arrival of Bishop Roberts, who seems to be a man of God, and is apostolic in his appearance, gave a deeper interest to the meeting until it closed. On Monday the sacrament was administered; about twenty were baptized; forty united with the Church, and the meeting closed. I accompanied the Bishop to Brother Hawks, at Phelps."[39]

Aurora here compressed considerable information, which yields valuable insights when rounded out. "Palmyra" no doubt indicates Palmyra Village, meaning that the meetings were held nearby, since a camp meeting was by definition in a wooded area, and he was one of the regional ministers gathering to assist. This full town (or township) was a strip of land ten miles by twelve miles, but the campsite would normally be referenced by the nearest village, which in this case had the same name as the township. As mentioned, on June 28, 1820, the editor of the *Palmyra Register* reported an unfortunate death of a man who supposedly got drunk at "a camp-meeting which was held in this vicinity." Some Methodists complained, to whom the editor apologized in the next issue, indicating that the man had come to the village to stay overnight.

Orsamus Turner, a young village printer discussed in the appendices of this article, knew Joseph personally before 1822 and said that Joseph caught "a spark of Methodism in the camp meeting, away down in the woods, on the Vienna road."[40] That road connected Palmyra Village to Vienna Village (now Phelps Village), a dozen miles southeast; Turner's point was that Joseph was nearly converted near Palmyra in a Methodist meeting in a forested section of the road running to Vienna. In 1877, Professor W. H. McIntosh reviewed the beginnings of Methodism in Palmyra, citing their 1822 Palmyra charter and reporting that they "erected their first edifice on Vienna street, near the cemetery, in the eastern part of the village."[41] Moreover, the huge 1826 Palmyra camp meeting at the Genesee Conference took place "in a most beautiful and picturesque grove, near the village."[42] Some of these locations on the east of Palmyra Village may be identical; all are in general proximity, showing a Methodist continuity in this area, probably some four miles by indirect road from the Smith farm.

As mentioned, young Joseph Smith turned twelve just before 1818, the year he named as the start of serious investigation of major Palmyra churches. That alone makes his attendance expected at the known special Methodist meetings in 1818–19. His mother and his printing acquaintances indicate that Joseph regularly came into Palmyra Village from the Smith farm, two miles south. In fact, in that period the Smiths probably continued selling homemade refreshments by cart at public occasions, as editor Pomeroy Tucker said, "on Fourth of July anniversaries, and on military training days."[43] In a society seeking religion, a camp meeting drew similar crowds that attracted vendors, as discussed in the appendices under the Pomeroy Tucker heading.

The 1818 Palmyra camp meeting followed a well-used weekend pattern.[44] Seager and certainly other ministers arrived on Friday or before. Also attending was Robert Roberts, one of the three bishops of the Methodist Church, who was traveling toward the annual Genesee Conference meeting scheduled the next month at Lansing, New York, outside of Ithaca. Roberts was tall and heavy-built, unaffected, with a frontier background.[45] A fellow preacher recalled his "plain, practical sermon" at the Sunday preaching to crowds at the 1818 Genesee Conference the following month.[46] His unusual presence at the June camp meeting near Palmyra certainly drew a greater crowd. Roberts's devout preaching was described by attorney Richard W. Thompson, who later heard Bishop Roberts open in "conversational style" and then develop his topic in "terse" language, at the same time portraying "the majesty, power and love of God."[47]

Numbers at the June 1818 Palmyra Camp Meeting

Preachers' writings usually evaluate camp meetings by the smaller number of those accepting Christ rather than by estimating full attendance, which included up to a score of ministers, volunteer laymen, hundreds of tent residents, and rotating visitors each day from surrounding villages and farms.

Over half of the audience would already be Christian (regularly called "professors of religion"[48]), maybe a fourth would be serious seekers, and the rest the curious and the skeptical. Young people are mostly praised as pious, but guards were set up for contingencies. Seager wrote that "forty united with the Church" at the 1818 Palmyra camp meeting, which suggests an above average audience. For instance, in 1835 in southern Michigan, three circuit conferences were merged as a camp meeting, which perhaps totaled a thousand, termed by the presiding elder, "much people on the ground," with a final result: "There were it was supposed between 40 and 50 converted."[49] This identifies the numerical ingredients of the 1818 Palmyra camp meeting in New York's Genesee Conference. In that summer, Charles Giles was shifted from presiding elder of the Oneida District to the same position over the more eastern Chenango District. He remembered how camp meetings drew "thousands into the tented wilderness."[50] He described two 1818 camp meetings in the township of Manlius, around sixty miles east of Palmyra. In the first meeting, emotional cries rose from "a multitude of pious worshippers, and many curious attendants." After preaching "from day to day," there were "many . . . yet unconverted, besides we gathered up fifty happy converts."[51] In a few months, another camp meeting was opened on the same ground, which "was soon swarming with life. . . . Tent after tent arose in order, encircling the hallowed spot." This second encampment brought another fifty converts, who stood beside the earlier fifty as the second set of meetings closed.[52] Giles reminisced about his vigorous voice, which rang "in the open air in quarterly meetings, and on camp grounds, where thousands frequently assembled . . . so that five or six thousand could hear distinctly."[53]

At this time, George Peck was entering the ministry in the Genesee Conference, in the Broome and Cortland Circuits of the Chenango District, and he pictured some early, successful camp meetings, including the following prototype:

> Those having charge of the preparations would select a spot in the dense woods, and proceed to clear away the bushes and small trees, putting the brush around the encampment, and forming with it an impassable fence sometimes ten or twelve feet high. Within this enclosure the tents, perhaps a hundred in number, would be pitched. When the meetings began great multitudes of people would throng the place. Among these would come an occasional party of wild young men. . . . To keep such as these in awe, "guards" were appointed, whose duty it was to . . . keep the whole encampment in good order. . . . [T]he preachers and the Church-members carried on the campaign, preaching, exhorting, singing, praying, with a zeal that never cooled, and lungs that seemed never to grow weary.[54]

Even in the "cold summer" of 1816, camp meetings were held in Peck's area, one of them near Norwich, about ninety miles southeast of Palmyra. He and another circuit minister cleared the forest, after which Bishop M'Kendree was present and "spoke with great energy," during which "the multitudes hung upon his lips as if entranced." This camp meeting began as "feeble," but vivid warnings of hellfire caused "hundreds" in the crowd to offer pleas for mercy, which joined with piercing prayers of the faithful to produce an "unbroken roar." A relief squad of experienced preachers concluded this series of meetings, and many converts are implied by speaking of their "influence upon the Church and the whole community."[55] The following year, George Peck came back to the Broome Circuit for another camp meeting, which included days-long instruction and exhortation, when "many penitents cried for mercy."[56] The summer of 1818 Peck helped to rough out a camp space at Truxton Township, near Cortland, some sixty miles east of Palmyra. In spite of a punishing heat wave, he says, "we had a goodly number of souls converted."[57] The Giles and Peck memoirs in this period help to estimate numbers at the 1818 Palmyra camp sessions, as well as understand its aftermath, which includes the doctrinal competition that so offended Joseph Smith (see vv. 6–8). At Truxton, one of the rougher circuit preachers downgraded Methodist backsliders, as well as ordinary Baptists and Presbyterians, in praying and speaking, and afterward a "Baptist preacher" visited the homes of camp meeting converts, "misrepresenting the Methodists . . . turning aside a few." Peck later overcame his indignation but felt the pain of seeing "a portion of the fruit of our labors lured from us and borne off in other directions."[58]

In post-pioneer New York, there were normally large turnouts for these "forest gatherings," and success kept them vigorous for decades. Even before the Erie Canal was built, cumulative attendance from Friday to Monday at the 1818 Palmyra campground should have been about two thousand, since Palmyra Village was a trade center drawing on the township of that name and bordering ones. In 1820–21 census statistics, the adjoining east-west townships of Palmyra and Macedon contained 3,724, and those on the land running south to prosperous Canandaigua would double that figure. On the other hand, Palmyra Village then only had "125 houses . . . and about 1000 inhabitants," so anyone moderately informed there would know of the Methodist crusade from Friday through Monday in late June 1818.[59] The physical preparation of the site as well as Methodist announcements in meetings and by word of mouth would herald the coming event.

Western New York sources give a context to the 1818 Palmyra journal of Aurora Seager. His figure that "forty united with the Church" is about average for camp meeting conversions in two of the six districts (Oneida and Chenango) in the Genesee Conference from about 1816 to 1818. Seager says the

Palmyra preaching closed on Monday, June 20, when "about twenty were baptized; forty united with the Church." The latter figure was more significant, since baptism was not regularly given on Methodist conversion, but when requested. Accepting Christ was the public mark of conversion. These forty new believers came out from a much larger group of spectators. Charles Giles spoke about a "multitude" or even "thousands" in his audiences when fifty converts pledged faith. Peck spoke of "many penitents" or a "goodly number" of converts called out from assemblies of "hundreds" or "multitudes." As stated, Palmyra Village produced an estimated camp meeting of ten thousand in 1826.[60] But even the 1818 Palmyra camp meeting was successful in gathering an average number of converts for that period. Outdoor audiences in similar western New York meetings then reached estimated highs well beyond two thousand.

Giles and Peck furnish many broad estimates of camp meeting attendance and quite regularly add specific numbers of conversions. Their overall ratios are about 1 or 2 percent of Christian converts to each camp meeting audience in western New York. This means that those forty 1818 camp meeting converts at Palmyra would be drawn from a pool of roughly two thousand spectators. So the Prophet's phrasing is apt, calling the pre-1820 initiating Methodist meeting an "unusual excitement" (v. 5). Right afterward, the Prophet's large historical estimates really refer to converts in the expanding circles surrounding Palmyra Village, which, as noted, had a population then of "about a thousand inhabitants."[61] A camp meeting or quarterly district conference in Palmyra would draw a great but temporary crowd. As discussed above, "great multitudes" of converts are mentioned in Joseph's history only after he notes what was happening in "the whole district of country" (v. 5). Just before that, the Prophet's history said that the Methodists created a heavy impact on society in "the place where we lived" (v. 5), the beginning of religious agitation dated as 1818 by his 1832 history. After the above comparative analysis, the contemporary journal of Rev. Aurora Seager should shift historical perspective to greater respect for Joseph's 1838 history of the First Vision. A concrete source now locates a camp meeting in Palmyra in the summer of 1818, large enough to unsettle that upstate area socially and religiously. It at least doubled the population for a long weekend, added one of the three Methodist bishops to its list of distinguished visitors, and left behind changed lives and ongoing religious discussion that would materialize into a new and significant restoration church. Joseph Smith perhaps met fellow seekers at this camp meeting, and he may have questioned some of the forty new believers about their convictions and how they could be sure.

Joseph's Attendance at the 1818 Palmyra Camp Meeting

Interlocking sources indicate that Joseph Smith attended at least some sessions of the June 1818 camp meeting at Palmyra. One dependable observer is Orsamus Turner, who was slightly older than Joseph and was a Palmyra printer's apprentice during part of the first six years of Smith family residence in that vicinity. Later a successful small-town editor, he also became a major western New York historian and gave several memories of Joseph as "distinct ones." Though writing of Joseph Smith with disdain, Turner admits that Joseph "occasionally" showed his "mother's intellect" when "he used to help us solve" ethical questions in the "juvenile debating club" in the village, likely before the Smiths started clearing their land before 1820. Turner concludes this section about Joseph's youth with grudging praise: "And subsequently, after catching a spark of Methodism in the camp meeting, away down in the woods, on the Vienna road, he was a very passable exhorter in evening meetings."[62] Very likely this is the same experience that Joseph shared with Alexander Neibaur in Nauvoo: "The first call he had a Revival meeting his mother & Br & Sist got Religion, he wanted to get Religion too wanted to feel & shout like the Rest but could feel nothing."[63] In addition to the Turner and Neibaur accounts of Joseph's near-conversion at an outdoor Methodist revival, the Seager journal notes an important Methodist camp meeting near Palmyra in June 1818 with forty converts. This unusual event in Joseph's village was sure to attract him, judged by his assertion of active church shopping about this time (see v. 8). Thus we have three good sources about a Methodist revival or camp meeting near Palmyra, harmonious in time but dated by the Seager journal of June 1818. The statistics show it was a major event in the community that certainly came to Joseph's attention and almost certainly compelled his attendance. These three sources evidently report the same Methodist camp meeting and match Joseph's 1838 history that his boyhood quest for the true church began with a local "unusual excitement" generated by "the Methodists" (v. 5). By itself, the Seager journal of June 1818 establishes the high probability of Joseph's presence there, which is historically strengthened by Joseph's memory of being present in a Methodist revival meeting with family members (Neibaur Journal) and by his teenage acquaintance's report that Joseph caught "a spark of Methodism in the camp meeting away down in the woods, on the Vienna road" (Orsamus Turner).

The Smith family arrived from Vermont in late 1816 or early 1817, and in her dictated manuscript Mother Smith contrasted their migrating poverty with their later security: "In two years from the time we entered Palmyra strangers . . . we were able to settle ourselves upon our own land [in] a snug comfortable though humble habitation built and neatly furnished by our own industry."[64] Pomeroy Tucker, a Palmyra editor who knew Joseph in this early period, states that the Smiths lived in Palmyra Village for "some two and a half years" and "in 1818" moved two miles south to the uncleared farm, where they constructed their "original log hut"—"occupying as their dwelling-place, in the first instance, a small, one-story smoky log-house, which they had built prior to removing there."⁶⁵ Lucy and lifelong Palmyra resident Tucker agree that the first (and only) log house of the Smiths was self-built to be ready for their move to the farm about 1819. Orsamus Turner agrees on this pre-1820 chronology, since he remembered "to have first seen the [Smith] family, in the winter of '19, 20, in a rude log house with but a small spot underbrushed around it."⁶⁶ The normal settler's routine was to replace a simple log structure with a later frame home. These observers describe but one log home as the Smith's residence before the surviving frame home was built, which was well under way by Alvin's death in late 1823. Joseph's own history picks up his religious narrative at the point of settling on the farm, when the Methodists initiated "an unusual excitement," and he began to favor them (see v. 8). The above three camp-meeting accounts center in a close window of time, dated as June 1818 in the Seager journal. This is a few months after Joseph Smith's twelfth birthday, a time when his 1832 memoir says he was beginning to investigate the area churches. This 1832 history clarifies that his seeking lasted "from the age of twelve years to fifteen," though the vision in early spring 1820 cut off seeking for the rest of that year (see v. 14). Moreover, Joseph's youthful church investigation could begin as early as mid-1818, according to clues in this 1838 account of the First Vision. These outdoor services were normally organized in the milder seasons, late spring through early fall, so the religious controversies as Joseph turned fourteen in late 1819 (see v. 7) definitely allow a local camp meeting during the warmer months of 1818 or 1819 as the "unusual" event that first caught young Joseph's religious attention. The known 1818 Palmyra camp meeting fits Joseph's chronology and also fits the Turner Methodist camp meeting context.

Walters has passed on, and he has loyal defenders. But the old claims do not stand against careful study of the 1818 camp meeting in Palmyra. As an intense seeker with Methodist inclination, Joseph would certainly be at some of the six-odd meetings over four days of this major Christian gathering only a few walkable miles from his home. Very likely there also to sell food at public events, the youth was personally seeking his own salvation and how to resolve the family division developing concerning the right church. Vogel doesn't want to mix the scriptural 1838 account and the simple 1832 history penned by Joseph Smith, since he thinks the latter leaves out "a revival and confusion over which sect to join as motivation for praying." Instead, Vogel believes that Joseph "was motivated by a need for salvation and forgiveness of sins."[67] Though some others share this view, it is a distinction without a difference. Both the 1832 and 1838 accounts merge different aspects of the same thing.[68] Early western New York literature contains autobiographies in which juveniles seek God's church and God's forgiveness at the same time.

In 1819, normal Methodist quarterly conferences were held in Palmyra's Ontario Circuit, the northern part of the original large Ontario County. In 1819 this circuit included nearly seven hundred members in an area roughly equal to the western two-thirds of Wayne County today, so the circuit conferences drew a crowd of at least three hundred that assembled several times that year—circuit preachers, visiting officials, local and visiting members, and serious investigators. Yet the big 1819 event in the area was the Annual Genesee Conference, held for a week beginning July 1. Although an annual meeting of delegates of the Methodist Episcopal Church was held on the Eastern Seaboard, preaching and administrative assignments were mostly supervised by the bishops as they attended the eleven United States and Canadian conferences divided on sectional lines. So in 1819 the Genesee Conference hosted a visiting bishop, the presiding elders of its six circuits, and about a hundred circuit preachers from the whole conference, stretching across western New York west of Albany, and including adjoining sections of northern Pennsylvania and Canada.[69] In 1819 this event was held in Vienna Village, noted then as twelve miles southeast of Palmyra, in the town or township of Phelps, a prosperous farming area with good roads.[70] It opened on July 1 for a week of business and assignments, but preaching was expected on the Sabbath from the array of experienced and persuasive ministers there. Preacher-historian George Peck comments on the Sabbath meetings of some Genesee conferences in the years just before. Although held in the country area of Genoa (east of Cayuga Lake) in 1818, only a "neighboring grove" could accommodate "the crowds which gathered from far and near" for general services.[71] In 1816 in the Paris locality (south of Utica) there were between three and four thousand spectators, which is some measure of the 1821 gatherings in the same place, where "sermons in the grove" were given "before a crowded congregation."[72]

Details on the 1819 sermons at Vienna Village are not available, but the above meetings are prototypes for this period. Did Joseph Smith take the twelve-mile journey to Vienna, motivated to hear men of faith who had collectively moved mountains of doubt? That possibility is likely but not yet proved. He may have joined other Methodists traveling to the Sabbath preaching by wagon, carriage, or horseback. The legendary preacher George Lane attended the Vienna conference, and young Joseph may have heard him there, possibly because the family sent Joseph to sell food at this publicized event. According to Joseph's 1838 history, Methodist meetings first raised questions of authority and forgiveness, after which the quest for answers steadily intensified in Joseph's thinking, in large or small meetings, in discussion or meditation (see vv. 8–10). Whether the youth was present at Vienna preaching sessions or only discussed them with Palmyrans who attended, the Genesee Conference intensified family and local church discussions concerning church and salvation.

First Vision Circumstances in Palmyra Memories

As the only human witness of the First Vision, Joseph Smith left behind invaluable direct accounts. Next in significance are Joseph's comments remembered by close associates. His mother's published history has a chapter on the First Vision because her editors copied it from Joseph's 1838 history, giving him credit, as it was borrowed from the first publication in the Nauvoo *Times and Seasons*. Though she adds further details about the early dynamics of Joseph's family, she does not directly incorporate the First Vision in her narrative. Joseph's 1838 story of the First Vision had a preface and fade-out in Lucy's edited manuscript and first printing; these words may seem to come from her, but on closer study, they are paraphrases of Joseph's 1838 language. So Lucy's published history generally contains Joseph's 1838 dictation of the First Vision, and there is not now evidence that her son told her of the event before the early 1830s.[73] Joseph later said that right after the vision he told his mother that he had learned that Presbyterianism was not true (see v. 20), but this may be sharing a conclusion without explaining its basis.[74]

Joseph Smith discussed the First Vision with some acquaintances. He shared this experience with a Methodist minister but was rebuffed, which discouraged him from publicizing his story at that time (see v. 21).[75] He also reported "persecution," evidently what professionals now call "verbal abuse" of a sensitive teenager. This led to scorn from "professors of religion," a phrase for anyone who publicly professed belief, some of whom were evidently reacting directly to Joseph's "telling the story" (v. 22).[76] Pomeroy Tucker was a Palmyra native, three years older than Joseph, and claimed to know what Joseph told his Methodist probationary class as he withdrew after he had found answers: "The final conclusion announced by him was, that all sectarianism was fallacious, all the churches on a false foundation and the Bible a fable."[77] There is a corrosive undercurrent in the Tucker-Turner reporting and in the Palmyra-Manchester affidavits on Joseph and his family, all of which confirm what Joseph claims about "bitter persecution and reviling" by many respectable members of his society (v. 23).[78]

One disappointing source is William Smith, Joseph's younger brother born in Royalton, Vermont, in March 1811. He came to Palmyra at about age five, when mother and children reunited with Joseph Smith Sr. in the winter of 1816–17. As discussed, the years 1818 and 1819 were those of Joseph's intense seeking for a church authorized by God, when William was age seven and eight, with a next birthday about the time Joseph received the First Vision (see v. 14). As illustrated in the appendices of this article, William Smith's memories of his brother's visions begin with evening family gatherings, when Mother Smith tells of Joseph's descriptions of Moroni's coming and the assignment to obtain and translate the plates. In his *Early Mormon Documents*, Vogel published all or the main parts of seven family recollections by William Smith of varying lengths. However, William does not tell a First Vision story about Joseph Smith seeing the Father and Son, the main point of Joseph Smith's First Vision accounts.[79] William states or implies 1822–23 for the revivals he remembers, stating that Joseph was "about seventeen" (between December 1822 and December 1823) when he saw the earliest vision, after which Joseph shared this revelation with his assembled family.[80] At this point William's dates correlate somewhat with those given in Joseph's 1838 history for Moroni's appearances, including the delay of four years for Joseph to get the plates after the angel first appeared in 1823. Yet William seems to have little memory of Joseph's religious experiences before that, as shown in the appendices of this article. William is inconsistent in relating the coming of the angel. As William relates the story, Moroni once came in the sleeping chamber, but in several accounts William says that the angel appeared in the woods. In William's accounts, the angel might give one or more of these messages: answer which church was true, describe Joseph's future mission, instruct him about the plates and translation. Yet William's Book of Mormon story is premature by three years, compared with Joseph's accounts.

Thus William's version of Joseph's First Vision is unreliable. What he says about secular family history generally parallels what Joseph and Mother Smith say, but William's early history of Joseph's visions is skewed. William follows Joseph in his account of revivals, the prayer in the grove, and the brilliant glory, all of which is followed not by Joseph's vision of the Father and Son but by the appearance of an angel. It is as though William remembered hearing the latter story but failed to realize that there were two early visions, one in 1820 and one in 1823. In several documents William remembered Joseph's telling the family about Moroni when William was twelve (mostly 1823). But as he moved back in time, William became more dependent on others' records. In his major memoir, *William Smith on Mormonism*, he proves himself a secondhand witness on key issues by largely copying Oliver Cowdery's account of the 1820 period revivals and then borrowing from Orson Pratt to narrate the First Vision.[81] So William's account of Joseph's earliest visions is not independent recollection, but he has often lifted from others the information that earlier came from the Prophet. Matthew B. Brown, an admired researcher, died from an untimely heart attack October 5, 2011, but had published a short but important chart of a half-dozen phrases that William borrowed and remodeled from Orson Pratt's 1840 *Remarkable Visions*.[82] They are rearranged here in the following table.

Pratt's *Remarkable Visions* (1840)[83]	William Smith on Mormonism (1883)[84]
He . . . retired to . . . a grove . . . and knelt down, and began to call upon the Lord. . . .	He accordingly went out into the woods and falling upon his knees called for a long time upon the Lord. . . .
He, at length, saw a very bright and glorious light in the heavens above. . . . The light appeared to be gradually descending towards him. . . . By the time that it reached the tops of the trees, the whole wilderness . . . was illuminated. . . . He expected to have seen the leaves . . . consumed. . . .	A light appeared in the heavens, and descended until it rested upon the trees where he was. It appeared like fire. But to his great astonishment, did not burn the trees. . . .
He . . . saw two glorious personages. . . . He was informed, that his sins were forgiven . . . and he received a promise that the true doctrine . . . should . . . be made known to him.	An angel then appeared to him. . . . He told him that . . . the true way should be made known to him; that his sins were forgiven, etc.

The First Vision Gap in Oliver's Serial History

This article stresses that trustworthy history must come from firsthand observers or from those who reliably preserve what firsthand observers say. This means that the real story of the First

Vision must come from Joseph Smith's narratives, either from what he said or what a dependable person reported that he said about it. Some critics interpret later disclosures as inventions, but fuller details of important events often come out later. The Restored Church was officially organized on April 6, 1830, and on April 10, 1830, John Whitmer copied its founding constitution, which listed one major spiritual event preceding the coming of Moroni in 1823.[85] The early verses of this founding revelation stated that a mighty angel revealed the Book of Mormon "after that it truly was manifested unto this first Elder, that he had Received a remission of his sins." Some accounts of the First Vision, especially that of 1832, stressed that the First Vision assured Joseph that his sins were forgiven through Christ.[86] And the longer First Vision accounts describe an interim during which Joseph sinned again and repented and prayed for forgiveness, after which the angel Moroni appeared with a second message of acceptance while revealing the existence of an ancient buried record. Joseph's 1838 history says the angel came on the night of September 21, 1823 (see vv. 27–29), which is confirmed by Mother Smith's detailed story of the event and how it impressed oldest brother Alvin, who died prematurely on November 19, 1823.[87] Thus Joseph's early Church history stressed three religious events: the First Vision, which Joseph said granted him forgiveness,[88] followed by human sin and repentance, followed by the first coming of Moroni in late 1823 with a second assurance of forgiveness.

William Smith, however, was ill informed on the history that his brother repeatedly gave in print. Perhaps William was confused by following Oliver Cowdery's serial narrative of Joseph's first visions, published in the *Messenger and Advocate* in 1834–35. Oliver said he consulted Joseph in this series, which broadly correlates with Joseph's later history started in 1838 and canonized in the Pearl of Great Price. Joseph there described his spiritual journey with the main points he had given earlier in the opening verses of D&C 20 and in his 1832 history: the pre-1820 Palmyra religious conflict, the First Vision ("early" spring 1820), succumbing to "temptations, offensive in the sight of God" (v. 28), sincere repentance again, then the first appearances of the angel Moroni, in 1823 (see vv. 27, 29). Informed students of Church history now know that in 1832, Joseph Smith produced a private, compact history and background of the founding visions, which confirms and supplements the above experiences. This 1832 document is in print and was recently republished in the initial history volume of *The Joseph Smith Papers*.[89] Joseph penned a preface to the 1832 history, stating that he would narrate the miraculous events that brought the Church into existence. He then described the pre-1820 Palmyra religious conflict and the First Vision, which added Christ's words assuring Joseph of forgiveness, as well as declaring the departure of Christian churches from the original faith. Then, similar to some other religious writings of this period, Joseph acknowledged his shortcomings: "I fell into transgressions and sinned in many things which brought a wound upon my soul." Next came the vision of Moroni "when I was seventeen years of age" (December 23, 1822, to December 23, 1823).

After the violent destruction of the Missouri press, and the Jackson County exodus, Oliver Cowdery was called to move to Ohio and in 1834 became the founding editor of the *Messenger and Advocate*, the replacement religious newspaper of the Church. Oliver began a series on Joseph Smith's earliest visions, stating, as noted, that Joseph would help him personally and allow access to Church documents.[90] This statement shows that Oliver used the 1832 history, which contained the only known account then of the First Vision. In fact, Oliver quoted from the 1832 history in relating young Joseph Smith's Palmyra religious conflict, as shown in the chart below. But unlike Joseph, who made his revival story a preface for the First Vision, Oliver told of an 1820 revival and afterward postdated this religious conflict, thus deleting the First Vision and transitioning into the narrative of Moroni coming several years later. It is a minor mystery in Church history why the careful Oliver would explain Joseph's need to pray about which church was true but then avoid giving the vision that Joseph said was the answer to that prayer. Oliver, who first came to Palmyra as a schoolmaster in 1828, made some mistakes in his piece on Joseph's religious seeking in Palmyra about 1820. Since he inaccurately introduced Methodist minister George Lane into the Palmyra religious scene about 1820, this possibly caused Kirtland leaders to jump to the coming of Moroni in the next episode without taking space to mention that Lane supervised the district including the Palmyra circuit for the second half of 1824.

In summary, Joseph was the only mortal witness of the First Vision, and in his 1832 history he described the Palmyra religious conflict and the divine vision that answered his prayer in the "wilderness," after intensely seeking from ages twelve to fourteen. Oliver stated that he had access to Joseph's documents, one of which was Joseph's 1832 history, which was then the only known document with descriptions of Joseph's religious history, moving through the founding chain of events: revival confusion, the First Vision, human transgression, and the vision of Moroni.[91] But Oliver, who virtually states that the 1832 history is in his possession, follows parts of Joseph's background of the First Vision but does not narrate the First Vision. By this silence he differs from the only detailed Church history model then in existence. Oliver had also edited the founding revelation of D&C 20 for publication in the first printing of the revelations, titled the Book of Commandments, with its early verse (present D&C 20:5–6) alluding to Joseph's manifestation of forgiveness, which in the 1832 history came as a direct statement of Christ in the First Vision. We know that Oliver examined Joseph's 1832 history, for he quotes phrases from it, especially several that relate to Joseph's confusion before the prayer in the grove. Literary pirates thrive because they don't tell where they found their lines, but Cowdery is a historian, explaining to readers that his material came from writings and conversations with Joseph: "With his labor and with authentic documents now in our possession, we hope to render this a pleasing and agreeable narrative."[92]

Thus Oliver knew about the 1832 narrative of the First Vision. Yet he deleted the First Vision from his history sequences in spite of knowing about it. There are two places in the Cowdery installments where Oliver closely follows the order of events and phrases of the Prophet's 1832 document. First, the final *Messenger and Advocate* installment (October 1835) depicted an incident that had not yet appeared in any Latter-day Saint writing except the 1832 manuscript history. This was the first view of the plates by the young Joseph, who was so overwhelmed with their value that he reached to take them for selfish motives, only to be checked and rebuked in a sudden appearance of Moroni. Both accounts (Cowdery's 1835 installment and Joseph's 1832 history) refer to the angel's original warning in identical words: the Prophet was directed to obtain the plates with "an eye single to the glory of God." Both accounts record the same question of frustration: "Why can I not obtain this book?" And the answer of the angel is identical in each account: "You have not kept the commandments of the Lord."[93]

Interrelationship is reinforced by comparing Joseph's early religious conflict in the two documents. Verbal correlations do not always prove dependence, since two similar phrases may come from an earlier written source, which does not exist in this case. Moreover, an additional tool is similar sequence of phrasing, in this case showing that Cowdery sometimes followed wording but also moved through the same succession of topics already written by Joseph Smith:

1832 Manuscript History[94]	December 1834, Cowdery Letter[95]
My mind became seriously imprest with regard to the all important concerns for the wellfare of my immortal Soul. . . .	His mind was led to more seriously contemplate the importance of a move of this kind.
I discovered that they did not . . . adorn their profession by a holy walk and Godly conversation agreeable to what I found contained in that sacred depository this was a grief to my Soul. . . .	To profess godliness without its benign influence upon the heart, was a thing so foreign from his feelings, that his spirit was not at rest day nor night.
There was no society or denomination that built upon the gospel of Jesus Christ as recorded in the new testament and I felt to mourn. . . .	To unite with a society professing to be built upon the only sure foundation, and that profession be a vain one, was calculated . . . to arouse the mind. . . .
Therefore I cried unto the Lord for mercy for there was none else to whom I could go.	In this situation where could he go?

The Palmyra Revival Periods Spanning 1820

In his revival installment (December 1834), Oliver dated the "excitement raised on the subject of religion" to the "15th year" of the Prophet's life, a time which is strictly December 23, 1819, to December 23, 1820. Oliver Cowdery included material in that issue that was never confirmed in any account of Joseph Smith, naming the leader in these revivals as "one Mr. Lane, a presiding Elder of the Methodist Church," and identified the scene of his labors as "Palmyra, and vicinity." The next history installment (February 1835) hit a huge bump in the road. Pleading "an error in the type," editor Cowdery said that the above events happened "in the 17th" year of Joseph Smith's life. According to Oliver's initial observation, this adjustment "would bring the date down to the year 1823," but the correction is confused, since "the 17th" year is strictly December 23, 1821, to December 23, 1822, whereas Joseph's specific date for Moroni's coming is September 21, 1823, almost a year later than Cowdery's first date (see JS—H 1:27, 29). "I do not deem it necessary," the editor told his audience, "to write further on the subject of this excitement." Yet this plan was not strictly followed, for Cowdery's narrative portrays Joseph as continuing to search for "assurance that he was accepted" by God until 1823, "while this excitement continued." Oliver then pictured Moroni appearing in the cabin loft for a message of acceptance, which corresponds to Joseph's histories of the appearances of Moroni in 1823. As Oliver methodically closed the angel's first instructions to Joseph, he added that he had given the essence of the story but not with perfect "arrangement," which might mean flawed dating or an imperfect order of events or both: "I have now given you a rehearsal of what was communicated to our brother, when he was directed to go and obtain the record of the Nephites. I may have missed in arrangement in some instances, but the principle is preserved."[96]

So Oliver opened Joseph's history with the boy's seeking in 1820 and corrected the date to 1823, admitting in closing that he perhaps was mistaken "in some instances." Joseph's 1838 history timed the First Vision as "early in the spring" of 1820 (v. 14), which would require a starting revival about a year earlier for Joseph's investigation period. And Joseph's 1832 history is explicit that his investigation period lasted at least two years, "from the age of twelve years to fifteen" (late 1817 to late 1820), apparently an inclusive approximation.[97] So the youth's period of seeking is 1818–19 in Joseph's histories but is delayed from 1820 to 1823 in Oliver's narration, when both men were in close touch in Kirtland. Though the sudden shift of Palmyra religious excitement from pre-1820 to 1823 was made in the February *Messenger and Advocate*, that issue was published on or after February 27, since a school notice of that date appeared on the last page. Joseph Smith was a strong administrator, and likely he directed Cowdery or agreed with him on whether to explain the mistakes made in the revival period in the previous December issue. We can identify these December errors but lack Joseph's journals or presidency records to explain why dates were changed with little comment. Administrative minutes in early Kirtland are limited to the first book of high council minutes, which show a high level of meetings and presidency activity in February 1835. The presidency and Kirtland high council were the chief authorities, and during that month the Twelve and many Seventies were chosen, with appointments discussed, instruction meetings held, and many ordinations and blessings given. One explanation of the narrative leap in Cowdery's narrative from 1820 to 1823 is the lack of time to fully explain corrections. After all, Joseph had already handwritten his 1832 account of the First Vision and Joseph's search beforehand for a Biblical church and divine forgiveness, which could later be edited and published. Yet the next stage in preparing a full history for printing was not made by the Prophet until mid-1838. Perhaps the Cowdery confusion in early 1835 convinced Joseph Smith that his personal history could be accurately written only by himself.

The most obvious chronological error in Cowdery's flawed revival installment (December 1835) is dating a Palmyra "great awakening or excitement raised on the subject of religion" in "the 15th year of his [Joseph's] life," which technically began December 23, 1819. And the most obvious personal error is crediting the leadership of this local revival to Elder George Lane, whereas he was not assigned as presiding elder of the circuit including Palmyra until the summer of 1824. Methodist and community records furnish a good survey of Lane's life, the topic of Professor Porter's reprinted article in this volume. As a young man, Lane was a circuit minister assigned to scattered congregations in huge western New York areas, but he retired from itinerancy during 1810–19, during which time he was in business and local government in the Wilkes-Barre vicinity, in Pennsylvania's upper Susquehanna Valley, roughly two hundred miles southeast of Palmyra. He returned to the traveling ministry in mid-1819, journeying from upper Pennsylvania to the 1819 Genesee conference sessions in Vienna (later Phelps), New York, a dozen miles from the Smith farm, as discussed above. Lane's name appears in the minutes, and a fellow minister remembered that "he and I set off together on horseback" for the gathering.[98] Joseph Smith's proximity to this impressive occasion and his proven connection with Methodism about this time make it possible that the religious youth heard Lane preach at the 1819 conference, though Lane's northeast route to the 1819 Vienna gathering was direct and evidently not close to Palmyra, as far as possibly attending outdoor meetings in that vicinity before the annual conference. At this 1819 Genesee Conference, Lane was appointed presiding elder of one of the six districts, the Susquehanna District, and he took a direct path back to upper Pennsylvania, again making a camp meeting near Palmyra unlikely. In fact, Lane was assigned within the Susquehanna District until 1824, when he was made presiding elder of the large Ontario District encompassing Palmyra. Early the next year, he wrote a detailed report of his ministry at Palmyra and his circuit conferences in that area and then left the traveling ministry because of his wife's serious illness, afterward residing in Pennsylvania and preaching only in that locality for a few years. In 1836 he began administrative assignments in New York City as Methodist assistant book agent and then as book agent until his retirement in 1852 and death in Wilkes-Barre, Pennsylvania, in 1859.[99]

As Larry Porter notes in his careful research on Lane, Joseph may have heard George Lane preach at Vienna Village, a dozen miles from the Smith farm, at the Genesee Conference in July 1819. Otherwise, this minister had no extended contact with Joseph Smith in any official assignment until Lane visited Palmyra after appointment as presiding elder of the Ontario District, after midyear 1824.[100] It is most unlikely that young Joseph went to hear Lane preach in 1824, since he told his mother at that time that he could learn more spending time alone with his Bible than by hearing preaching in Palmyra meetings.[101] However, hearing Lane preach at Sabbath sessions of the 1819 weeklong Genesee conference is possible, as well as hearing other devout circuit riders then. A younger historian-preacher was at a camp meeting held a couple of months after the Vienna Conference and gave his impression of Lane's preaching then: "The exhortations of the presiding elder, George Lane, were overwhelming. Sinners quailed under them, and many cried aloud for mercy."[102] Historians have recently learned that Lane participated in a camp meeting in July 1820, near present Honeoye, some twenty-two miles southwest of the Smith farm, but it seems a little too far and definitely too late to be relevant for the First Vision early that spring.[103]

Oliver accurately described Lane personally but placed him in Palmyra years before his assignment there. Oliver came into Palmyra as a teacher in the fall of 1828 and boarded with the Smiths that winter. Memories of Lane no doubt lingered from the minister's 1824 presidency of the new Ontario District, but Joseph Smith had no known contact with Lane at Palmyra before the 1820 First Vision. Moreover, Joseph never mentioned Lane in the several accounts he left of the First Vision. At the end of his life, William Smith credited Lane with preaching on James 1:4–5, thus suggesting the scripture that moved the youth to pray for God's direction on which church to join.[104] What basis William had for this claim is not known, though he depended on Oliver for his Lane story and on Orson Pratt for his First Vision account, as charts above and in the appendices show. Joseph mentions James 1:4–5 in all but one First Vision account and generally states that he discovered the verse providentially in opening his Bible.[105] Perhaps Joseph wanted a more accurate account (without Lane) because he so strongly felt that God alone directed him to pray at this crucial moment in his life. Lane was a devout man and could easily deliver a message to ask of God, but Joseph's hearing about James 1:4–5 from Lane before the First Vision is not historically established. The theory that Joseph heard Lane preach on this topic at the 1819 western New York conference seems to contradict the self-discovery of the 1838 history (see v. 11) and its several parallels. Since Oliver's narrative of Joseph's early visions placed Lane in Palmyra prior to the First Vision, Oliver confessed his chronological mistake, but simply moved the story ahead to Joseph's next vision, without further comment on Reverend Lane.

Smith Presbyterian Conversions before Early 1820

This study opened by questioning the First Vision relevance of Palmyra area revivals that brought about four hundred into the Methodist, Presbyterian, and Baptist churches in the 1824–25 period. Revisionist scholars concluded that this was the revival that Joseph described in his 1838 history, claiming Joseph had dated it too early. But the forepart of this article analyzed the four-day Palmyra camp meeting of late June 1818, which harvested forty converts from one or two thousand in attendance. This fills all the conditions that Joseph recalled in his 1838 history except "great multitudes" of converts in "that district of country," which on its face is a much larger group within a larger slice of territory than the more constricted environs of Palmyra. The 1824–25 Palmyra area revival doesn't measure up to "multitudes" either. In looking for correlations to Joseph's 1838 history, an open-minded reader should look for a Methodist event described by "unusual excitement," which sounds more like a special event, like a camp meeting, rather than meetings programmed in a regular schedule. A four-day meeting bringing forty immediate converts fits Joseph's "excitement" as much as the 1824–25 revivals, whose four hundred converts were spread over many months. The historical record now includes both this mini-revival with spreading effects before the First Vision, and a community revival of hundreds starting about six years later. Merely quoting the more numerous conversions in the 1824–25 Palmyra area is no reason to ignore the 1818 journal entry recording the forty Methodist converts from the 1818 Palmyra camp meeting, backed up for that period by Joseph Smith's 1832 and 1838 histories and the memories of Palmyra apprentices who were Joseph's peers. Joseph's histories picture religious enthusiasm spreading in his area before 1820, and Mother Smith's history includes an 1818 anxiety dream of Father Smith with a revival setting, about being in a church building too late but seeking Christ's mercy to forgive his sins.[106]

Smith family materials confirm the increased religious activity at Palmyra before 1820. Joseph's 1838 history relates that he was fourteen ("in my fifteenth year") when his family (his mother, his sister Sophronia, and his brothers Hyrum and Samuel) "was proselyted to the Presbyterian faith" or "joined that church" (v. 7). Palmyra Western Presbyterian Church records are missing, but family history shows that several Smiths were seeking a true church before 1820, as was Joseph. Early in her marriage, Lucy had received believer's baptism without commitment to a specific church, later commenting that she retained this status "until my oldest son attained his 22nd year."[107] She refers to the oldest living son, Alvin, who died of a doctor's folk remedy in late 1823 but had started his twenty-second year on February 11, 1820.[108] Here she agrees with Joseph's 1838 history that she made a Presbyterian commitment by early 1820. Moreover, Joseph recalled at Nauvoo that he came from the 1820 vision in the grove and told Mother Lucy that he had learned for himself that "Presbyterianism is not true" (v. 20). Thus the older Smiths were investigating Palmyra churches on a parallel track to Joseph prior to the First Vision. The Neibaur journal, discussed above, has Joseph recalling a Methodist "Revival meeting," likely the June 1818 camp meeting in the Seager journal, where "his mother & Br & Sist got religion."[109] As Joseph says in the 1838 history, he was fourteen at the end of 1819, the period when his mother and three siblings chose Presbyterianism, and afterward Alvin received a Presbyterian funeral in 1823.[110]

On which level were Lucy and three children Presbyterians? This could be Presbyterian attendance, attendance on formal probation, or full membership, with right of the Lord's Supper. Yet historians following Walters have tried to merge revivals dated around 1820 with those after Alvin's death by claiming (without direct evidence) that Lucy became a Presbyterian member in her grief about 1824. Mother Smith does describe a Palmyra awakening then, when her hopes were raised by a minister who sought cooperation from local denominations, though she could not influence her husband or son Joseph to attend these meetings. However, Lucy's history does not say she joined a church in the surge of religion at Palmyra after Alvin's late 1823 death.[111] A later religious conflict throws light on the intervening years. In March 1830, Lucy and sons Hyrum and Samuel were served notice of a church hearing for nonattendance and were then visited by officials of the Palmyra Presbyterian Church.[112] Lucy's history gives her version of the conversation with visiting Presbyterian elders, when the Smiths defended the Book of Mormon vigorously, which was significant, since the Smith men were two of the Eight Witnesses, who had seen and handled the plates. The hearing minutes still exist, indicating that the Smiths "did not wish to unite with us anymore." The defendants avoided the hearing, which charged them with "neglect of public worship and the Sacrament of the Lord's Supper for the last eighteen months." Instead of being cut off, the three were disfellowshipped, "suspended from the Sacrament of the Lord's Supper."[113] These records are also significant for what charges were not filed against the Smiths. Over several years, charges appear for serious moral infractions, but the Smiths were disciplined for inactivity, an important counterbalance to community affidavits later taken against them, which were selectively obtained with negative labels such as laziness, a charge which is objectively incorrect. Moreover, the charge of church inactivity probably indicates that the Presbyterian Smiths had fairly regularly attended preaching and communion meetings during the early 1820s, or the nonattendance charge would have been filed earlier.

Conclusions: Joseph's Accuracy on the First Vision Setting

This paper presents the following sequences and historical judgments, listed somewhat in the order of the above discussion:

1. Understanding the historical background of the First Vision has been obstructed by poor recognition of how early young Joseph Smith started to search for true religion and the true church.

2. A correlation of Joseph's accounts indicates that he actively investigated Protestant groups in his area during the years 1818 and 1819 (1832 account), or "in process of time" prior to receiving the First Vision in "early" spring 1820 (JS—H 1:8, 14).

3. By Joseph's accounts (e.g., v. 8) and those of two contemporary Palmyra printers' apprentices, Joseph developed a preference for Methodism in the above years and some degree of Methodist activity.

4. Joseph's 1838 history says that his intense searching began after Methodists started a "religious excitement" in "the place where we lived" (v. 5). This has drawn claims that there is no 1820 Palmyra revival evidence, and that the Palmyra area revival of about four hundred converts in 1824–25 is the only historic match.

5. This article focuses on a Palmyra camp meeting of four days in late June 1818, documented at the time by the journal of Aurora Seager, a Methodist traveling elder who died at the end of the following year. This camp meeting was attended by one of the three American Methodist bishops and about a dozen circuit preachers, resulting in forty conversions, which, in comparison with other contemporary camp meetings in western New York, would come from an estimated crowd of one to two thousand. This gathering precisely fits the local conditions before the First Vision as described by Joseph Smith's 1838 history and his other accounts. This huge assembly near a village of one thousand would certainly arrest the attention of the young seeker Joseph Smith and morally compel him to attend meetings because of documented personal zeal and additionally because of the family business of selling refreshments at public gatherings.

6. Orsamus Turner, Palmyra printing apprentice and early editor-historian, said his memories of young

Joseph Smith were "distinct ones" and that Joseph caught "a spark of Methodism in the camp meeting, away down in the woods, on the Vienna road," which ran through the east side of Palmyra Village and past a Methodist campground further south that was reused in later Methodist meetings.

7. In 1844 Joseph Smith's Hebrew tutor, Alexander Neibaur, wrote details in his journal of a conversation on the First Vision, with Joseph Smith stating, "The first call he had a Revival meeting his mother & Br & Sist got Religion, he wanted to get Religion too wanted to feel & shout like the Rest but could feel nothing . . . went into the Wood to pray. . . . After a wile a other person came to the side of the first Mr Smith then asked must I join the Methodist Church = No = they are not my people, all have gone astray . . . but this is my Beloved son harken ye him."[114] This Neibaur journal and editor-printer Turner's "distinct" memories (point 6 above) establish Joseph's presence in an early Methodist camp meeting, likely the one reported by the Aurora Seager journal (point 5 above), which is dated June 1818 and located near Palmyra Village, with a crowd probably larger than that settlement.

8. Parts of Joseph Smith's 1832 handwritten Church history were copied and paraphrased by Oliver Cowdery in his 1834–35 *Messenger and Advocate* series on Church history, which began with his version of the Palmyra religious "excitement" when Joseph was fourteen. Although the First Vision was narrated in Joseph's 1832 history that Oliver examined, Oliver did not mention it, evidently because

he dropped further discussion of the early Palmyra revival because of mistakes. One major mistake was describing Methodist elder George Lane as a local revival leader about 1820, though Lane was not assigned there until appointed presiding elder of the district including Palmyra in mid-1924, when he became prominent in later church expansion there.

9. William Smith also reported George Lane as participating in the pre-1820 Palmyra revival, though William's First Vision accounts are unreliable, borrowing revival phrasing directly from Oliver Cowdery's serial Church history and First Vision material from Orson Pratt's 1840 pamphlet, *Remarkable Visions*.

10. The 1838 Joseph Smith history has been faulted because local history did not record "great multitudes" as converted "in the place where we lived" (v. 5) before the First Vision in early spring 1820. But this reading shrinks Joseph Smith's narration of time, for his 1832 account describes the full years of 1818–19. This narrow reading also shrinks location, for the 1838 history narrates the beginning, local event as a Methodist "unusual excitement," which progressed from "the place where we lived" to all major denominations "in that region of country" and in "the whole district of country" (v. 5). Such "great multitudes" of Christian converts come at the end of a progression of events, not at the beginning, as Joseph perceived it. His slice of Church history began with the local Methodist "unusual excitement." And Joseph quickly identified the crescendo of growth as the "whole district of country," which may be a general term for

his large area or his technical term for the whole Methodist Genesee District, which the earlier chart shows as then comprising about ten preaching stations in each of thirteen circuits stretching across upper New York from the mid-Finger Lakes to Buffalo. This multicounty Methodist "District" increased by 1,187 in the conference year ending July 1819, and Joseph included "all the sects in that district of country" (v. 5), which means that he has in mind perhaps three thousand Christian converts in his general area during the year before the First Vision.[115]

11. The most recent evaluation of Joseph Smith's multiple accounts of the First Vision concludes, "They combine impressively to give a consistent and coherent picture."[116] This article broadens that conclusion to note that Joseph's accounts coalesce not only with each other but also with family, local, and revival records, showing that his First Vision setting is historically authentic.

Appendices: Palmyra Memories about Young Joseph Smith

The following profiles are reprinted with some changes from my spring 1969 article, "Circumstantial Confirmation of the First Vision through Reminiscences" (*BYU Studies* 9, no. 3: 373–404). The present article builds on this information, which shows that William Smith relies on secondary information about Joseph's First Vision, though he has some independent recollections of the pre-1820 period. The reminiscences of two young Palmyra printing apprentices who knew Joseph Smith are historically important. Thus full information appears here on Orsamus Turner and Pomeroy Tucker, who gave sparse but important religious information about him, though slanted negatively.

Appendix A: William Smith's Memories of Events Prior to 1823

As the last surviving brother of Joseph Smith, vocal William Smith gave several apparent memoirs of his brother's reports of early religious experiences. But are they memories from William's early childhood or things he only heard about later? Joseph's religious investigations probably peaked in 1819, soon after William turned eight years of age.[117] An example of William's defective early memory is his claim that the family moved from Palmyra Village to the rural Manchester Township "in 1821."[118] This is factually in error because an official survey of June 13, 1820, "taken by the poor old town compass" begins on the south county line and locates the starting point "three rods fourteen links southeast of Joseph Smith's dwelling house."[119] Orsamus Turner remembered seeing this self-built log structure the previous winter, which was on the edge of Palmyra Township but adjoining the Manchester farm on the north. According to Mother Smith and Palmyra resident Pomeroy Tucker, the Smith family moved to their farm two years after moving to Palmyra Village, the year that William turned seven.[120]

Up to 1823, William resisted spiritual instruction, since he was "quite young and inconsiderate";[121] during the years 1823–27, he paid "no attention to religion of any kind."[122] William left two extended narrations of his early life. In both, the earliest point regarding Joseph's religious experience is the appearance of the angel in 1823: "I remember when Joseph called his father's family together and told them that he had seen an angel, and what this angel had told him."[123] Lucy and William Smith report Joseph's announcement to the family similarly. Mother Smith draws the vivid image of several family sessions, "all seated in a circle," giving "the most profound attention" to the young Prophet.[124] William underlines the first reaction: "The whole family were melted to tears, and believed all he said."[125] The mother and brother agree that Joseph shared the coming of Moroni with them in 1823.

There is an informative corollary to William's lack of firsthand information prior to 1823. His published memoirs depend heavily upon the Cowdery account for background of Joseph's vision. William's narrations follow the same sequence as the Cowdery installments of December 1834 and February 1835 in the *Latter Day Saints' Messenger and Advocate*, though Oliver's ornate style is considerably condensed by William. The Prophet's brother copies Oliver Cowdery quite directly, with the intervening quotation of Matthew 7:13–14 used similarly by both writers:

Oliver Cowdery in 1834	William Smith in 1883
If he went to one he was told they were right, and all others were wrong—If to another, the same was heard from those:	If he went to one he was told they were right, and all others were wrong. If to another, the same was heard from them.
All professed to be the true church. . . .[126]	Each professed to be the true church. . . .
But if others were not benefited, our brother was urged forward and strengthened in the determination to know for himself of the certainty and reality of pure and holy religion. . . .	All this however was beneficial to him, as it urged him forward, and strengthened him in the determination to know for himself of the certainty and reality of pure and holy religion.
He continued to call upon the Lord in secret for a full manifestation of divine approbation . . . to have an assurance that he was accepted of him.[127]	He continued in secret to call upon the Lord for a full manifestation of his will, the assurance that he was accepted of him.[128]

Significantly, William Smith relied heavily upon his own memories of what Joseph said to the family about Moroni's coming, but he relied upon Oliver's published series for the background of the vision. As explained in this article, this produced a mismatch, for Oliver described the 1820 period Palmyra religious "excitement" and then skipped over to the 1823 coming of Moroni. This suggests that William had no memory of hearing about the First Vision. By his own performance, William is not likely to remember Joseph's consecutive religious story before late 1823, although he appears to have valid personal memories before then. He admitted that his repetition of Joseph's early visions was inferior to the firsthand narration of his older brother: "A more elaborate and accurate description of his vision, however, will be found in his own history."[129]

Appendix B: Biographical Sketch of Pomeroy Tucker

Joseph Smith had a double reason to attend any camp meeting in his vicinity, religious investigation and the family refreshment business. The main evidence for the latter comes from a former printer's apprentice in Palmyra, Pomeroy Tucker. Tucker's career was remarkably like Orsamus Turner's, whose biography follows this account. Born in Palmyra August 10, 1802, Tucker evidently remained there until the time of his apprenticeship at the *Palmyra Register* around 1820.[130] After serving as a journeyman printer at Canandaigua, he returned to Palmyra to purchase and manage the *Wayne Sentinel* in the fall of 1823.[131] His professional life as a journalist continued over thirty years, mostly with that paper, though he was also a public servant at various levels and author of a book on Mormonism in 1867, three years before his death.

From the point of view of history, Tucker's *Origin, Rise, and Progress of Mormonism* is a disappointing performance. With access to the generation that remembered the establishment of the Prophet's work, the experienced editor is content to quote the Hurlburt-Howe affidavits, to repeat common gossip, and to quote extensive portions of the Book of Mormon and articles about Brigham Young for the bulk of the book. Although but weakly living up to the subtitle ("Personal Remembrances and Historical Collections Hitherto Unwritten"), Tucker does relate valuable information concerning the period of the publication of the Book of Mormon. He also claims knowledge of the Smiths "since their removal to Palmyra from Vermont in 1816, and during their continuance there and in the adjoining town of Manchester."[132] There is no reason to question this firsthand contact, provided one is on guard not to take his western New York prejudice for fact. It is to his credit that he could at least distinguish between the two. He repeats tattered stories about Joseph Smith's dishonesty, only to admit in "common fairness" that such allegations were "not within the remembrance of the writer."[133] Although Tucker is content to repeat the armchair observations about the laziness of the Smiths, his specific descriptions prove the opposite. Most of Tucker's unattributed particulars of the Smiths' early Palmyra life are probably based on his observation. Much of his negative material from Palmyra is traceable to published statements, and the "hitherto unwritten" incidents are typically details of human interest. The descriptions of the Smiths in Palmyra prior to 1820 tend to belong to this category.

Tucker is particular with regard to the Smiths' arrival at Palmyra in 1816 and removal to the uncleared land in Manchester in 1818; moreover, he has a fairly accurate knowledge of their physical and financial arrangements, evidently quite independent of the earlier published details of Lucy Smith. There is no reason to question the picture of the refreshment

Orson Pratt's pamphlet Remarkable Visions *tells of how Joseph Smith's "remarkable vision" came in response to his prayer "in the wilderness." (Photo from a video created by the Church Audiovisual Department, © 2001 Intellectual Reserve, Inc. All rights reserved)*

shop of the Smiths in Palmyra, which catered to holiday crowds. Even after the move to the farm, there was "the continued business of peddling cake and beer in the village on days of public doings." Tucker remembers Joseph in particular "as a clerk" in such selling.[134] This activity, somewhat attested in Palmyra sources, provides a practical reason for camp meeting attendance.[135] Such meetings were notable as places of socializing and festivity. De Witt Clinton left a classic description of the typical campground of that decade, featuring not merely the preaching and the crowds but the "persons with cakes, beer, and other refreshments for sale."[136] It appears to be the Smiths' business and Joseph's special charge to be present at such public events in the vicinity.

Pomeroy Tucker also verifies the circumstances of the First Vision, all the more important because the editor's positive views seem unintended. Assuming 1827 as the beginning of Joseph Smith's revelations, the editor relates the "remarkable vision" that came "about this time" in response to the youth's prayer "in the wilderness." The words of this experience are generally placed in quotation marks, and the phrases are borrowed in sequence from Orson Pratt's pamphlet *Remarkable Visions*.[137] Tucker depends verbally on this written source, although he seems to have some memory of what young Joseph Smith said about the First Vision while still in Palmyra. But in Tucker's first chapter, where Mormon writings are not in evidence and the editor's recollections are concentrated, the following description of the early religious life of the Prophet is given:

> Protracted revival meetings were customary in some of the churches, and Smith frequented those of different denominations, sometimes professing to participate in their devotional exercises. At one time he joined the probationary class of the Methodist Church in Palmyra, and made some active demonstrations of engagedness, though his assumed convictions were insufficiently grounded or abiding to carry him along to the saving point of conversion, and he soon withdrew from the class. The final conclusion announced by him was, that all sectarianism was fallacious, all the churches on a false foundation, and the Bible a fable.[138]

No other Palmyra source identifies young Joseph Smith as a member of the Methodist "probationary class." Since Tucker immediately follows with a reference to "all the early avowals and other evidences remembered," he apparently claims firsthand knowledge of Joseph's temporary religious affiliation and reason for its abrupt termination: he publicly "announced ... that all sectarianism was fallacious." A study of Turner requires a date of about 1820 for this tentative Methodist association, and Tucker emphasizes that "he soon withdrew from the class," a specific description that explains Turner's metaphor, "a spark of Methodism." This evidence indicates that about 1820 Joseph Smith was openly expressing the identical convictions that he later maintained came at that early time through the First Vision. Since such negative attitudes could have brought only scorn upon him, it is unlikely that a fourteen-year-old boy would take this extreme position without some religious experience to solidify his personal convictions.

The historical reconstruction of Joseph's announcement about 1820 that the churches were wrong throws a different light on subsequent community opinion. The Hurlburt-Howe affidavits generally do not reach back to Joseph's early religious investigations, so they are suspect on the ground of merely reporting public reaction to Joseph's religious explanations. Mrs. Brodie stated a thesis that is found in Palmyra sources in several contradictory forms. By this theory, the earlier Joseph Smith was a seeker of buried treasure, not the sincere religious investigator that he describes himself to be in all of his vision accounts. Supposedly the metamorphosis from adventuring to outward religion took place about 1827. A standard and crucial proof in building this image is satirical editor Abner Cole's 1831 summary of the evolutionary hypothesis, speaking of the angelic revelation of the Book of Mormon: "It however appears quite certain that the prophet himself never made any serious pretensions to religion until his late pretended revelation."[139]

Contemporaneous opinions may be factual or legendary. Cole was editor of the Palmyra *Reflector*, a satirical newspaper carrying his columns under the name of Dogberry. He attributes his information on the mother and father of the Prophet to others and implies secondhand information on Joseph Smith. In 1820 Abner Cole was middle-aged and a successful lawyer-entrepreneur with no reason to notice a teenager from rural Manchester. But the apprentices Tucker and Turner were near the young prophet's age level and moved in similar social and perhaps religious circles. Tucker's initial chapter of impressions about the Smiths is likely to be better informed than Cole's writing. Pomeroy Tucker portrays Joseph as a young man of unusual "taciturnity," speaking mainly to "his intimate associates" and generally ridiculed because he could relate a "marvelous absurdity with the utmost apparent gravity."[140] Is this the community response to Joseph's limited sharing of the First Vision? Palmyra editor Tucker has his own evolutionary theory of the young Prophet advancing from reading worthless fiction to serious study of the Bible. In fact, as a student of the scriptures, he became so capable that he could discuss texts "with great assurance" and with "original and unique" interpretations. What this proved to Tucker is highly instructive. Joseph Smith came to "disgustingly blasphemous" conclusions which, coupled with his religious investigation and announcement that he would join no sect, disclosed that he and his family "were unqualified atheists," an inevitable "hypothesis" based on "their mockeries of Christianity."[141]

Tucker's reasoning shows that most epithets applied to the Smiths may be grounded in the community disbelief of Joseph's visions. If Tucker equates unorthodoxy with atheism, then his readers know that this editor represents a rigid social structure whose labels on nonconformity cannot be taken at face value. Cole's report that the early Joseph Smith "never made any serious pretensions to religion" really means that Joseph declined to affiliate with any church. Paradoxically, Joseph's original announcement of religious convictions created a reputation for irreligion, and the closed society that so perceived the young prophet lost the memory of his earlier religious investigations and convictions about 1820, which were recorded by his acquaintances Turner and Tucker.[142]

Appendix C: Biographical Sketch of Orsamus Turner

Most statements from Palmyra-Manchester residents are more interested in ridiculing the Smiths than factually describing their life in the early 1820s. So the value of the affidavit format is limited because many statements are canonized gossip rather than balanced appraisals of real people. Orsamus Turner is not exempt from this criticism, but he differs from the majority who made anti-Smith affidavits in that he is capable of separating rumor from personal knowledge. Turner led a relatively short but distinguished life spanning the years 1801 to 1855. Born on the edge of civilization in western New York, he had a log cabin childhood and grew with the country to become a respected editor and author.[143] In 1852 he published a sketch of Joseph Smith and Mormonism in his *History of the Pioneer Settlement of Phelps and Gorham's Purchase*, which he partially drew from his own experience. Because the time of Turner's residence in Palmyra is fairly pinpointed, his recollections of young Joseph Smith can be dated. He remembers their Manchester "rude log house, with but a small spot underbrushed around it," in "the winter of '19, '20." He recalls the Wayne County countryside because he had been assigned during his apprenticeship "in a newspaper office at Palmyra" to accompany a blind newspaper carrier "in the years 1818, '19."[144] This employment did not begin before October 1818, when the *Palmyra Register* was first issued by Timothy S. Strong, who moved away from Palmyra in 1823.[145] Turner says that Strong's apprentices were Luther Tucker, Pomeroy Tucker, and "the author of this work." But young Turner did not serve his whole time in Palmyra, for he also notes that he was an apprentice under James Bemis at Canandaigua.[146] Since he expressed a great admiration for Bemis based on intimate contact, he probably spent the years 1821 and 1822 at Canandaigua, where he "finished his apprenticeship."[147]

Turner later recounted that he heard of the need of a printer-editor at Lockport, about a hundred miles west of Palmyra, where he had evidently returned from Canandaigua for a brief period of school. He traveled to the new locality, arrived "but a few days after we had reached the age of 21 years" (about August 1, 1822), and purchased the new *Lockport Observatory*.[148] Concerning the year 1822, Turner recalled, "The author . . . became the editor and publisher of the paper, in August, of that year."[149] In 1847 a fellow editor summed up his career in Lockport as continuous to that time: "Either as publisher, editor, or assistant editor, [he] has continued at his post from 1822, to the present time."[150] Turner's personal recollections of Joseph Smith of necessity refer to the period prior to the late summer of 1822 and are probably no later than 1820, the latest date of Palmyra memoirs in his writings.

Orsamus Turner declined to dignify Mormonism with serious treatment. Instead he preferred sarcasm, admitting that his sketch was made "lightly—with a seeming levity." Although it relies heavily upon community hearsay and in irony reads like Gibbon on Christianity, certain portions of the sketch bring the early life of the Smiths into the focus of personal contact. One conclusion is based on "those who were best acquainted with the Smith family" and reports that "there is no foundation for the statement that their original manuscript was written by a Mr. Spaulding, of Ohio."[151] But the most notable break in derisive tone is the early introduction of Joseph Smith into his narrative. At this point Turner gives glimpses of Joseph's early life, prefacing them with these remarks: "The author's own recollections of him are distinct ones."[152] A series of vignettes follows, portraying the young farmer's son bringing small loads of wood into the village, doing odd jobs, and performing errands, one of which was to get the weekly paper. On one occasion Turner and another apprentice inked Joseph's face for his curiosity about the press. The sketch lapses back to derision after this final paragraph of personal recollection:

> But Joseph had a little ambition; and some very laudable aspirations; the mother's intellect occasionally shone out in him feebly,

especially when he used to help us solve some portentous questions of moral or political ethics, in our juvenile debating club, which we moved down to the old red school house on Durfee street, to get rid of the annoyance of critics that used to drop in upon us in the village; and subsequently, after catching a spark of Methodism in the camp meeting, away down in the woods, on the Vienna road, he was a very passable exhorter in evening meetings.[153]

From his personal contact, Turner gives the time, place, and nature of the Prophet's early Methodist attraction. The time is probably during the editor's Palmyra apprenticeship, presumably 1820 or before, and is certainly no later than the summer of 1822, when he settled at Lockport. The semi-conversion is to Methodism, precisely the belief that Joseph Smith said attracted him. Turner's "Vienna road" plainly means the road running diagonally between Palmyra Village and Vienna Village (renamed Phelps), about a dozen miles away. The road is still identified by that name, and Turner's local association is shown by his location of a mill site "a mile east of the village [of Palmyra], on the Vienna road."[154] "Away down in the woods" on this road is not a considerable distance from Palmyra, for this campground was reused and understood as near Palmyra.

Itinerant Methodist preachers were at the peak of their influence in Joseph Smith's youth, and their rural protracted meetings were so common that they were taken for granted. Preachers' diaries and memoirs of this period are filled with references to these "forest gatherings," which drew their audience from the countryside, up to a dozen miles' radius. This gathering is incredible to many now locked into a sedentary culture, but the pioneer's life was lonely, and he paid the price of travel for his religious and social meetings. Turner remembers an eight-mile trip by ox sled as nothing unusual for "an evening's visit," and he quotes a settler as recalling the "itinerating Methodist ministers; we used to go through the woods, generally on foot, whenever we heard of one of their appointments."[155]

Notes

Thanks to able research assistant Elizabeth Pew for locating sources for this article and to the Mormon Historic Sites Foundation for help in producing it. Thanks also to BYU professor Steven C. Harper and to BYU Religious Studies Center executive editor Devan Jensen for their encouragement and patience.

1. Wesley P. Walters, "New Light on Mormon Origins from the Palmyra Revival," *Dialogue* 4 (Spring 1969): 67, claimed that there was no mention of Palmyra revivals in denominational magazines in these years, nor in the "Palmyra newspaper" for 1819–20.

2. Unless otherwise noted, all scripture citations are from Joseph Smith—History.

3. Joseph left a number of First Vision accounts. In 1838 he began dictating his formal history, now canonized in the Pearl of Great Price, where he asks the Lord "which of all the sects was right . . . for at this time it had never entered into my heart that all were wrong" (JS—H 1:18). Yet in his 1832 private history, Joseph had concluded before praying, "There was no society or denomination that built upon the gospel of Jesus Christ as recorded in the new testament." But a claimed contradiction here is superficial, for most devout people would see the difference between a tentative human judgment and the "certain conclusion" from God that Joseph Smith prayed for. In fact, the 1832 account implies the same prayer question as the 1838 account, for the Lord's answer written in 1832 answers the question of which church is true: "None doeth good. . . . They have turned aside from the gospel." Dean C. Jessee, "The Earliest Documented Accounts of Joseph Smith's First Vision," in John W. Welch and Erick B. Carlson, eds., *Opening the Heavens* (Provo, UT: Brigham Young University Press, 2005), 7. Also, if Joseph was asking about only Christian churches in his

region, he made a negative decision on perhaps a dozen groups. His question was really whether a true church existed any place on earth. Since the Pearl of Great Price generally follows Joseph's 1838 history manuscript faithfully, the canonized version is quoted here if accurate. The text used for Joseph Smith's 1832 handwritten account is found in Jessee, "The Earliest Documented Accounts of Joseph Smith's First Vision," in Welch and Carlson, *Opening the Heavens*, 4–7. Other First Vision accounts discussed also appear there. Both the 1832 and 1838 vision texts also appear in Dean C. Jessee, *Personal Writings of Joseph Smith*, rev. ed. (Salt Lake City: Deseret Book, 2002) and will reappear in the *Joseph Smith Papers*, Histories series 1.

4. "Joseph Smith's Experience of a Methodist 'Camp-Meeting' in 1820," *Dialogue Paperless*, E-Paper 3, Expanded Version (Definitive), December 20, 2007, 23–25.

5. Several scholars have written on the integration of First Vision accounts, principally Milton V. Backman Jr. in his First Vision article in the *Encyclopedia of Mormonism* and in his book *Joseph Smith's First Vision*, 2nd ed. (Salt Lake City: Bookcraft, 1980), 112–13. For bibliography to 2000, see James B. Allen, Ronald W. Walker, and David J. Whittaker, *Studies in Mormon History, 1830–1997* (Urbana: University of Illinois Press, 2000), 933. For updated bibliography and discussion, see Matthew B. Brown, *A Pillar of Light* (American Fork, UT: Covenant Communications, 2009). For recent source studies, see the two opening articles in Welch and Carlson, *Opening the Heavens*: Jessee, "The Earliest Documented Accounts of Joseph Smith's First Vision"; and James B. Allen and John W. Welch, "The Appearance of the Father and the Son to Joseph Smith in 1820." Internet resources are uneven, but see the websites of Brigham Young University's Maxwell Institute and of the Foundation for Apologetic Information and Research (FAIR).

6. This article updates my earlier contribution, "Circumstantial Confirmation of the First Vision through Reminiscences," *BYU Studies* 9, no. 1 (Spring 1969): 373–404. Some paragraphs are revised and reprinted here, especially those evaluating data

furnished by Oliver Cowdery, William Smith, and two Palmyra printers' apprentices, Pomeroy Tucker and Orsamus Turner.

7. Walters, "New Light on Mormon Origins," 67.

8. Walters, "New Light on Mormon Origins," 61.

9. Compare JS—H 1:59, where "at length" covers the four years between the coming of Moroni and the reception of the plates.

10. 1832 History, in Jessee, "Earliest Documented Accounts," 5; Walters, "New Light on Mormon Origins," 70.

11. Walters, "New Light on Mormon Origins," 73. This conclusion is basically unchanged; witness H. Michael Marquardt and Wesley P. Walters, *Inventing Mormonism* (Salt Lake City: Smith Research Associates, 1998), 15, claiming that publications and records show "no significant gains in church memberships or any other signs of revival in Palmyra in 1820." In Marquardt's *Rise of Mormonism: 1816–1844* (Longwood, FL: Xulon Press, 2005), 13, this sentence is repeated, denying "any other signs of excitement or revival in Palmyra in 1820."

12. See Marquardt and Walters, *Inventing Mormonism*, 29, after an obscure mention of the 1820 Palmyra camp meeting: "Camp meetings were often held by Methodists but did not often spark a significant revival."

13. Lucy is explicit on living in their own cabin on the edge of their farm in "2 years from" entering Palmyra. Lavina Fielding Anderson, *Lucy's Book* (Salt Lake City: Signature Books, 1853), 321. For agreement of Palmyra resident Pomeroy Tucker, see Richard Lloyd Anderson, "Alvin Smith," in Kyle R. Walker, ed., *United by Faith* (American Fork, UT: Covenant Communications), 88–91.

14. Walters, "New Light on Mormon Origins," 66; Marquardt and Walters, *Inventing Mormonism*, 27.

15. "Scarcely overstatements" and "matching" are used by Marquardt and Walters, *Inventing Mormonism*, 27.

16. See the appendices to this article under the headings of Pomeroy Tucker and Orsamus Turner.

17. See the accompanying Methodist Membership Chart, 1817–19. Comparable figures are not possible in 1820, a year after the Genesee District was bisected into western and eastern

sections, with the Palmyra area remaining in the older Ontario District. Numbers taken in mid-1820 (for the twelve months before) are flat or somewhat depressed after 1819, affected by possible Methodist restructuring, possible population shifts due to canal construction, and westward migration. For instance, Charles Giles was presiding elder of the Oneida District when he complained about fluid population: "One thousand members have been added to the church this year on our district; but in consequence of numerous removals to the western country, the Minutes will show an increase of only seven hundred and forty." Giles to *Methodist Magazine* editors, Utica, NY, August 2, 1817, in Charles Giles, *The Pioneer: A Narrative of the Nativity, Experience, Travels, and Ministerial Labours* (New York: G. Lane and P. P. Sanford, 1844), 264.

18. See Richard Lloyd Anderson, "Joseph Smith's Testimony of the First Vision," *Ensign*, April 1996, 16–19; see also Backman, *Joseph Smith's First Vision*, 84–88.

19. Backman, *Joseph Smith's First Vision*, 84–85.

20. John H. Wigger, *Taking Heaven by Storm: Methodism and the Rise of Popular Christianity in America* (New York: Oxford University Press, 1998), 3.

21. From annual *Minutes Taken at the Several Annual Conferences of the Methodist Episcopal Church in the United States of America*, figures gathered for the year prior to each annual conference of the major American Methodist sections, called annual conferences. The Genesee Conference recorded new membership at each annual session, held about each July.

22. The village of New Amsterdam was assimilated into Buffalo by final lot sales in 1822, as described in O[rsamus] Turner, *Pioneer History of the Holland Purchase* (Buffalo, NY: Jewett, Thomas & Co., 1849), 499–503.

23. For issues in this decision, see John Matzko, "The Encounter of the Young Joseph Smith with Presbyterianism," *Dialogue* 40 (Fall 2007): 68–84.

24. Alexander Neibaur journal, May 24, 1844, in Jessee, "Earliest Documented Accounts of Joseph Smith's First Vision," 25.

25. *Pittsburgh Weekly Gazette*, September 15, 1843, in Jessee, "Earliest Documented Accounts of Joseph Smith's First Vision," 25.

26. Alexander Neibaur journal, May 24, 1844, in Jessee, "Earliest Documented Accounts of Joseph Smith's First Vision," 26.

27. Wigger, *Taking Heaven by Storm*, 97.

28. Wigger, *Taking Heaven by Storm*, 92.

29. Giles, *Pioneer*, 212–13.

30. Michael Quinn's recent study of Palmyra camp meetings is insightful on the patterns of the Methodist outdoor gatherings that supplemented regular worship. As this article explains, however, local history matches just what Joseph describes, that is, Joseph's sustained anxiety from the conflicting views he observed after attending Protestant gatherings, moving into serious inquiry from 1818 to his First Vision, which Joseph dated about late March 1820. I disagree with Quinn's logic of postponing the "early" spring theophany because it was supposedly too cold then for a farm boy's outdoor prayer. "Joseph Smith's Experience of a Methodist 'Camp-Meeting' in 1820," 23–25. Dan Vogel also questions that thinking in his letter, "What Is a Revival?," *Dialogue* 41 (Winter 2008): viii–ix.

31. See this article's appendices for full discussion of these Palmyrans who recalled Joseph's First Vision years.

32. Backman referred to Seager's 1818 camp meeting journal entry, citing correct data from P. Blakeslee's secondhand summary in "Notes for a History of Methodism in Phelps, 1886"; see Backman's reprinted 1969 article, "Awakenings in the Burned-Over District," in this volume, and his *Joseph Smith's First Vision*, 74n34. Michael Quinn quoted the printed copy of the 1818 journal, emphasizing its importance ("Joseph Smith's Experience of a Methodist 'Camp-Meeting' in 1820," 2–3), as did Mark L. Staker, *Hearken, O Ye People* (Salt Lake City: Gregg Kofford Books, 2009), 128. Stephen C. Harper also mentions Seager's journal in his early Mormonism presentations. The present article reviews Seager's entry in the light of regional camp meeting insights from other Methodist circuit riders.

33. See E. Latimer, a later Genesee Conference minister who knew the Seager family, *The Three Brothers: Sketches of the Lives of*

Rev. Aurora Seager, Rev. Micah Seager, Rev. Schuyler Seager, D.D. (New York: Phillips & Hunt, 1880), and W. C. [William Case], "Account of the Life and Death of Rev. Aurora Seager," *Methodist Magazine*, October–December, 1821, 367–71, 406–12, 449–55.

34. Horatio Gates Spafford, *Gazetteer of the State of New-York* (Albany: B. D. Packard and author, 1824), 411; emphasis in original.

35. Latimer, *Three Brothers*, 17.

36. Aurora Seager, April 7, 1817, Windsor, CT, in W. C. [William Case], "Account of . . . Rev. Aurora Seager," *Methodist Magazine*, November 1821, 411–12.

37. Latimer, *Three Brothers*, 21.

38. At the Genesee Annual Conference, starting July 16, 1818, Aurora was assigned to the Clarence (NY) Circuit with a companion (*Minutes Taken at the Several Annual Conferences of the Methodist Episcopal Church, 1818*, 44); at the Genesee Annual Conference, starting July 1, 1819, Aurora was assigned alone to the Montreal Circuit, under the District Presiding Elder William Case (*Minutes . . . 1819*, 52). Aurora died in Montreal of lung involvement December 21, 1819, in a scene of "triumphant death." W. C. [William Case], "Account of . . . Rev. Aurora Seager," *Methodist Magazine*, December 1821, 454–55.

39. Latimer, *Three Brothers*, 22.

40. *History of the Pioneer Settlement of Phelps and Gorham's Purchase* (Rochester, NY: William Alling, 1851).

41. W. H. McIntosh, *History of Wayne County, New York* (Philadelphia: Everts, Ensign & Everts, 1877), 148. Two similar certificates of incorporation (July 3, 1821, and February 14, 1822) of the "first Methodist Episcopal Church of Palmyra" are recorded, Miscellaneous Records, Bk. C, Ontario County, NY, 385–86, 397–98, perhaps in connection with erecting a meetinghouse.

42. *Methodist Magazine*, August 1826, 313.

43. Pomeroy Tucker, *Origin, Rise, and Progress of Mormonism* (New York: D. Appleton, 1867), 19. See Tucker's profile in the appendices to this article for full treatment. The Palmyra road list was made each April and can be analyzed for years that the Smith family lived together in Palmyra Village (1817–19), the time when Alvin

continued living in the village and the family (judged by the father's residence) had already moved to the farm (by April 1820 and an undetermined time before), and the years the family lived together on the farm (1821–22). Later years in the village and double residence years were evidently the time of constructing the only log home known. The road records appear in Dan Vogel, *Early Mormon Documents* (Salt Lake City: Signature Books, 2000), 3:411–14, along with his theory of two log homes, which I consider not justified by observer evidence. Lucy Smith and Palmyra resident Pomeroy Tucker agree that the Smiths had only two houses in the countryside, a log house they began to build during 1818–19 and then a frame house nearly finished when Alvin died in 1823. See discussion under the subhead "Joseph's Attendance at the 1818 Palmyra Camp Meeting."

44. See the 1815 Tennessee schedule for five days, starting Friday (half-day) and ending Tuesday (half-day), with four extended meetings on Saturday, Sunday, and baptisms and the Lord's Supper administered on Monday. The formal "invitation to the altar" came on two designated days. Charles A. Johnson, *The Frontier Camp Meeting* (Dallas, TX: Southern Methodist University Press, 1955), 90–91.

45. Abel Stevens wrote of the bishop's "large person—corpulent and nearly six feet in height . . . and manners of extreme simplicity and cordiality." *Sketches and Incidents* (New York: Carlton & Phillips, 1853), 2:130. For the bishop's life, see *American National Biography* 18 (New York: Oxford University Press, 1999): 616–17.

46. George Peck, *Life and Times of Rev. George Peck* (New York: Nelson & Phillips, 1874), 93.

47. In Worth Marion Tippy, *Frontier Bishop: The Life and Times of Robert Richford Roberts* (New York: Abingdon, 1958), 151–52. Thompson was a congressman and later secretary of the Navy.

48. See the variation of "old professors" for ordinary Methodists revitalized at a camp meeting. *Methodist Magazine*, July 1826, 373. See Peter Cartwright's more usual reference to believers as "two hundred who had professed religion, and about that number joined the Church," in Abel Stevens, *History of the Methodist Episcopal*

Church in the United States of America 4 (New York: Eaton & Mains, 1864): 347–75.

49. James Gilruth journal, June 5–9, 1835, transcription in Johnson, *Frontier Camp Meeting*, 112.

50. Giles, *Pioneer*, 234.

51. Giles, *Pioneer*, 267–69.

52. Giles, *Pioneer*, 270–71.

53. Giles, *Pioneer*, 279.

54. *Life and Times of Rev. George Peck*, 48.

55. *Life and Times of Rev. George Peck*, 60–64.

56. *Life and Times of Rev. George Peck*, 82.

57. *Life and Times of Rev. George Peck*, 87.

58. *Life and Times of Rev. George Peck*, 88, 90.

59. See Horatio Gates Spafford, *Gazetteer of the State of New York* (Albany: B. D. Packard, 1824), 4 (statistics used), 376 (township populations in Ontario County, with Wayne County created in 1823 [586]), 401, left column (Palmyra Village).

60. Backman, *Joseph Smith's First Vision*, 2nd ed., 73.

61. The source for the Palmyra Village population is Spafford, *Gazetteer of the State of New York* (1824), 401; "125 houses . . . and about 1000 inhabitants."

62. *History of the Pioneer Settlement of Phelps and Gorham's Purchase*, 213–14. For full background on Turner, see his profile in the appendices of this article.

63. Jessee, "Earliest Documented Accounts," 25. The Neibaur account tells of a "Revival meeting," near Palmyra (mother and two brothers present, in home area) but outdoors (large crowd shouting) in Methodist context (virtual camp-meeting description and Joseph's question, "Must I join the Methodist church?").

64. Lucy Smith, 1844–45 manuscript, in *Lucy's Book*, 321, left column. The Walters-school researchers developed a theory that the log house the Smiths first occupied was of unknown origin. It did stand on the property of Samuel Jennings, who owned the land in Palmyra Township adjoining the Smith farm on the north. Lucy Smith says quite a bit about her rural homes but only mentions living near Palmyra in one modest log house that her family built,

followed by their frame house, finished on the exterior by Alvin before his death in late 1823. As the text here shows, Palmyra editor Tucker also gives this sequence of two dwellings (see his section in the appendices to this paper), as does William Smith, who, though young, lived in both homes. Handwritten "Notes," in Vogel, *Early Mormon Documents*, 1:486.

65. Tucker, *Origin . . . of Mormonism*, 13. The Walters-theory scholars speculate that the log house that the Smiths first occupied was not built by the Smiths, since it stood on the adjacent land of Samuel Jennings, who owned the farm in Palmyra Township adjoining the Smith farm, which was just south across the border line of Manchester Township. Lucy Smith's history has a domestic subtheme, making the reader conscious of the family's move to the farm and the first log house and the long-term plan to replace it with the sided house nearly finished by Alvin before his death in late 1823. Palmyra editor Tucker also knows only these two houses, and both say that the original home was self-built. Walters and those following him have relied on the Manchester assessment rolls, which value the Smith farm (south of the log house) at $700 in 1821 and 1822 but raise the value to $1,000 in 1823, when the frame home was under construction within the border of Manchester Township. These revisionary scholars claim the frame home had not been started before the summer assessment of 1823, so the increased value came from building a second log home on Manchester land, no trace of which has been found. Yet the first country dwelling appears as a point of measurement in an 1820 highway survey, and archaeology has verified the site, which is some twenty-five yards north of the Palmyra-Manchester Township border on the Jennings property. Explanations have included using a log dwelling already built (seemingly the Walters theory) or the Smith's ignorance of the property line when they began their log house. In my view, more thought should be given to the Smith's deliberately building close to their prospective farm, with Jennings's permission (with whom they had work and business dealings in the 1820s), against the contingency the Smiths might not be able to raise cash to purchase the Manchester farm. The argument is made that the land agent,

Zachariah Seymour, did not register his power of attorney from the Evertson estate until mid-1820, so the Smiths could not contract for their Manchester farm until then. Yet Seymour was a seasoned land agent in the area and had a trusted relationship with the New York City Evertson estate before 1820, so the Smiths may have had a tentative agreement to buy their farm before Seymour was formally authorized to sell it. So they perhaps agreed with Jennings to build on his land, with some possible provision for buying the self-built cabin if their plans succeeded. Like many settlers, the Smiths could not move forward until they saved the cash to make a binding contract, and there are variations of the above strategy, which I have probed somewhat in my longer biography of Alvin Smith, in Kyle Walker, *United by Faith: The Joseph Smith Sr. and Lucy Mack Smith Family* (American Fork, UT: Covenant Communications, 2005). Besides arguing from a supposed 1820 time contract, revisionists contend that Lucy Smith places beginning the frame home as early November 1823: "When the month of November, 1822 [1823] arrived the House was raised and all the Materials procured for completing the building" (preliminary MS, in *Lucy's Book*, 349, left column, 1844–45). The revisionists arbitrarily take one meaning of this sentence, insisting that Lucy is saying that the Smiths began the frame house in November 1823. Yet construction materials for the existing medium-large frame house were obviously not assembled in the short three weeks when Alvin faded and died. I think Lucy means that the clapboard house had been framed and all construction materials were on site by early November 1823, when Alvin's symptoms of abdominal pain began. After his wrenching death, Lucy continues her narrative that the finished carpenter was soon hired to complete the house, meaning Alvin had probably taken the summer and fall to manage raising the frame, roofing, and enclosing by siding before his death. This means the county appraisers could well increase the 1823 valuation because the new house was partly in place, not because of the illogical replacement of another settler's cabin by a duplicate. The inferences made to justify the two-cabin theory are discussed in Vogel, *Early Mormon Documents*, 1:415–21.

66. Turner, *Pioneer History*, 212n, which describes the Smiths living in their log home in the winter of late 1819, closely surrounded by forest and underbrush. Turner apparently intended to indicate that the Smiths themselves had built this log dwelling, since it had no other purpose in a sea of trees but as a base for clearing the land. Turner knew quite a bit about the Smiths but did not mention a second log home.

67. Dan Vogel, "What Is a Revival?," *Dialogue* 41 (Winter 2008): ix.

68. Readers of multiple news reports of the same incident must decide whether to take them as contradictory or supplementary. Two seasoned historians give the latter answer to this question in regard to Joseph's reports of the First Vision: "No single account tells the whole story. At the same time, all the details in each of the accounts add significantly to the entire picture." James B. Allen and John W. Welch, "The Appearance of the Father and the Son to Joseph Smith in 1820," in Welch and Carlson, *Opening the Heavens*, 37.

69. For basic information on the 1819 conference, see F. W. Conable, *History of the Genesee Annual Conference of the Methodist Episcopal Church* (New York: Philips and Hunt, 1876), 158–61. The statistics of the ministers obligated to attend are found in the 1818 and 1819 *Minutes Taken at the Several Annual Conferences of the Methodist Episcopal Church in the United States of America*.

70. Spafford, *Gazetteer of the State of New York* (1824), 401.

71. *Life and Times of Rev. George Peck*, 93.

72. *Life and Times of Rev. George Peck*, 65, 93, 122. The rivalry for proselytes at conversion appears regularly in the memoirs of Methodist preachers. For instance, Peck comments (p. 110): "When conversions began to occur among us, the Baptists, by whom we were surrounded, began to practice their usual strategy. . . . Two preachers of that persuasion . . . were very attentive to our converts."

73. Orson Pratt obtained a finished manuscript of Lucy's history and (without radical editing) published it as *Biographical Sketches of Joseph Smith, the Prophet, and His Progenitors for Many Generations* (Liverpool: Orson Pratt, 1853). Chapter 18 (17 in some later editions) copied Joseph Smith's 1838 record of the First Vision "from

his history" (74), and at the end credited this installment as originally appearing in the Nauvoo *Times and Seasons*, and reprinted in the *Millennial Star* (78). In my earlier article ("Circumstantial Confirmation of the First Vision," *BYU Studies* 9, no. 1 [Autumn 1968]: 391–93), I misinterpreted editorial comments before and after (paraphrases of Joseph Smith's 1838 history) as Lucy Smith's direct comments. However, present manuscript and printed versions of her history do not show her early knowledge of Joseph's First Vision. See the similar explanation in Richard Lloyd Anderson, *Joseph Smith's New England Heritage*, rev. ed. (Salt Lake City: Deseret Book, 2002), xvii–xviii.

74. Joseph Smith added this episode of talking with his mother in supplementary dictation to Willard Richards in 1842. See Jessee, "Earliest Documented Accounts," in Welch and Carlson, *Opening the Heavens*, 15, 32n22.

75. In the Neibaur account of the aftermath of the First Vision, Joseph again recounted the story of the Methodist minister who told Joseph that his vision was not of God: "Told the Methodist priest, said this was not a age for God to reveal himself in Vision Revelation has ceased with the New Testament." Jessee, "Earliest Documented Accounts," 26.

76. Some earlier critics of the First Vision assumed that Joseph Smith recalled physical persecution, but Joseph's explanations (see JS—H 1:21–23) pertained to public and private scorn ("reviling"), which left its legacy in many overdone affidavits later taken against the Smith family in the Palmyra region. On the meaning of "professor," see contemporary examples in Brown, *Pillar of Light*, 70, 83n32. Also see similar usage at note 42 above.

77. Tucker, *Origin . . . of Mormonism*. Though, the idea of the Bible as a fable contradicts Joseph's documented statements on that book. See the appendices to this article for data on Tucker.

78. The community bias is discussed in Richard Lloyd Anderson, "Joseph Smith's New York Reputation Reappraised," *BYU Studies* 8 (Spring 1968): 277–93. Disagreement on some issues is registered in Dan Vogel and literature he cites, *Early Mormon Documents* 2:13–21. One pseudo-issue is the sincerity of those

making affidavits on the character of Joseph Smith and his family. Statements based on hearsay or group prejudice are not more accurate if sincere.

79. Vogel, *Early Mormon Documents*, 1:475–513.

80. William Smith, *William Smith on Mormonism*, 6–7, also in Vogel, *Early Mormon Documents*, 1:494–95.

81. For William Smith's borrowing from Oliver Cowdery's 1820 period revival history, see the appendices to this article concerning William Smith.

82. Brown, *Pillar of Light*, 241.

83. Orson Pratt, *Interesting Account of Several Remarkable Visions* (Edinburgh: Ballantyne and Hughes, 1840), 5; also in Jessee, "Earliest Documented Accounts," in Welch and Carlson, *Opening the Heavens*, 20–21. After building up to the need of a divine answer on the right church, Oliver simply skipped over the answer and in the continuation described Moroni's appearance with the message about the Book of Mormon. So later in the century, William Smith did not find Joseph's account of the First Vision in Oliver's early Church history series. Thus he turned to an alternative account, written by Orson Pratt as the first in his 1840 pamphlet, *Remarkable Visions*.

84. *William Smith on Mormonism*, 8–9.

85. See the facsimile and transcription of the revelation copy of the above date in Robin Scott Jensen, Robert J. Woodford, and Steven C. Harper, eds., *Manuscript Revelation Books*, facsimile edition, first volume of the Revelations and Translations series of the Joseph Smith Papers, ed. Dean C. Jessee, Ronald K. Esplin, and Richard Lyman Bushman (Salt Lake City: Church Historian's Press, 2009), 74–77.

86. Jessee, "Earliest Documented Accounts," in Allen and Welch, *Opening the Heavens*, 5–7.

87. Background and a photo of the original gravestone is in Anderson, "Alvin Smith," in Walker, *United by Faith*, 99. A more legible photo appears in Vogel, *Early Mormon Documents*, 3:450.

88. These earliest Joseph Smith events (First Vision and message of forgiveness, falling into sin and seeking forgiveness,

Moroni's coming and renewal of forgiveness) are found in all versions of D&C 20:5–6, and in Joseph Smith's 1832 history and journal narration of early visions to Joshua in 1835. See Jessee, *Personal Writings of Joseph Smith*, 11–12, 104–5; *Joseph Smith Papers, Journals* 1:87–88, 90–91.

89. Jessee, *Personal Writings of Joseph Smith*, 9–14.

90. *Latter Day Saints' Messenger and Advocate*, October 1834, 13. Cowdery confessed his personal incompetence on the early life of the Prophet but stressed, "With his labor and with authentic documents now in our possession, we hope to render this a pleasing and agreeable narrative."

91. The preface of Joseph's 1832 history also makes the restoration of each priesthood a major founding event, seeming to promise detail that was not included because the document was not finished.

92. *Messenger and Advocate*, October 1834, 23.

93. Cowdery differs from the 1832 account in the quoted phrases only by the substitution of "this book" for "them," whose antecedent is "the plates." The phrases are found in *Messenger and Advocate*, February 1835, 80, and *Messenger and Advocate*, October 1835, 198.

94. Jessee, "Earliest Documented Accounts," in Welch and Carlson, *Opening the Heavens*, 4–5.

95. *Messenger and Advocate*, December 1834, 43.

96. *Messenger and Advocate*, April 1835, 112.

97. Jessee, "Earliest Documented Accounts," in Welch and Carlson, *Opening the Heavens*, 5.

98. *Life and Times of Rev. George Peck*, 104.

99. George Peck, *Early Methodism within the Bounds of the Old Genesee Conference* (New York: Carlton and Porter, 1850), 492.

100. Larry C. Porter examined Lane's life in two publications, the shorter being *A Study of the Origins of the Church of Jesus Christ of Latter-day Saints in the States of New York and Pennsylvania* (Provo, UT: Joseph Fielding Smith Institute, Brigham Young University, 2000), 19–23. See also his "Rev. George Lane—Good 'Gifts,' Much 'Grace,' and Marked 'Usefulness,'" 199–226 of the present volume.

101. Anderson, *Lucy's Book*, 358.

102. *Life and Times of Rev. George Peck*, 109.

103. Handwritten journal of Genesee circuit rider Benajah Williams, who with Lane stopped over at Richmond Township, New York, on the way to the 1820 Genesee Conference, that year in Canada somewhat near Niagara Falls. With other Mormon historians, I have had access to transcripts and photocopies of this section of the lengthy journal, which in 2011 was in possession of Michael Brown of Philadelphia, according to Steven C. Harper's "Seeker's Guide to the Historical Accounts of Joseph Smith's First Vision," n. 18 (electronic copy of BYU Religious Studies Center occasional paper). Staker, *Hearken, O Ye People*, 128–29, incorrectly dates this camp meeting as 1818 instead of the summer of 1820.

104. Edmund C. Briggs and John W. Peterson interview with William Smith (1893), in Vogel, *Early Mormon Documents*, 1:513.

105. See the chart including using James 1:4–5 and its mention in the various accounts, in the beginning articles of Jessee, and Allen and Welch, in Welch and Carlson, *Opening the Heavens*, 56, with accounts on 3–26.

106. *Lucy's Book*, 324, left column, indicating the preliminary MS dates the dream to "the same year that Carlos was 2 years old," which began March 25, 1818.

107. *Lucy's Book*, 281, both versions and n. 103.

108. *Lucy's Book*, 264n102.

109. See Jessee, "The Earliest Documented Accounts," in Welch and Carlson, *Opening the Heavens*, 25.

110. *Lucy's Book*, 264n103.

111. *Lucy's Book*, 357–58, left column (preliminary MS).

112. Sophronia had married Calvin Stoddard in late 1827, which may be one reason why she was not included in the disciplinary hearing, minutes of which are reproduced in Backman, *First Vision*, 2nd ed., Appendix K, and in Vogel, *Early Mormon Documents*, 3:496–501. The original manuscript is on a BYU microfilm in L. Tom Perry Special Collections, Harold B. Lee Library, Brigham Young University, Provo, UT.

113. This time of inactivity has been used as a measure of when the mother and sons joined the Presbyterian Church, but there are

other cases in these records taking action on the basis of two years' inactivity or less. These times seem to be based on taking action soon after inactivity rather than measuring the number of years of membership.

114. Jessee, "Earliest Documented Accounts," in Welch and Carlson, *Opening the Heavens*, 25–26.

115. See Anderson, "Joseph Smith's Testimony of the First Vision," *Ensign*, April 1986, 17–19.

116. Allen and Welch, "Appearance of the Father and Son," in Welch and Carlson, *Opening the Heavens*, 20, and reprinted in this volume. For similar conclusions of Joseph's consistency in his accounts and with history, see Backman, *Joseph Smith's First Vision*, 2nd ed., Appendix Q.

117. He furnishes his birth date in *William Smith on Mormonism* (Lamoni, IA, 1883), 5. It is also found in Lucy Smith, *Biographical Sketches*, 41, as March 13, 1811.

118. *William Smith on Mormonism*, 5; also in Vogel, *Early Mormon Documents*, 1:493.

119. Palmyra Town Record, book 1, 221, reproduced in Vogel, *Early Mormon Documents*, 3:420–21, along with his case for this being an existing, not a self-built, cabin of the Smiths, which is argued at length but not proved.

120. See Tucker, *Origin . . . of Mormonism*. "Smith and his household continued their residence in Palmyra village . . . for some two and a half years. In 1818 they settled . . . about two miles south of Palmyra."

121. *William Smith on Mormonism*, 6; also in Vogel, *Early Mormon Documents*, 1:495.

122. *William Smith on Mormonism*, 10; also in Vogel, *Early Mormon Documents*, 1:496.

123. Sermon on June 8, 1884, Deloit, Iowa, *Saints' Herald*, October 4, 1884, 643; also in Vogel, *Early Mormon Documents*, 1:503.

124. Lucy Smith, *Biographical Sketches*, 83–84.

125. *William Smith on Mormonism*, 9; also in Vogel, *Early Mormon Documents*, 1:496.

126. *Latter Day Saints' Messenger and Advocate*, December 1834, 43. See also Brown, *Pillar of Light*, 240, for this direct borrowing.

127. *Latter Day Saints' Messenger and Advocate*, February 1835, 78. See also Brown, *Pillar of Light*, 240, for this direct borrowing.

128. *William Smith on Mormonism*, 7–8. See also Brown, *Pillar of Light*, 240, for this direct borrowing.

129. *William Smith on Mormonism*, 9; also in Vogel, *Early Mormon Documents*, 1:495.

130. Turner, *History of . . . Phelps and Gorham's Purchase*, second supplement, 499.

131. Tucker's first issue of the *Wayne Sentinel* (October 1, 1823) still exists. Information on his apprenticeship at Canandaigua appears in the best sketch of his life, written as an obituary for the *Troy Times* by his son-in-law, John M. Francis, copied in the *Palmyra Courier*, July 8, 1870, and the *Rochester Union and Advertiser*, July 2, 1870. See also Follett, *History of the Press in Western New York*, 63, and Hamilton, *Country Printer*, 303–4.

132. Tucker, *Origin . . . of Mormonism*, 4.

133. Tucker, *Origin . . . of Mormonism*, 15.

134. Tucker, *Origin . . . of Mormonism*, 14. Tucker's summary of the Smiths' Palmyra-Manchester holiday business stresses that young Joseph was regularly vending and sometimes tricked by "the boys of those by-gone times."

135. In 1831 young James Gordon Bennett wrote his tongue-in-cheek impressions of the Smiths from interviews with some who had known them. It is probably better-than-average hearsay when he reports the father as a former "country pedlar" dealing in "the manufacture of gingerbread and such like domestic wares." His son Joseph is portrayed as being "a partner in the concern," who aimlessly hung around the "villages," perhaps an indication of selling at public gatherings that Tucker specifically mentions. See *New York Courier and Enquirer*, August 31, 1831. One of Bennett's sources was E. B. Grandin, who was closely associated with Tucker in business and social affairs, so it is perhaps no accident that the story of the Smiths' holiday business should be similar from Bennett's contacts and the editor Tucker. His fullest description of the Smiths' goods

for sale is in the setting of the Palmyra residence: "gingerbread, pies, boiled eggs, root-beer, and other like notions of traffic." *Origin . . . of Mormonism*, 12.

136. The citation of Clinton's "Private Canal Journal, 1810" is found in William W. Campbell, *The Life and Writings of De Witt Clinton* (New York: Baker and Scribner, 1849), 107. Increasing population makes such activity even more likely for camp meetings in 1820.

137. Tucker, *Origin of Mormonism*, 28. Compare the descriptions of the First Vision and the angel's first revelation of the Book of Mormon in any of the editions of Orson Pratt, *An Interesting Account of Several Remarkable Visions*. Proof that this source was used over other possibilities with the same phrasing is Tucker's quotation of Pratt's narration of the Moroni visitation. Compare Turner's quotation of the closing portion of *Remarkable Visions*, 139–45.

138. Tucker, *Origin of Mormonism*, 17–18. Tucker is the origin of derivative material in McIntosh, *History of Wayne County*, 150.

139. *The Reflector*, Palmyra, NY, February 1, 1831.

140. Tucker, *Origin . . . of Mormonism*, 16.

141. Tucker, *Origin . . . of Mormonism*, 17–18. The knowledge of the Bible attributed to Joseph Smith by Turner makes suspect his remark that Joseph announced the "Bible a fable." The memoirs of Lucy, Joseph, and William all agree that reverence for scripture characterized the Smith home.

142. Tucker's chapter immediately following Joseph's announcement that the churches stood on a "false foundation" is a recital of the community tradition of his money-digging activities. This repetition adds nothing, for he is merely warming over "affidavits" in print thirty years before his book. But the Palmyra editor repeatedly insists that Joseph's deceptions began late in 1819 and continued "from 1820 to 1827" (p. 22). If these stories originated in community prejudice after the Smiths began telling of Joseph's revelations (as William Smith spiritedly insists), then the existence of the rumors dates the early religious claims of the Smiths around 1820. Tucker accepted this same chronology a decade before his book, as shown in his newspaper recollections of June 11, 1858, in the

Palmyra Courier. Talking then about "the origin of Mormonism," he dates Joseph's "gift of supernatural endowments" as beginning "as early as 1820." His odd identification of Joseph Smith as then "at the age of about 19 years" may be accounted for by the young prophet's large physical stature.

143. The two most extensive biographies of Turner are Morley B. Turpin and W. De Witt Manning, "Orsamus Turner," *Rochester Historical Society Publications* 17 (1939): 273–90; Harry S. Douglass, *Historical Wyoming* 12, no. 2 (January 1959): 33–46.

144. Turner, *History of the . . . Phelps and Gorham's Purchase*, 213, 400.

145. Strong suspended publication of his Palmyra newspaper in the spring of 1823, judged by existing issues. Turner recalls the date of his move away from Palmyra as 1823 (499), which appears in two other works: Arad Thomas, *Pioneer History of Orleans County, New York* (Albion, NY: H. A. Bruner, 1871), 111–12; Milton W. Hamilton, *The Country Printer, New York State, 1785–1830*, 2nd ed. (Port Washington, NY: Ira J. Friedman, 1964), 302.

146. Turner, *History of the . . . Phelps and Gorham's Purchase*, second supplement, 459, 499.

147. This phrase is from John Kelsey, who wrote his sketch while Turner was still alive, *The Lives and Reminiscences of the Pioneers of Rochester* (Rochester, NY: J. Kelsey, 1854), 71.

148. Orsamus Turner, "Then and Now—1822, 1854," *Niagara Democrat*, ca. May 4, 1854, cited in *Lockport Daily Courier*, May 5, 1854, copy furnished by Chester O. Lewis, former Niagara County Historian. Turner was born July 23, 1801. Turner's complete words pertaining to his pre-Lockport life show that he did not stay long in Palmyra after completing his Canandaigua apprenticeship: "Resuming . . . a position . . . which had a commencement, but a few days after we had reached the age of 21 years.—(32 years ago) . . . *Then*, just out of our apprenticeship, and at school, we heard that a place called 'Lockport' . . . had been made the county seat . . . and hearing further that a printer was wanted there, we journeyed from Palmyra passing through Rochester."

149. Turner, *Pioneer History of the Holland Purchase of Western New York* (Buffalo, NY: Jewett, Thomas & Co., 1849), 655.

150. Frederick Follett, *History of the Press of Western New York* (Rochester, NY: Jerome & Brothers, 1847), 65. Cf. Hamilton, *The Country Printer*, 304.

151. Turner, *History of the... Phelps and Gorham's Purchase*, 214.

152. Turner, *History of the... Phelps and Gorham's Purchase*, 213.

153. Turner, *History of the... Phelps and Gorham's Purchase*, 214. Although the Methodist records of the period in Palmyra are not now available, Turner's early history of that denomination shows that he personally knew more about its history in Palmyra than about any other church there: "The Methodist Church was organized in 1811. At first, few in number, and feeble in resources, its places of worship alternated from school house to school house; sometimes in an apartment at a private dwelling; at others in a vacant log dwelling;—until having largely recruited its numbers, it emerged from its feeble condition, and in 1821 erected its present church edifice."

Early existence of the "juvenile debating club" at the "old red school house on Durfee Street" is confirmed by periodic newspaper notices to "the young people of the village of Palmyra and its vicinity" inviting attendance at a "debating school at the school house near Mr. Billings" (*Western Farmer*, January 23, 1822). The similarity of later notices shows that this notice does not mark the beginning of the society.

154. *History of the... Phelps and Gorham's Purchase*, 389. Compare a traveler's sarcastic reaction to an obstruction blocking this well-traveled highway "as I was entering your village, on what I understood to be the Vienna road." *Wayne Sentinel*, April 7, 1826. Also compare the complaint of the later deterioration of "the road between this village and Vienna." *The Reflector* (Palmyra, NY), September 23, 1829.

155. Turner, *Pioneer History of the Holland Purchase*, 542, 555.

Joseph Smith was one who was spiritually quickened while living in the Burned-Over District. He became keenly interested in organized religion during one of the higher waves of revivalism which swept across western New York. (Lewis A. Ramsey, Joseph Smith Jr., *Courtesy of Church History Museum)*

Awakenings in the Burned-Over District: New Light on the Historical Setting of the First Vision

Milton V. Backman Jr.

This essay was among several included in this volume that were originally published in BYU Studies 9, no. 3 (Spring 1969): 301–20.

The six decades preceding the Civil War were years of intense religious activity in many sections of the United States. During this second great awakening, sporadic spiritual quickenings erupted throughout the new nation; and many Americans living in the rugged frontier communities, in the rapidly growing urban areas, and in the villages and towns of the northern and southern United States turned their attention to organized religion. Subsequently, church membership and religious zeal soared. Although in 1800 there were fewer church members in this country than in any other Christian land and active church membership had dropped to about 7 percent of the population, the lowest in the history of this land, this decline was arrested; and in 1850, 17 percent of Americans were churched. By 1860, membership in religious societies increased to about 23 percent of the rapidly expanding American population.[1]

One of the regions in the new nation that was in an almost constant state of revivalism was western New York. During the first half of the nineteenth century, revivals were so habitual and powerful in the area west of the Catskill and Adirondack Mountains that historians have labeled this ecclesiastical storm center the "Burned-Over District."[2]

As in Kentucky, the winter of 1799–1800 was the era of a "Great Revival" in western New York. Since an innumerable series of spiritual quickenings followed this first major wave of enthusiasm, this powerful awakening initiated a new religious epoch in that region of America. Although one can locate evidence of spiritual enlivenment in a number of New York communities every year of the early 1800s, peak periods occurred when revivals erupted in more than the customary number of towns and villages and unprecedented numbers joined the popular churches of that age. One of these apexes of religious fervor followed the low ebb which occurred during the War of 1812. Between 1816 and 1821, revivals were reported in more towns, and a greater number of settlers joined churches than in any previous period of New York history.[3] After a brief calm in which awakenings continued in a less spectacular manner, the grand climax in the "series of crests in religious zeal" occurred between 1825 and 1837.[4]

Joseph Smith in the Burned-Over District

One who was spiritually quickened while living in the Burned-Over District was Joseph Smith the Prophet. Joseph became keenly interested in organized religion during one of the higher waves of revivalism which swept across western New York. Approximately eighteen years after witnessing this spiritual phenomenon, Joseph recalled his experience from a distant vantage point. The Prophet asserted that in the second year after his removal to Manchester (a town, or sometimes called township in some states, which in the period immediately preceding the spring of 1820 had not been separated from the town of Farmington),[5] an "unusual excitement on the subject of religion" occurred in "the place" where he lived. "It commenced," he said, "with the Methodists, but soon became general among all the sects in that region of country." Then probably placing this religious quickening in an enlarged historical setting, Joseph declared, "Indeed, the whole district of country seemed affected by it, and great multitudes united themselves to the different religious parties."[6]

Although the tools of a historian cannot be employed to either verify or challenge Joseph's testimony concerning the remarkable vision which occurred during this awakening,

On Wesley Walters

While I was teaching at BYU, Truman Madsen invited me into his office and said that a number of people were concerned because Wesley Walters, a Presbyterian minister, had published a pamphlet saying that Joseph did not write an accurate or reliable account of the background of the First Vision—that there was no evidence of a great revival in Palmyra in 1819 or 1820, that the great revival took place a few years later. We didn't really have an answer to that question because no one had done serious research on the historical setting of Mormonism or on events that took place in the Palmyra area at the time of the First Vision. So I was invited to be one of five individuals to gather information on conditions that existed at the time of the First Vision. . . . I decided that I would spend my time in the Palmyra area going from library to library, from historical society to historical society, checking all of the churches, gathering everything I could about conditions that existed there—the churches, membership of the churches, revivals. The result was the publication of my first book on LDS Church history—*Joseph Smith's First Vision*. As a result of that research, I found out that Joseph was a very reliable historian. He wrote a very accurate account of the historical setting of the First Vision. (Milton V. Backman Jr., interview by Samuel Alonzo Dodge, August 12, 2009, Provo, UT) records of the past can be examined to determine the reliability of Joseph's description regarding the historical setting of the First Vision.

Joseph Smith stated that the Methodists initiated the religious excitement which took place in the neighborhood where he lived during the months preceding the First Vision. At that

The Towns of Palmyra and Farmington 1820

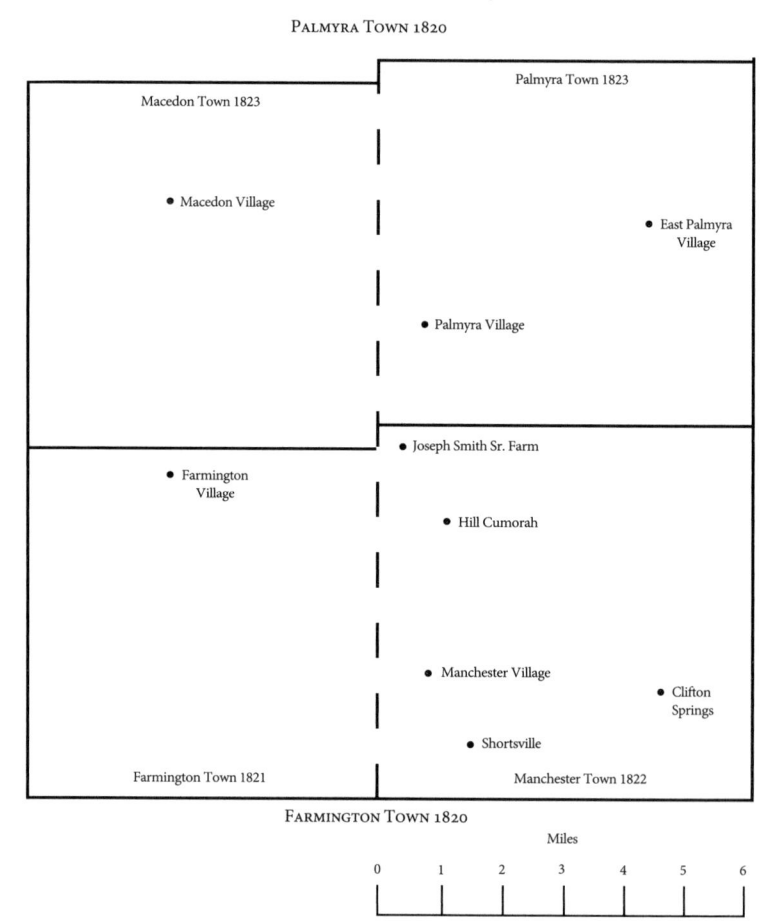

PALMYRA TOWN 1820

Macedon Town 1823	Palmyra Town 1823
• Macedon Village	• East Palmyra Village
	• Palmyra Village
	• Joseph Smith Sr. Farm
• Farmington Village	• Hill Cumorah
	• Manchester Village • Clifton Springs
	• Shortsville
Farmington Town 1821	Manchester Town 1822

FARMINGTON TOWN 1820

Miles
0 1 2 3 4 5 6

In 1821 Farmington Town was divided. One approximate six-mile square area retained the name Farmington Town, and the other section was called Burt Town and was renamed Manchester Town in 1822.

In 1823 Macedon Town was formed from the western section of Palmyra Town.

time, Methodism was replacing the Baptist faith as the largest religious society in America, numerically speaking, and was the fastest-growing religion in the early republic. These ambitious Protestants had initiated the most effective missionary program existent in the young nation. They, in part, solved the problem of the shortage of ministers by not requiring their preachers to be college graduates, and a great many dedicated Americans sacrificed many comforts of life to serve as Methodist itinerants. The Methodists, moreover, divided the country into conferences and districts and then subdivided the districts into stations and circuits. In areas where there was a Methodist meetinghouse, stationed preachers were appointed who in most instances derived much of their support from their own industry. But most communities, such as the towns of Palmyra and Farmington, were served by traveling ministers who had no secular employment. Preaching locations were determined within the circuits, and itinerant ministers were appointed to preach regularly in the designated places of worship. The circuits were called two-week circuits, three-week circuits, or four-week circuits depending on the period required to preach at each location. Ministers were usually assigned to a circuit for only one or at the most two years, and the presiding elders of each district were usually assigned to a region for no longer than four years. By this ingenious system, vast numbers of Americans living in rural communities received regular spiritual edification.[7]

Palmyra Methodists until 1823

Since there were no Methodist meetinghouses in the towns of Palmyra and Farmington prior to 1823, Methodists residing in the neighborhood where Joseph lived worshiped in the homes of the settlers, in school buildings, and in and near the beautiful virgin groves.[8] About every two weeks, a Methodist itinerant would contact the settlers in the towns of Palmyra and Farmington and would preach, exhort, and counsel those who gathered. The Smith farm was located near the border of the Ontario and Lyons Circuits (probably within the Ontario Circuit) of the Ontario District of the Genesee Conference, and from the summer of 1819 to the summer of 1820 these circuits were served by two active itinerants; William Snow and Andrew Peck visited the people residing in the Ontario Circuit, and Ralph Lanning and Isaac Grant traveled the Lyons Circuit.[9] Since Joseph Smith considered joining the Methodist Church, he probably listened to one or more of these ministers preach and was impressed by the message of salvation which they proclaimed.

One of the most effective missionary programs adopted by the Methodists to promulgate their faith was the camp meeting. Although Baptists, Presbyterians, and members of other

Camp meetings and other types of religious services were conducted regularly by Methodists in the community where Joseph Smith lived during the era of the First Vision. (Lithograph of a ca. 1829 religious camp meeting, Library of Congress)

religious societies also sponsored such meetings and while Christians of various faiths participated in these gatherings, the Methodists in western New York conducted more camp meetings in the early nineteenth century than did members of any other denomination. These meetings were usually held on the edge of a beautiful grove of trees or in a small clearing in the midst of a forest. After traveling many miles along dusty or waterlogged roads, the settlers would locate their wagons and pitch their tents on the outskirts of the encampment. Farmers' markets and grog or liquor shops often sprung up near the campgrounds, thereby providing some farmers with unusual economic opportunities. The meetings frequently continued for several days, and sometimes one session would last nearly all day and into the night. Ministers would rotate preaching assignments so that one minister would immediately be followed by another, and at times two or three ministers would preach simultaneously in different parts of the campground. Ministers not only preached lengthy sermons but devoted much of their time in counseling and directing prayer circles and group singing.[10]

The numbers who attended camp meetings held in New York about 1820 varied considerably. There were times when only a few hundred gathered, and on other occasions thousands witnessed the proceedings.[11] In a camp meeting held in Palmyra in 1826, one reporter estimated that ten thousand people gathered on the grounds to behold the spiritual drama.[12]

In some sections of early America, camp meetings frequently erupted into exciting spectacles in which enthusiasts demonstrated their emotional aspirations with a variety of physical demonstrations. During these exuberant meetings, people went into trances, jerked, rolled and crawled on the ground, barked like dogs, and fell to the ground as though they had been hit by a piercing cannonball, remaining unconscious for minutes or even sometimes for hours. In western New York, however, at the time of the First Vision, physical demonstrations were rarely manifest, except for the occasional practice of falling to the ground and crying out for mercy. Nevertheless, some settlers who were attending these New York meetings for the first time were alarmed by the piercing, dissonant commotions that would occasionally erupt. Some viewed with mixed emotions the weeping, the crying, the mourning, and the sighing which created loud noises in the encampment.[13]

Camp meetings and other types of religious services were conducted regularly by Methodists in the community where Joseph Smith lived during the era of the First Vision, and many of these meetings undoubtedly could have been considered by an attender such as Joseph Smith as the beginning or the continuation of an unusual religious excitement. On June 19, 1818, for example, a camp meeting was held near Palmyra which, according to one report, resulted in twenty baptisms and forty conversions to the Methodist society.[14] The following summer, many memorable Methodist services were held in Phelps, a town located near Manchester. These meetings precipitated a powerful spiritual awakening in that section of western New York.

The historic gatherings which led to a great revival and created such an impression on the settlers in the town of Phelps began in July 1819, when the Methodists of the Genesee Conference held their annual meetings in Phelps Village, which was then called Vienna. Approximately one hundred Methodist ministers gathered in this small village during that summer to deliberate, to develop programs, to resolve controversies, and to receive edification, instruction, and annual appointments. The sessions of this conference were held in a yellow clapboard meetinghouse, a newly completed Methodist church which was painted with yellow ochre and crowned with a diminutive cupola. Although this building contained no classrooms, carpets, or cushions, fairly comfortable seats with backs were installed shortly before the conference began.[15]

In addition to the special services which were held in connection with this conference, camp meetings were conducted following the deliberations; and during the ensuing twelve months (from the summer of 1819 to the summer of 1820), a "flaming spiritual advance" occurred in that region. In the 1880s, one convert of that impressive revival, Mrs. Sarepta Marsh Baker, described this momentous awakening in a manner that resembled Joseph's testimony. The revival, she observed, was a "religious cyclone which swept over the whole region round about and the kingdom of darkness was terribly shaken."[16]

Since the boundaries of the Genesee Conference stretched from the Catskill Mountains in the east to Detroit in the west, a distance of about five hundred miles, and from Upper Canada in the north to central Pennsylvania in the south, a distance of about three hundred miles, many itinerant preachers—from western New York, northwestern Pennsylvania, portions of Canada, Ohio, and other western regions—traveled through or near Palmyra and Farmington in the summer of 1819. It was common for those ministers to preach and participate in camp meetings while they were traveling to and from their annual conferences. It is not unreasonable, therefore, to assume that Joseph Smith might have attended meetings convoked by ministers of this conference held immediately before, during, or shortly after the deliberations which took place in Phelps; and it might have been in connection with this event that Joseph Smith turned his attention to organized religion.

A contemporary of Joseph Smith, Orsamus Turner, concluded that the Mormon Prophet became excited about religion while he was attending a camp meeting held "away down in the woods, on the Vienna road," a road that led from Phelps Village.[17] This report of Joseph's catching a "spark of Methodist fire" while attending a camp meeting near Phelps has been repeated by several town and county historians and interpreted as a meeting held in and near Phelps and in Oaks Corners, a small community located southeast of Phelps Village in the town of Phelps.[18]

In the neighborhood where Joseph lived, camp meetings and other services conducted by Methodists were held so frequently at the time of the First Vision that notices of such gatherings seldom appeared in the local newspapers except when an unusual event occurred in connection with a particular meeting. In June 1820, the *Palmyra Register* reported on a Methodist camp meeting in the vicinity of Palmyra because an Irishman, James Couser, died the day after attending the gathering, at which he became intoxicated. "It is supposed," the editor commented, that Couser "obtained his liquor, which was no doubt the cause of his death, at the Camp-ground, where it is a notorious fact, the intemperate, the lewd and dissolute part of community too frequently resort for no better object, than to gratify their base propensities."[19] A quasi-apologetic clarification of this report was printed in a later edition of this paper in which the editor stated that when he wrote that Couser "obtained his liquor at the Camp-ground," he did not mean that the Irishman "obtained it within the enclosure of their [Methodist] place of worship, or that he procured it of them, but at the grog-shops which were established at, or *near* if you please, their camp-ground."[20]

Records Reveal Religious Excitement

Not only is historical evidence available to support Joseph Smith's testimony that an unusual excitement on the subject of religion commenced with the Methodists in the vicinity where he lived, but many records also reveal that the excitement "soon became general among all the sects in that region of country." There were three Presbyterian churches in the towns of Farmington and Palmyra in 1820: one located in or near the village of Farmington, one in East Palmyra, and another in Palmyra Village. The Western Presbyterian Church was the only meetinghouse located in the village of Palmyra at the time of the First Vision and was the congregation with which Lucy, Samuel, Hyrum, and Sophronia were affiliated until shortly before The Church of Jesus Christ of Latter-day Saints was organized.[21] There were also two Baptist meetinghouses in that area in 1820: one was located two miles west of Palmyra Village (the Palmyra Baptist Church) and one near Manchester Village (the Farmington Baptist Church). Members of the Society of Friends had erected three meetinghouses, one north of Palmyra Village and two near the village of Farmington. The Methodists had one house of worship, a church which they purchased from the Episcopalians in the village of Clifton Springs, and Methodist classes were being held in or near Palmyra and Manchester villages at that time. In adjoining towns, other Protestant denominations such as the Freewill Baptists, Episcopalians, Congregationalists, and Eastern Christians were worshipping.[22]

An examination of Presbyterian church records reveals that between the summer of 1819 and the summer of 1820, its members participated in the upsurge of spiritual fervor which took place in the region of country where the Smith family lived. In the fall of 1819, a great awakening erupted in the village of Geneva, a community located near Phelps and adjacent to Seneca Lake. Whereas the average increase in membership of the Presbyterian Church in Geneva by examination (admission of new converts) had been only nine annually from 1812 to 1819, the increase in membership by examination from July 1819 to July 1820 was eighty. In September 1819, twenty-three adults were baptized, and in October 1819, approximately fifty new members (who had not previously been Presbyterians) were received into this church.[23]

182   ☞   Exploring the First Vision

The Great Revival of 1819–20 in Western, Central, and Upstate New York

●   Towns or villages where there were reports of "unusual religious excitement" and/or significant increases in church membership in 1819–20.

◆   Towns or villages located near the Smith farm where there were reports of "prospects of revivals" in 1819–20.

△   Indicates location of other landmarks of New York.

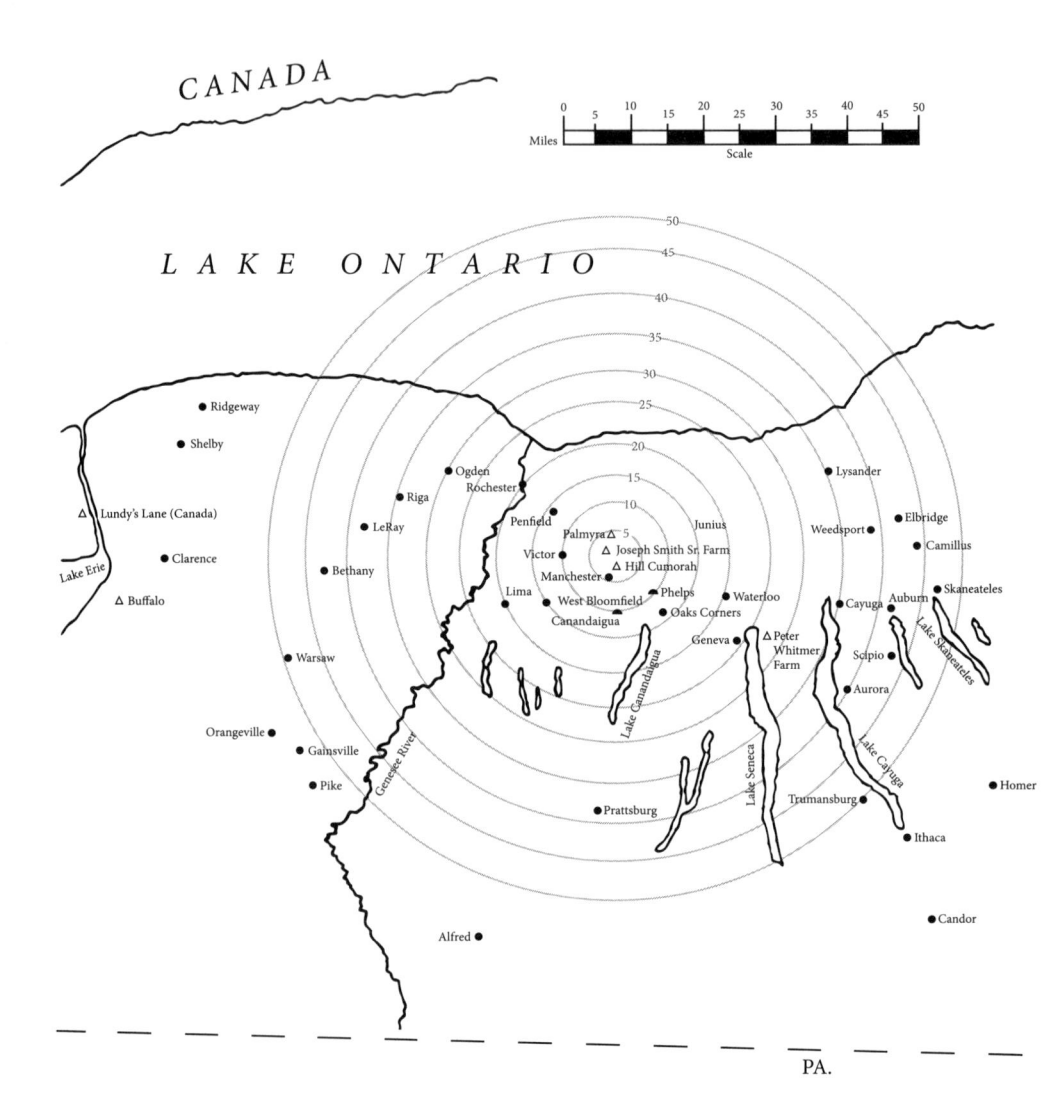

An examination of the session records of the Presbyterian Church located at Oaks Corners provides further evidence that an unusual awakening was occurring in the region where Joseph lived during the months immediately preceding the First Vision. The average annual increase in membership of this church between 1806 and 1819 had been only five, with no more than nine new members being admitted by profession in any single year prior to 1820. In 1820, however, seven were admitted by profession in January, fifteen in April, six in August, and two in November, making a total of thirty additions to this small congregation.[24]

Not only did revivals among Presbyterians erupt in the village of Geneva and the town of Phelps in 1819 and 1820, but during these years awakenings occurred in Penfield, Rochester, Lima, West Bloomfield, and Junius, towns or villages located within a radius of twenty-five miles of the Smith farm. Within a radius of forty-five miles of Joseph's log cabin home, other significant "ingatherings" of Presbyterians occurred in Cayuga, Auburn, Aurora, Trumansburg (Ulysses), Ogden, East and West Riga, Bergen, and Le Roy; and prospects of revivals were reported in Waterloo and Canandaigua, meaning that in these areas there was probably an unusual religious excitement.[25]

Although membership records of the Presbyterian church of Farmington and Palmyra Villages dating back to 1820 have not been preserved and membership figures are not available for the Methodist classes held in the neighborhood where Joseph lived, presbytery records and reports of growth in Methodist circuits are available. When representatives of the Presbyterian churches assembled in Phelps in February 1820, members of the presbytery of Geneva reported that "during the past year more have been received into the communion of the Churches than perhaps in any former year," and the word "perhaps" has been crossed out in the original record. At this meeting it was

> ### "Which Church Should I Join?"
>
> Thousands asked the question "Which church should I join?" And they were joining many churches. Probably more people joined the Methodist Church than any other church at this time. But they were joining the Presbyterian Church, they were joining the Baptist Church. Consequently, it was interesting not only to identify the churches and their possible growth but also to locate the areas where there was the greatest religious excitement. The result was finding that one of the areas of greatest revivalism in the United States at that time was upstate New York.... As I continued to search the area of revivalism in upstate New York, I continued to return to Joseph Smith's account where he said that in the second year after he moved to Manchester, "there was in the place where we lived" unusual religious excitement that began with the Methodist "but soon became general among all the sects in that region of country." In fact in the whole region of country "great multitudes united themselves to the different religious parties" (Joseph Smith—History 1:5). And I noticed that the Reverend Wesley Walters had misrepresented Joseph Smith. Joseph Smith never wrote that there was a great revival in Palmyra. He was living in Manchester and he said that the revival was in the whole region of country. I found the local newspapers that described hundreds of people joining churches in upstate New York. The name of the churches were identified, the number of people who were joining the church in 1820 were identified. So Joseph became aware of many, many people joining churches throughout the area where he lived....
>
> In fact, on one occasion I was at Phelps doing research and reading their newspapers when one of the directors invited my wife and me to her home for lunch. So we went to the home and had a nice lunch, and then while I was in her home I saw a picture. It had a grove, and in the picture it said, "Where Joseph got religion." And I asked the lady, "Well, what does this mean? Here you have a picture in your home of a grove where Joseph got religion." And she said, "That's my backyard. Tradition says that Joseph Smith came here, attended these revivals, then became all excited, and then went back home and claimed to have had a vision." (Milton V. Backman Jr., interview by Samuel Alonzo Dodge, August 12, 2009, Provo, UT)

also reported that two hundred were added to the churches by examination and eighty-five by certificate (transfer of membership); and only sixteen of the twenty-three churches in this presbytery reported, Palmyra and Farmington being two of the seven churches which failed to report.[26] Even though Methodist records indicate that there was no increase in the Ontario Circuit in 1820, in that year membership in the Lyons Circuit doubled, increasing from 374 to 654.[27]

Evidence that Baptists in the region of country where Joseph lived prospered from the religious stirrings is found in the membership reports of the Baptist Church of Farmington located a few miles south of the Smith farm. Baptist Church membership figures indicate that twenty-two converts were added to this congregation in 1819, which was a significant growth for a church consisting of only 87 members in 1818.[28]

Freewill Baptists also reported an advancement of spiritual sensitivity in the vicinity of New York where Joseph lived at the time of the First Vision. A quarterly meeting of members of this society was held in Phelps in July 1819, at which time "a profitable season was enjoyed" and five were added to their society. A few months later, Freewill Baptists in Junius, a town located east of Phelps, reported a revival in their community; and in the autumn of 1820, fifteen were added to their society. Strife and contention, however, erupted among these Protestants; and some of the newly awakened souls were dismissed from the Baptist society, forming a nondenominational church in Junius and "taking the Scriptures for their only rule of faith and practice."[29]

In the fall of 1819, Bishop John Henry Hobart, an Episcopalian bishop, visited western New York and received "encouraging reports" from missionaries laboring in Phelps, Waterloo, Bergen, Le Roy, and many other towns of western New York.[30]

Eastern Christians also benefited from the increased religious fervor which excited many settlers in western New York following the War of 1812. One of the leaders of this restorationist movement, David Millard, preached frequently in West Bloomfield and organized a church in that village in October 1818 with sixteen members. A few months after the inception of this religious society, membership increased to about fifty.[31]

Revival Is Conversion from Darkness to Light

Although membership records provide one indication of religious activity in a community, occasionally an unusual religious excitement occurred in a neighborhood without resulting in an immediate increase in church membership. Periodically, there was a renewal of religious fervor among church members. Sometimes many seekers were converted to the basic teachings of Christianity but postponed uniting with one of the religious societies located near their homes, and some converts never discovered what they regarded as God's true church. Some "outpourings of the Spirit" have vanished from mankind's memory because a contemporary failed to record the "extension of the power of godliness" or because the primary source was not preserved. As one American of the early Republic asserted, a "revival of religion" is "the translation" of a considerable number of souls in the same congregation or neighborhood "from darkness to light, and from bondage of iniquity to the glorious liberty of the sons of God," which is "attended with an awakening sense of sin and with a change of temper and conduct, which cannot be easily concealed."[32]

Many valuable ecclesiastical records dating back to the early nineteenth century have also been preserved that vindicate Joseph Smith's testimony concerning the "whole district of country" being affected by the spiritual awakening of 1819–20 and "great multitudes" uniting "themselves to the different religious parties." A careful reading of the Prophet's account

> ### "Thy Sins Are Forgiven Thee"
>
> I have two favorite accounts—the 1832 and the 1838. You cannot fully understand what happened without combining those two major accounts. But in the 1835 and the 1842 there is information that's not available in others. I especially like what Joseph included in his 1842 account regarding the churches....
>
> One reason I like the 1832 account is that it talks about Joseph's long quest for religious truth. He didn't just read James 1:5 and go into the grove. For three years he was seeking and searching and investigating. And then his big concern was that he was a sinner. He would have been asking ministers not which church to join, but what is the means of salvation? He was looking for the minister that could tell him the true path toward securing a forgiveness of sins. He wanted to be saved. Then he went to the grove, and that's the account that said, "Joseph thy sins are forgiven thee.... Behold I am the Lord of glory I was crucifyed for the world that all those who believe on my name may have Eternal life." *The Personal Writings of Joseph Smith*, comp. and ed. Dean C. Jessee (Salt Lake City: Deseret Book; Provo, UT: Brigham Young University Press, 2002), 11. That's just beautiful....
>
> The 1838 account is officially written for the history of the Church, so that includes probably more details than any other accounts. It's one of the most complete accounts, and there it says the Father appeared. It's the only account where Joseph identifies the Father. I just love that one personage said to him, "Joseph, this is my Beloved Son. Hear him." (Milton V. Backman Jr., interview by Samuel Alonzo Dodge, August 12, 2009, Provo, UT)

indicates that the great increase in membership occurred in "the whole district of country," meaning possibly western New York or eastern and western New York and not necessarily Palmyra, Farmington, or just the neighborhood where he lived. Joseph undoubtedly learned that many revivals were occurring in New York in 1819 and 1820. Accounts of the most impressive and productive religious quickenings were widely circulated by preachers, traveling merchants, and newspapers. In the summer and early fall of 1820, for example, descriptive accounts of awakenings occurring in central and upstate New York were published in the *Palmyra Register*, a paper which, according to Orsamus Turner, the Smith family obtained regularly.[33] The June 7, 1820, issue carried a brief report of "Great Revivals in Religion" in the eastern part of the state. This revival was more fully reported on in a later issue. In this later report, the Palmyra paper announced that "the face of the country has been wonderfully changed of late." Last summer, as a result of a powerful revival, 40 were added to the church at Saratoga Springs. Shortly thereafter, an awakening kindled the settlers of Malta and Stillwater, where in the latter town about 200 were converted. At Ballston, 118 were added to the church during two communion services. At East Galway, within two months, at least 150 were "hopefully" converted; at Amsterdam, 50 members had been added recently to the church; and, the report concluded, at Nassau, 30 settlers had been converted in less than three weeks.[34] And in still a different article, the readers of the *Palmyra Register* learned that more than 200 people had been converted since the first of the year during a great spiritual vitalization which was animating the settlers of Homer.[35]

Presbyterian church records provide one of the most valuable insights into the extent and numerical consequences of the great awakening which transformed New York into an ecclesiastical storm center during the years following the termination of the War of 1812, including the years 1819 and 1820. After delegates from Presbyterian churches located throughout the United States gathered in Philadelphia in May 1820, they prepared their annual report on the state of religion for the preceding year. "It is with gratitude and heart-felt joy," the delegates asserted, that "the past has been a year of signal and almost unprecedented mercy" as far as "genuine religious revivals" are concerned. When the committee enumerated the areas where "the most copious of these effusions of the Spirit" had been experienced, they specified eight presbyteries, six of which were located in New York.

Then they described the congregations where the most significant revivals were occurring. Twenty-two congregations were listed, nineteen of which were located in New York, including Geneva, Homer, Smithfield, Utica, Whitesboro, New Hartford, Clinton, Cooperstown, Sherburne, Pleasant Valley, Stillwater, Malta, Ballstown, Galway, Schenectady, Amsterdam, Marlboro, and Hopewell.[36]

Revival "Fruits" in 1820

The report of the General Assembly for the year ending 1820 indicates that the great New York revival continued during the year of the First Vision. In fact, the "fruits" of the 1820 revivals were considered more "numerous, extensive, and blessed" than in any previous year. Awakenings occurring in fifty-four congregations in New York were specifically mentioned, and this enumeration did not include a special report on the revivals in the presbytery of Albany, where "one thousand four hundred" were added to the Presbyterian churches.[37]

Presbyterian church membership figures compiled by the General Assembly also reveal not only that there was a significant increase in membership in New York in 1819 but that there was a greater increase there than in any other state. During the year preceding the First Vision, the national increase in Presbyterian Church membership was approximately 6,500, and the increase in New York State alone was 2,250, representing 35 percent of the national total. But what is most significant here is the fact that more than 67 percent or 1,513 of the 2,250 New York converts came from the Burned-Over District. This is 23 percent of the national total.[38]

Membership summaries for the Presbyterian Church in western New York for 1820 indicate a decline in membership; the decline is probably due to failure of many Presbyterian churches to report. Although Methodist reports for the region show a decline in 1819, probably because of the reorganization of the Methodist circuits, Methodist membership figures for 1820 indicate that during the year of the First Vision there was an increase of 2,256 members in western New York. This was the largest annual increase reported by this group for that region of America.[39]

The Baptists were also increasing rapidly in membership in western New York at the time Joseph beheld his remarkable vision. At a triennial meeting of the Baptists held in Philadelphia in 1820, 83 of the 145 associations reported baptisms for the year 1819. Although only ten associations or 12 percent of the alliances of churches which reported were located in New York, these groups recorded 26 percent of the baptisms. In the Empire State, the most significant increases were noted by associations located west of the Catskill Mountains. Madison disclosed 506 baptisms (more than any other Baptist association); Cayuga, 474; Holland Purchase, 262; Franklin, 183; and Genesee, 147. Consequently, in five western New York Baptist associations, there was an increase of more than 1,500 for the year 1819.[40]

When Calvinist Baptists described the region where some of the most powerful revivals occurred in 1820, they reported a profound enhancement of religious sensitivity in Madison, Onandaga, Cortland, and Chenango counties, where Baptists of central New York had formed the Madison Association. About January 1, a spiritual enlivenment commenced in Homer and continued during much of the year. By August, more than one hundred converts had joined the Baptist society in Homer, about one hundred had united with the Baptists in Truxton, and other significant additions were made in the societies located in Nelson, Virgil, Preble, and Scipio. Another "extensive revival" which reached a peak in the spring of 1820 took place in the town of Smithfield, where eighty-four joined the Baptist society in Peterboro and fifty-four in Siloam. The Baptists also reported that many converts were joining Congregational and Presbyterian churches located in central New York. The Seventh-day Baptists noted that great numbers were joining their society in Alfred, a community located southwest of Joseph's home.[41]

One witness of the great awakening which erupted in Homer wrote a colorful description of this movement in which he testified that all classes in society were affected by the great and powerful work which had broken forth. Some, he said, who had previously made a confession of religion again searched their hearts, resulting in second rebirth. Others for the first time "fell under the power of truth and exclaimed, 'What shall we do?' Of this class," he observed, "were a great company of the youth of both sexes. The principal means of awakening," he continued, were the "exhortations of the pious, the pathetic expostulations of young converts, and the preaching of the Gospel." The revival, he added, was distinguished by its great solemnity and order, for there was "scarce a feature of enthusiasm or blind zeal visible. . . . It ought to be recorded," this witness concluded, "to the honor of Divine grace, that in many instances prayer" was "most signally and speedily answered; whether it was for the conversion of a sinner, or the comfort of a saint under peculiar trials. It has been fully manifested, that those who asketh, receiveth."[42]

Church records, newspapers, religious journals, and other contemporary sources clearly reveal that great awakenings occurred in more than fifty western New York towns or villages during the revival of 1819–20. Primary sources also specify that great multitudes joined the Methodist, Presbyterian, and Calvinist Baptist societies in the region of country where Joseph Smith lived; and significant additions were also made in western New York communities by the Congregational Church, the

Christian denomination, the Freewill and Seventh-day Baptist societies, and other Protestant faiths.[43]

Summary

While summarizing the spiritual quickenings that awakened America into a new reality of the divinity of Christ, one editor declared in 1820 that there were currently more reports of revivals in religious publications than in any previous era.[44] Although this spiritual phenomenon was certainly not limited to New York, this state, especially the area stretching from Albany to Buffalo, was the ecclesiastical storm center of America at the time one of the most remarkable visions was unfolded to mankind.

The most reliable sources of the early nineteenth century show that Joseph Smith's brief description of the historical setting of the First Vision is in harmony with other contemporary accounts of the religious excitement which took place in the area where he lived and of the great revival which continued in New York in 1819 and 1820. Indeed, the Mormon Prophet penned a reliable description of an awakening which occurred in the Burned-Over District at the time he launched his quest for religious truth.

Notes

1. Milton V. Backman Jr., *American Religions and the Rise of Mormonism* (Salt Lake City: Deseret Book, 1965), 283, 308–9.

2. Whitney R. Cross, *The Burned-Over District* (Ithaca, NY: Cornell University Press, 1950), 3–4.

3. Cross, *Burned-Over District*, 9–11; P. H. Fowler, *Historical Sketch of Presbyterianism within the Bounds of the Synod of Central New York* (Utica, NY: Curtiss & Childs, 1877), 167–68. Presbyterian church membership in western New York (based on the

membership reports of the Geneva, Cayuga, Oneida, Onondaga, Ontario, Niagara, Rochester, Genesee, and Bath presbyteries) increased slowly from 1812 to 1816, the average annual increase being about five hundred members per year. In 1816, Presbyterian membership in western New York increased by 1,050; in 1817, the increase was 1,989; in 1818, 1,516; and in 1819, 1,513. Since the report for 1819 did not include the membership of the Genesee presbytery, the increase in 1819 was probably greater than any previous year except for 1817. Methodist increase in membership in approximately the same region (based on membership reports of the Chenango, Oneida, and Genesee districts and the districts formed from these bodies) indicates that there was an increase in membership of 1,873 in 1816; of 1,613 in 1817; and of 2,154 in 1818. After a major realignment occurred in the districts in 1819, membership reports reveal that during the year 1820 another significant increase in membership took place, there being an increase of 2,256. *Minutes of the General Assembly of the Presbyterian Church in the United States of America from its Organization, A.D. 1789 to A.D. 1820 Inclusive* (Philadelphia: Presbyterian Board of Publication, 1847), 516, 574–75, 634–35, 667, 696, 742; *Minutes Taken at the Several Annual Conferences of the Methodist Episcopal Church* (New York: Methodist Episcopal Church, 1816), 34, hereafter referred to as *Methodist Minutes*; *Methodist Minutes* (1817), 29; *Methodist Minutes* (1818), 30; *Methodist Minutes* (1819), 36; *Methodist Minutes* (1820), 27; *Methodist Minutes* (1821), 27–28.

4. Cross, *Burned-Over District*, 13.

5. The town of Manchester was formed from Farmington on March 31, 1821. It was originally named "Burt," but the name was changed to Manchester on April 16, 1822. Horatio Gates Spafford, *A Gazetteer of the State of New York* (Albany, NY: B. D. Packard and Troy, 1824), 302–3; Hamilton Child, *Gazetteer and Business Directory of Ontario County, New York, for 1867-8* (Syracuse, NY: printed by author, 1867), 49.

6. Joseph Smith—History 1:5.

7. An excellent description of the Methodist circuit-rider system is found in an article relating the history of Methodism in

Connecticut. The program adopted in Connecticut was similar to the system existent in New York at the time of the First Vision. See William Thacher, "A Sketch of the History and Present State of Methodism in Connecticut," *Methodist Magazine*, January 1822, 33–38.

8. *Palmyra Courier*, August 17, 1866; *Palmyra: Wayne County* (Rochester, NY: Herald Press, 1907), 51; G. A. Tuttle, "Historical Sketch of the Palmyra Methodist Episcopal Church," copy located in the Palmyra King's Daughters Free Library; Files of the Shortsville Enterprise Press, November 24, 1883; December 19, 1902, located in Shortsville, NY.

9. *Methodist Minutes* (1819), 51. From July 1820 to July 1821, the Ontario Circuit was supplied by Thomas Wright and Elihu Nash. *Methodist Minutes* (1820), 44.

10. Charles Giles, *Pioneer: A Narrative of the Nativity, Experiences, Travels, and Ministerial Labours of Rev. Charles Giles* (New York: G. Lane & P. P. Stanford, 1844), 266–70; "Religious and Missionary Intelligence," *Methodist Magazine*, December 1819, 474–76; Eben Smith, "Progress of the Work of God on Hudson-River District," *Methodist Magazine*, December 1822, 474–75; *Palmyra Register*, June 28, 1820; July 5, 1820.

11. Theophilus Armenius, "Account of the Rise and Progress of the Work of God in the Western Country," *Methodist Magazine*, July 1819, 272; Thomas Madden, "Good Effects of Campmeetings," *Methodist Magazine*, June 1818, 152–53.

12. "Genesee Conference," *Methodist Magazine*, August 1826, 313.

13. Giles, *Pioneer*, 268; R. Smith, *Recollections of Nettleton, and the Great Revival of 1820* (Albany, NY: E. H. Pease, 1848), 31–33, 71, 74, 123; T. Spicer, "A Short Sketch of the Revival of Religion in the City of Troy, A.D. 1816," *Methodist Magazine*, June 1818, 152–53.

14. M. P. Blakeslee, "Notes for a History of Methodism in Phelps, 1886," 7, copy located in the Harold B. Lee Library, Brigham Young University, Provo, UT.

15. Blakeslee, "History of Methodism in Phelps," 6–7; "Journal of the Genesee Conference, 1810 to 1828," 76–84, copy located in the Harold B. Lee Library; Helen Post Ridley, *When Phelps Was Young*

(Phelps, NY: Phelps Echo, 1939), 55; [W. H. McIntosh], *History of Ontario Co., New York* (Philadelphia: J. B. Lippincott, 1876), 170.

16. Blakeslee, "History of Methodism in Phelps," 7–8.

17. O. Turner, *History of the Pioneer Settlement of Phelps and Gorham's Purchase, and Morris' Reserve* (Rochester, NY: W. Alling, 1852), 214.

18. Child, *Gazetteer*, 52; Mabel E. Oaks, *History of Oaks Corners Church and Community* (Phelps, NY: Wilson, 1954), 11.

19. *Palmyra Register*, June 28, 1820.

20. *Palmyra Register*, July 5, 1820.

21. "Records of the Session of the Presbyterian Church in Palmyra," 2:11–12, located in the Western Presbyterian Church, Palmyra, NY; Pearl of Great Price, 47; [Sarah Lines], *One Hundred and Twenty-Five Years of the Western Presbyterian Church* (Palmyra, NY, 1942), 1–2; McIntosh, *History of Ontario County*, 195.

22. *Minutes of the Fifty-Eighth Anniversary of the Ontario Baptist Association* (Canandaigua, NY, 1871), 13–16; *Wayne County Journal*, June 6, 1872; Fred G. Reynolds, *One Hundred Years' History of the First Baptist Church of Macedon, N. Y.* (Macedon, NY, n.d.), 4–5; McIntosh, *History of Ontario County*, 111–13, 176, 180–82, 194, 221, 264; Marilla Marks, ed., *Memoirs of the Life of David Marks* (Dover, NH: Free-will Baptist, 1846), 26.

23. "Records of the Church of Christ in Geneva, State of New York," 136–38, 146–56, 158–59, located in the First Presbyterian Church, Geneva, NY; "Minutes of the Session, 1819–26," 260–86, located in the First Presbyterian Church, Geneva, NY.

24. "Session Book of the First Presbyterian Church in Phelps," book 2, 11–19, located in the Presbyterian Church, Oaks Corners, New York.

25. *Extracts from the Minutes of the General Assembly, of the Presbyterian Church, in the United States of America* (Philadelphia, 1821), 22; "Records of the Synod of Geneva (1812–1835)," 183, 220–21, copy located in the Harold B. Lee Library; "Records of the Presbytery of Geneva," Book C, 37, copy located in the Harold B. Lee Library; John Jermain Porter, *History of the Presbytery of Geneva, 1805–1889* (Geneva: Courier Job Department, 1889), 25.

26. "Records of the Presbytery of Geneva," book C, 37–38.

27. *Methodist Minutes* (1820), 27; *Methodist Minutes* (1821), 27.

28. *Minutes of the Ontario Baptist Association* (Canandaigua, NY: Messenger Office, 1818), 3; *Minutes of the Ontario Baptist Association* (New York: Messenger Office, 1819), 2.

29. Marks, *Memoirs of the Life of David Marks*, 26.

30. Charles Wells Hayes, *The Diocese of Western New York* (Rochester, NY: Scrantom, Wetmore, 1904), 53.

31. McIntosh, *History of Ontario County*, 221.

32. William Neill, "Thoughts on Revivals of Religion," *Christian Herald*, April 7, 1821, 708–11.

33. Turner, *History of the Pioneer Settlement*, 214.

34. *Palmyra Register*, September 13, 1820.

35. *Palmyra Register*, August 16, 1820.

36. *Extracts from the Minutes of the General Assembly* (1820), 321–22.

37. *Extracts from the Minutes of the General Assembly* (1821), 22–23.

38. *Minutes of the General Assembly* (1820), 742–43.

39. Although there were significant increases in 1820 in the Onondaga and Oneida presbyteries, the report of the General Assembly for that year indicates a combined decline of more than 2,584 in the Cayuga and Geneva presbyteries with only a reduction of two churches in these presbyteries, indicating that many churches in these presbyteries failed to submit reports in 1821; and two presbyteries, Genesee and Niagara, failed to report. *Minutes of the General Assembly* (1820), 742; *Minutes of the General Assembly of the Presbyterian Church in the U.S.A., from A.D. 1821 to A.D. 1835 Inclusive*, 4; *Methodist Minutes* (1821), 27–28.

40. *Proceedings of the Baptist General Convention in the United States, at their Second Triennial Meeting, and the Sixth Annual Report of the Board of Managers* (Philadelphia, 1820), 308–9.

41. "Revivals of Religion," *Western New York Baptist Magazine*, August 1820, 60, 90–94, 119–23; *Minutes of the Seventh-day Baptist General Conference* (New Brunswick, 1820), 5; "Revivals of

Religion," *Religious Intelligencer*, February–May 1820, 570, 668, 699, 717, 751, 770, 822–23; September 1820, 218, 222.

42. Alfred Bennet, "Revival of Religion in Homer," *Western New York Baptist Magazine*, November 1820, 119–21.

43. For additional information on the Great Revival of 1819–20 in New York, see R. Smith, *Recollections of Nettleton*; P. H. Fowler, *Historical Sketch of Presbyterianism*; Joshua Bradley, *Accounts of Religious Revivals in Many Parts of the United States from 1815 to 1818* (Albany, NY: G. J. Loomis, 1819); and James H. Hotchkin, *History of the Purchase and Settlement of Western New York* (New York: M. W. Dodd, 1848).

44. "Revivals of Religion," *Western New York Baptist Magazine*, August 1820, 91.

Like Joseph, many asked the question "Which church should I join?" And they were joining many churches. (Sandra B. Rast, Ask of God, *www.sandrarastart.com, rast_sandra@hotmail.com)*

Rev. George Lane—Good "Gifts," Much "Grace," and Marked "Usefulness"

Larry C. Porter

This essay was among several included in this volume that were originally published in BYU Studies *9, no. 3 (Spring 1969).*

Many of the personalities who touched early Mormonism have drifted into comparative obscurity, their initial roles ill remembered or undefined. Such has been the lot of the Methodist Episcopal Church minister the Reverend George Lane (1784–1859), a figure who, according to certain accounts, was one of those instrumental in moving Joseph Smith to make his epic inquiry of the Lord with the attendant vision of the Father and Son. The renewed research on Mormon origins has generated interest in Lane's activities and his contact with Joseph Smith. This new interest has pointed out how very little we know of the Reverend George Lane, which has motivated this study of the man and his relationship to Mormonism.

The writer enjoyed conducting original research in the area concerned here during the summer of 1968 and searching for the records that yielded the information contained in this article. The experience was made doubly enjoyable by the excellent assistance of Ralph Hazeltine, director of the Wyoming Historical and Geological Society at Wilkes-Barre, Pennsylvania; Luke A. Sarsfield, a doctoral candidate doing research at the society; Harrison Harvey Smith, editor of the *Wilkes-Barre Record* and a descendant of Sarah Harvey Lane, first wife of the Reverend George Lane; and Miss Marion Disque, Wyoming Seminary, Kingston, Pennsylvania. Each of these perceptive individuals generously shared information and materials helpful to this project.

George Lane was born near Kingston, Ulster County, New York, on April 13, 1784.[1] His birth apparently occurred "not far from the Hudson, after his parents set off from Massachusetts for the wilds of Susquehanna."[2] He was the sixth child of Nathan Lane (b. Attleboro, Massachusetts, March 20, 1750; d. Lanesboro, Pennsylvania, March 17, 1817) and Dorcas Muscroft (b. March 1, 1751; md. 1772; d. September 8, 1839).[3] His brothers and sisters were Daniel, Irene, Betsey, Nathan, David, Asa, Charles, and Dorcas.[4]

Lane's father remained for a short time in Ulster County and then moved to Broome County, New York, where he enjoyed the distinction of being the first white settler in Onaquaga, Windsor Township.[5] Similarly, he became the first town supervisor and erected the first gristmill in the area in about 1797. His sons, Nathan Jr. and David, were still listed as residents in the 1820 census.[6]

George Peck, a fellow preacher and intimate of George Lane, describes the circumstances of his friend's youth in these terms:

> The early history of George Lane was marked by the toils, hardships, and exposure common to the life of a boy in a new country. The simple food, often deficient in quantity, and few of the means and appliances of intellectual improvement. In those disadvantages

our subject shared a common lot with his fellows. The Puritan morals, piety, books, and reading of his excellent mother exerted a strong moral influence upon his mind while very young.[7]

Early in the nineteenth century, the Lanes settled in what is now Harmony Township, Susquehanna (then Luzerne) County, Pennsylvania, "at a place which was afterwards called Lane's Mills, or Lanesville, and is now Lanesboro. This is in the territory which was known as the 'Wyoming region,' and was claimed by the Connecticut Susquehanna Company."[8] It is not certain whether George went to Harmony Township with his family at the time of their removal. He may have taken up "school-keeping" at this juncture. While in Windsor Township, he had attended school in the settlement of Windsor, New York, where he made "good proficiency" studying his spelling book, reading book, and arithmetic. His highest ambition, subsequently, was to be a schoolteacher, a person much in demand in the new settlements. In the summer of 1802, he was engaged to teach by Putnam Catlin, Esq., at Great Bend (Pennsylvania). During the winter of 1802–3, he taught in the vicinity of where the community of Kirkwood, New York, is presently located. It was here that George Lane joined the Methodist Episcopal Church. An account of his conversion has been preserved by Rev. William Round:

> Mrs. Moore, of Kirkwood, says that she experienced religion and joined the Methodist Episcopal Church while George Lane was teaching school near where Kirkwood now stands in 1803. Brother Lane experienced religion himself during that winter. He was absent from the school a few days, and when he returned he told his scholars that he had experienced religion, and exhorted them and prayed with them, and a great revival broke out immediately.[9]

Lane was apparently "awakened" through the preaching of James Herron and was received into the church by Samuel

Budd.[10] Lane reacted favorably toward his religious experience, and "the fervor of his spirit, and his gifts in prayer and exhortation, soon indicated that he was a chosen vessel, destined to be heard at the division of God's sacramental host, then doing battle valiantly upon the frontiers."[11]

In 1804, George Lane was employed by the presiding elder of the Genesee District as an assistant preacher on the Tioga circuit.[12] The following year he was admitted on trial in the Philadelphia Conference and appointed to the Scipio circuit (New York) with Johnson Dunham.[13] "The circuit was characterized by what was nothing very peculiar for those times, poverty, bad roads, long rides, small congregations, and a sad deficiency of all the comforts of life. Here he found hospitality, and here God gave him seals to his ministry."[14] As an indication of the tremendous distances traveled by this pair of itinerants, the Scipio circuit was six hundred miles in circumference.[15]

Lane remained on trial in 1806 and was appointed by the Philadelphia Conference to the Pompey circuit (New York) with Benjamin Bidlack. "Here also he labored hard and was blessed with fruit."[16] In 1807, he was admitted into "full connexion" and ordained a deacon by Bishop Francis Asbury.[17] His appointment was to the Accomac circuit on the eastern shore of Virginia: "Here he labored as he was able, amid death-camps, for the salvation of the poor slaves and their masters, and was happy in witnessing the conversation of many of the poor degraded and downtrodden sons of Ham, and their union with the Church of Christ."[18]

George Lane was continued as a deacon in 1808 and assigned to the Holland Purchase Mission with Thomas Elliott. Their mission included all of New York State west of Canandaigua and extended along Lake Erie into Pennsylvania. In this unsettled area, Lane was often compelled to travel thirty to forty miles without seeing a house, and he frequently suffered from

A Man of Integrity

When I arrived in Pennsylvania back in 1968 and went to Wilkes-Barre, I had been alerted to be on the watch for records related to Rev. George Lane, a Methodist Episcopal minister in the early nineteenth century. Rev. Wesley P. Walters of the Presbyterian Church had recently published on the subject of Palmyra revivals and determined that Joseph Smith's First Vision really did not occur in 1820 and that there were no revivals in the Palmyra area during that time. It was likewise expressed that Rev. George Lane would not have ventured so far out of the Susquehanna District, where he served as presiding elder, to participate in such an alleged revival. Rather it was averred that he would have remained down in northeastern Pennsylvania and the southern tier of New York. I was invited to find out all I could about Rev. George Lane, so I went to the historical society in Wilkes-Barre. The director, Ralph Hazeltine, sent me in two directions. First of all, he said, "You ought to visit George Lane's final resting place. He's buried up in the Hollenback cemetery." The second place he directed me to was the Wyoming Seminary at Kingston, which was across the Susquehanna River from Wilkes-Barre, an old bastion of the Genesee Conference and a training ground for the ministry.

I went over to the Wyoming Seminary library, where I talked to the curator. I said I would like very much to see the Genesee Conference minutes in the old record book and wished also to gather certain information about some of the early Methodist ministers who were part of that conference. The curator said to me, "You need to go see the food services administrator." I thought he didn't hear me correctly, so I repeated what I had just said, but he said, "No, you really need to go over to the cafeteria." So I went over. The food services administrator's name was Miss Marian Disque. She got a ring of keys, and we walked down a long, dark hall. As she opened the door and turned on the light, I felt like I had stepped into a time warp. It was a museum for the old Genesee Methodist Conference. Before me were the saddles, the saddle bags, the hats, and the surtout coats, the outer coat that ministers wore in that period. And there were the minutes of the Genesee Conference, a copy of them, and a host of other documents including publications by the ministers. I couldn't believe my good fortune. At the end of the day, Marian came back and said, "I see you're interested." I said, "By all means." And she said, "If there's anything here that you would like to take back to your hotel room, please feel free to do so." She also said, "If there's anything there that you want to copy, the Ousterhout Library has a very fine Xerox machine." Well, that night I busted the copier making so many copies, and it's probably fortunate that I was able to make copies of certain records because in 1972 the Susquehanna overflowed its banks, and that basement room filled with water. It destroyed much, if not all, of the materials there. I found out later as I went to the courthouse at Wilkes-Barre that that same flood also got many of the old court records associated with the county itself. The documents that I had been able to copy at Kingston have proven invaluable to me over the years. From the minutes of the Genesee Conference, I could tell where Rev. George Lane was at conference time and where his assignments took him in the interim. I found out that he was involved in the camp meetings near Joseph's own Palmyra home when the annual conference was held at Vienna (later Phelps), Ontario County, New York, in 1819, and that he passed in the general vicinity of Palmyra to the south, preaching on his way, as he traveled to the annual Genesee Conference at Lundy's Lane, Upper Canada, in 1820.

As a historian, you try to investigate all of the documents and gather all of the evidence that you can find. In the process of examining the life experience of Joseph Smith at considerable length, I am completely satisfied that he was indeed the designated Prophet of the Restoration and was about his Father's business. I have been satisfied that Joseph Smith was speaking the truth concerning his revelatory experiences with the heavens. The historical documents that I have pieced together tell me that I am dealing with a man of integrity and that he accomplished the tasks which he has described. Many historians believe that the certainty of the evidence has to be tangible and cannot come from the spiritual realm. However, I can say, "Thank you, Lord, for the knowledge that I have from the available documents and from the confirmation of the Spirit that Joseph Smith was who he said he was, that he did what he said he did, and that he was a servant of the living God." Relative to his First Vision experience, he was stirred by the revivalist preaching in his neighborhood and directed by the Spirit of the Lord as he went out, knelt down, and offered up his prayer to God in the grove. Again, you can't necessarily measure Joseph's woodland theophany in terms of what documents you find in a library or courthouse, but you can measure the effects of that divine manifestation on yourself as witnessed by the Spirit. Joseph's humble prayer of faith was answered as the Father and the Son appeared before him in the early spring of 1820. (Larry C. Porter, interview by Samuel Alonzo Dodge, July 30, 2009, Provo, UT) hunger and cold.[19] While laboring under these conditions, Lane conducted the first camp meeting west of the Genesee River. This gathering was held in Caledonia, now Wheatland. As a result of this and other endeavors, he was able to report the activity of some ninety members.[20]

George Peck, in his biographical sketch of Lane, details for his readers the difficulties experienced by the itinerant in the Holland Purchase Mission during that eventful year of 1808. Of equal value to the researcher is Peck's preface to the account of those difficulties when he states, "The following extract from Mr. Lane's diary has been furnished us by his excellent lady [Lydia Bunting Lane, second wife of George Lane], and will give the reader a good idea of his labors and dangers on this new field, and the spirit in which he bore himself under them."[21] From this communication it becomes obvious that Lane maintained a diary of at least a part of his early ministry and that it was apparently available for reference as late as 1860 (the publication date of Peck's treatise). I have been unable to locate that diary or to determine whether there was another diary for the 1820s.

Bishop William M'Kendree ordained George Lane an elder in the Methodist Church in 1809.[22] Lane was appointed by the Philadelphia Conference to the Wyoming circuit (Pennsylvania), serving with Abraham Dawson. These ministers conducted the first camp meeting in Luzerne County, holding the event near the village of Wyoming. A graphic account of the proceedings has been recorded:

> A rough board stand was constructed, which was occupied by the preachers during Divine service, and a circle of tents was formed round about, composed of wagon and bed covers stretched over hooped saplings. The floors of the tents were the bare ground concealed by a sprinkling of straw, while the beautiful green foliage of the forest was spread out above them. Multitudes of people collected from far and near, attracted, many by novelty, and some by

a desire to do good and to get good.... The tremendous emotions of the speaker were communicated to his audience, and an excitement was produced of which we in this day can have but a faint conception. The cries of the penitent, and the shouts of rejoicing Christians, mingled with the deep tones of the preacher, produced a marked effect even on the most obdurate infidel.[23]

On July 20, 1810, the Genesee Conference, newly formed by a division of the Philadelphia Conference, held its inaugural gathering at Lyons, New York. The *Journal of the Genesee Conference* for July 23, 1810, specifies that Rev. George Lane was officially located as of that date.[24] Broken in health, because of his "former toils and exposure," he found himself under the necessity of retiring, for a season, from the itinerancy.[25] According to the records of the old *Steward's Book* of the Wyoming circuit, Lane had, in fact, located shortly after the quarterly meeting in December 1809. The account indicates that in March 1810 Samuel Carver received traveling expenses and one-fourth salary for one quarter of Lane's stead. From March to July 1810, Loring Grant traveled the Wyoming circuit in place of George Lane.[26]

Among the active adherents to the Methodist faith on the Wyoming circuit was Miss Sarah Harvey of Plymouth Township, daughter of Elisha and Rosanna (Jameson) Harvey. Evidence of Sarah's interest in religious matters is indicated by a remembrance from 1808:

> The stone church at Brier Creek was the rallying point for the Methodist people from Milton, Lewisburgh, Northumberland, Wyoming Valley and surrounding country. At the quarterly meetings, held at Christian and Thomas Bowman's, before the church was built, people came thirty-five miles, men and women, on horseback. From Wyoming Valley: Ann Denison, Sarah Brown, Sarah Harvey (afterward wife of Rev. George Lane), Eunice

Wakeman, niece of Mrs. Joseph Wright, a young woman of extraordinary mind and talents.[27]

While serving the Wyoming circuit, Lane became acquainted with Sarah and the couple were married at Plymouth, Luzerne County, Pennsylvania, on May 31, 1810. Six children were born to this union: Sally Ann, Harvey Bradburn, George Washington, Charles Asbury, Mary Butler, and Joseph Jameson.[28] Harvey Bradburn became professor of languages at Wesleyan University, Middletown, Connecticut, and a New York businessman.[29] George Washington was a licensed minister for the Methodist Church in Georgia and was subsequently called to the chair of ancient languages at Emory College, Oxford, Georgia.[30] Joseph Jameson became a minister of the Methodist Church and a teacher.[31]

When George Lane withdrew from the itinerancy, he entered the mercantile business in partnership with his youngest brother, Charles. They purchased a stock of general merchandise from Joseph Wright and set up operation in the storeroom formerly occupied by Mr. Wright at the lower end of the village of Plymouth. This partnership was dissolved by mutual consent on September 21, 1812, and George Lane continued alone until the early part of 1814, when Benjamin Harvey, his brother-in-law and clerk in the store, joined him as a partner. They then moved from the Wright storeroom "to a building which stood where Smith's Opera House now stands in Plymouth."[32] In October 1814, a second store was opened in Wilkes-Barre:

> The firm of Lane and Harvey opened a store "with a general assortment of goods suitable to the season," in Wilkesbarre at the stand formerly occupied by J. and W. Barnes, on north side of the Public Square, near the corner of West Market street, on land now covered by the large department store of Jonas Long's sons. Mr. Lane, having erected a dwelling-house between the store building and the

corner, occupied it with his family and managed the Wilkes-barre store, while Mr. Harvey took charge of the business at Plymouth. At these two stores business was carried on until April, 1816, when, the partnership having been dissolved, the store at Plymouth was closed, and Mr. Lane became sole owner of the Wilkesbarre establishment.[33]

Lane was collector of taxes for Plymouth Township in 1813, and in 1818 he was elected treasurer of the Wilkes-Barre Bridge Company.[34] He became a stockholder in that company, originally having twenty shares of stock which increased to forty by 1824.[35]

Despite his retirement from the itinerancy, Lane did not divorce himself from certain ministerial performances. He continued to preach occasionally and was called upon to address various congregations in Wilkes-Barre and surrounding communities. He also assisted other ministers: "In his house the preachers ever found a pleasant home, and in him a true friend and wise counselor."[36]

In 1818, George Lane participated in a camp meeting conducted in the mountains west of the valley. At the close of the gathering, and as the caravan was moving down the mountain, one Betsey Myers, pricked in her heart, "alighted from the wagon and fell upon her knees in the shade of a clump of oak and pine shrubs by the side of the road, crying, 'God have mercy upon me a poor wicked sinner!' The way was soon blocked up. The whole train was arrested, and the attention of all was attracted to a little group of young ladies."[37] For several hours the impromptu camp meeting proceeded while the cries of the penitents were followed by shouts of deliverance. Following this event, a strong religious influence pervaded the entire charge. Unfortunately, the preachers on the local and district levels were obliged to attend the annual Genesee Conference at Lansing, Cayuga County, New York, on July 16,

1818, and were unable to meet the demands for assistance created by "the little camp-meeting." However, Lane and other local preachers came to their aid:

> The cause was in good hands. The Rev. George Lane, who had rendered good service at the camp-meeting, and had been present and deeply interested at the wayside meeting, took charge of the work while the preachers were at conference. He was then a local preacher and resided in Wilkes-barre. "Father Bidlack" and "Brother Lane" did the preaching, while Darius Williams managed the prayer-meetings. Influential families became interested in the revival and were identified with the Methodist Episcopal Church. Mr. Lane took the names of those who wished to join the society and reported them to the preacher after conference.[38]

His health restored, and anxious to associate once again with the active ministry, Lane sold his stock at the Wilkes-Barre store in March 1819[39] and reentered the itinerancy. On Thursday, July 1, 1819, he was in attendance as the annual Genesee Conference convened in Vienna (afterwards Phelps), Ontario County, New York. The following day, Friday, July 2, at "9 o'clock AM. Conference met. George Lane, Gideon Draper, Wm. Snow and Thomas Wright were again received into the traveling connexion."[40]

The conference was in session over a period of eight days, July 1 to July 8, 1819. Abel Stevens gives us some appreciation of the general pattern which evolved at such conferences of the Methodist Church:

> These annual assemblies became imposing occasions. A bishop presided; the preachers from many miles around, usually including several states, were present; hosts of laymen were spectators. There was preaching in the early morning, in the afternoon, and at night. The daily proceedings were introduced with religious services, and were characterized by an impressive religious spirit. They continued usually a week, and it was a festal season, gathering

the war-worn heroes of many distant and hard-fought fields, renewing the intimacies of preachers and people, and crowned alike by social hospitalities and joyous devotions.[41]

The presence of some 110 ministers and their bishop, R. R. Roberts, at the Genesee Conference meetings, representing the New York, Pennsylvania, and Upper and Lower Canada districts, must have created at least a moderate stir in the immediate neighborhood.[42] This places Rev. George Lane within fifteen miles of Manchester, attending the largest Methodist meeting of the year in western New York, among a great number of Methodist ministers, at a time when Joseph Smith was aware of "an unusual excitement on the subject of religion" occurring "some time in the second year [1819] after our removal to Manchester" (Joseph Smith—History 1:5). At this time the Smiths were actually still living in Palmyra Township, not Manchester.

Whether or not Joseph attended some of these meetings cannot be determined from any records presently available, but the opportunity cannot be denied—if only to sell confectionaries.[43] To think that the Smiths would not have heard of the gathering is hardly believable.

Lane was appointed Presiding Elder of the Susquehanna District at the conference. He was so named because he was one "who incessantly travels his extensive territory, preaching, counseling the traveling and Local Preachers and Exhorters, meeting the official members of the circuit Societies, and promoting the interest of the Church in every possible way."[44] The circuits which comprised the Susquehanna District in 1819 were the Bald Eagle, Lycoming, Shamoking, Northumberland, Wyoming, Canaan, Bridgewater, Wyalusing, Tioga, and Wayne.[45] The following year, 1820, the Broome circuit was placed under Lane's jurisdiction.[46]

Lane's geographical assignment prompts some interesting speculation relative to his possible acquaintance with certain

Emma Hale, who became Joseph Smith's wife and whose family was devoutly Methodist. Reverend Lane probably became acquainted with the Hale family and other individuals who became prominent in Mormonism. (Lee Greene Richards, Emma Hale Smith, *© 1941 Intellectual Reserve, Inc.)*

individuals who were later to become principals in the advent of Mormonism. Living within the confines of the district at Harmony, Susquehanna County, Pennsylvania, immediately west of the community of Oakland on the Susquehanna River, were Isaac Hale, his wife, Elizabeth, and their nine children, among whom was Emma, future wife of Joseph Smith. The Hale family was devoutly Methodist, Isaac and Elizabeth being numbered among the members of the first class conducted at Lanesboro, Pennsylvania, some two miles east of their Harmony home: "The first class at Lanesboro was formed in 1810 by Mr. Grant, or in 1812 by Bro. King. It included John and Phoebe Gildersleeve Comfort, Isaac and Elizabeth Hale, Nathaniel and Sarah Lewis, Marmaduke and Clarisa Salsbury, and James Newman and Betsey Rouse; and if not at first, soon after, Mary Hilborn."[47]

The preachers on the Broome circuit in 1816 found a cordial reception at the Hale home, and one of their appointments was in a little log schoolhouse near the Hale homestead, "to a small but earnest congregation."[48] In the *Methodist Quarterly Review*, the content of an affidavit asserts that "Father Hale's house was the preacher's home."[49] Under these circumstances, it is a distinct possibility that Lane, in his capacity of "meeting the official members of the circuit societies," may well have known the Hale family. The prospect is heightened when we recall that George Lane grew up in Windsor Township, Broome County, New York, at a location some ten miles north of the Hales' place, and that his parents, Nathan and Dorcus Lane, lived for many years at Lanesboro, Pennsylvania, within a few miles of Isaac and Elizabeth Hale.

Lane would most assuredly have been acquainted with Isaac Hale's brother-in-law, Nathaniel Lewis. Nathaniel had married Sarah Hale and lived just across the Susquehanna River from Isaac. He was a deacon in the Methodist faith, having been ordained by Bishop Asbury on July 12, 1807.[50] "Nathaniel Lewis, an ordained local preacher, was deeply pious, shrewd, witty, and at home in the rough-and-tumble polemics of the time. He preached and formed classes at Jackson, Thompson, Starruca, and other places."[51] Lewis was one of those who strenuously challenged the validity of Joseph Smith's claims. He was still preaching in that vicinity as late as 1835, prior to moving west.[52]

On September 13, 1819, Rev. George Lane and Marmaduke Pierce preached with telling effect at a camp meeting held at Carpenter's Notch, Wyoming circuit. From the account, we derive some feeling for Lane's persuasive abilities from the stand:

> Marmaduke Pierce preached a short but mighty sermon, and closed with a perfect storm. He addressed the wicked with tremendous power, and then, exclaiming, "I feel the Spirit of God

upon me, Glory, halleluiah!" dropped down upon the seat behind him, shouting, weeping, laughing, wonderfully moved. The joyous responses from the preachers and the assemblage arose like the sound of many waters, while the whole congregation shook like the forest in mighty wind. The exhortations of the presiding elder, George Lane, were overwhelming. Sinners quailed under them, and many cried aloud for mercy. The meeting included the Sabbath, and continued about a week. Sixty persons professed to find peace, and thirty joined the church.[53]

The 1820 annual Genesee Conference convened at Lundy's Lane, Niagara, Upper Canada, on Thursday, July 20, 1820. Rev. George Lane was present at the gathering and on July 24 was examined and "passed."[54] Lane was an active participant in the proceedings of the conference, being named to at least two committees. In the first instance, July 20, he was elected to a three-man "committee of temporalities" with Abner Chase and Charles Giles.[55] George Lane reported to the conference the findings of that committee via the following resolutions:

> Resolved 1st. That this Conference highly disapproved of the departure of some of its members in the fashion of their coats and hats, and the manner of wearing their hair from the plainness of dress, which characterizes the great body of Methodist preachers.
>
> Resolved 2nd. That we use every consistent measure to bring back the members of our church, to that simplicity and plainess of dress, which we believe to be consistent with the Gospel and our Discipline.
>
> Resolved 3rd. That we inforce more thoroughly the rules of our Discipline, especially those that relate to class-meetings, Love feasts, the use of ardent spirits, and dress.
>
> The above resolutions were adopted.[56]

Lane also served on still another committee of three, which investigated the inroads of Free Masonry into the Methodist itinerancy in the Genesee Conference, and which committee formed these resolutions:

> Resolved, that this Conference consider it an impropriety for any of its members to attach themselves to, or attend the Masonic Lodge, inasmuch it is contrary to the Apostolic teaching, "to avoid every appearance of evil" and for as much as it grieves the feelings of a considerable number of our pious brethren.
>
> Resolved, Secondly, that if any traveling preachers belonging to this Conference, shall hereafter attach himself to, or persist in attending the Lodges, he be delt with as in other cases of imprudent conduct.
>
> Both resolutions adopted.[57]

Lane's service on the latter committee subsequently caused him considerable discomfiture. In his home community of Wilkes-Barre, where he had been affiliated with the Masons, certain persons proceeded to "implicate and assail his character." On September 24, 1823, Lodge No. 61, F. and A. M. (Free and Accepted Masons), having been appraised of the resolutions made at the Genesee Conference of 1820, and ascribing their authorship to Lane, formulated some resolutions of their own, calling for an investigating committee.[58] The efforts of the committee resulted in a carefully framed letter from George Lane to the members of the Free Mason Lodge. His detailed reply to the charges leveled against him is a classic representation of his powers of diplomacy in ameliorating a tense situation between the Methodist clergy and the Masonic Society.[59]

If the proceedings of the year 1820 were consequential in the life of George Lane, they were certainly no less momentous for Joseph Smith, residing at Manchester, Ontario County, New York. Joseph attested that early in the spring of 1820 he retired to a previously designed place of seclusion and knelt in prayer. His efforts culminated in a heavenly manifestation: "I saw a pillar of light exactly over my head, above the brightness of the sun; which descended gradually until it fell upon me. . . . When the light rested upon me I saw two personages (whose brightness and glory defy all description) standing above me in the air. One of them spake unto me, calling me by name, and said, (pointing to the other.) 'This is my beloved Son, hear him.'"[60]

Joseph asserted that his vision of the Father and the Son came from the motivation of an unusual excitement on the subject of religion, generated by various sects, and affecting "the whole district of country."[61] The question necessarily arises, was Rev. George Lane among the religionists promoting the revivalist excitement in the area, and in particular, was he a personal instigator of Joseph's design to pray?

In the pursuit of his ministerial duties, Lane was in the geographical proximity of Joseph Smith on a number of occasions between the years 1819 and 1825. The nature and degree, or indeed the actuality, of their acquaintanceship during this interval poses a number of interesting possibilities.

For eight days, from July 1, 1819, to July 8, 1819, George Lane was in attendance at the annual Genesee Conference at Vienna (now Phelps), New York, some fifteen miles southeast of the Smith farm at Manchester.[62] In July 1820, Lane would have had to pass through the greater Palmyra-Manchester vicinity on his way to Niagara, Upper Canada, to attend the conference held at Lundy's Lane, July 20 to July 26, 1820,[63] unless he went by an extremely circuitous route. Present records do not specify Lane's itinerary or exact route of travel to and from Niagara, but they do for Lane's friend, Rev. George Peck, who lived at Kingston, Pennsylvania, just across the Susquehanna River from Lane at Wilkes-Barre.

Reverend Lane's conference route took him north to Ithaca, then on to a camp meeting in the Holland Purchase, subsequently passing along the Ridge Road, and after two weeks he arrived at Lundy's Lane. His return journey was by way of the Ridge Road to Rochester and then on to Auburn, New York.[64] A quick look at the map of New York State will show that Palmyra is almost on a direct line between Rochester and Auburn. If Lane followed a similar avenue, it would have brought him very close to the neighborhood of the Smith home. As with Reverend Peck, he may even have stopped at a camp meeting somewhere along the way. A preacher of his standing would always be a welcome guest.

Conference Again in Phelps in 1822

The Genesee Conference of 1822 was again held at Vienna (now Phelps), Ontario County, New York, from July 24 to August 2, 1822. Lane was present and was examined and passed. He was also called to serve on two committees: one concerned the examination of manuscripts for publication, and the other, the receipt of communications relative to the establishment of auxiliary societies.[65] For some ten days, Lane was once again within a few miles of Palmyra Township.

From July 1819 to July 1823, Lane served as supervising elder of the Susquehanna District. During the interval from July 1823 to July 1824, his appointment was the Wyoming circuit.[66] In July 1824 he was once more assigned as a presiding elder, this time, however, to the Ontario District. The Ontario District then comprised the circuits of Lyons, Ontario, Seneca, Crooked Lake, Canandaigua and Geneva, Canisteo and Bath, and Prattsburgh.[67] For an entire year, then, July 1824 to July 1825, Lane presided over the district within the confines of which the Smith family resided. On January 25, 1825, Lane addressed a glowing letter to the editors of the *Methodist Magazine* in which he outlined the unusual successes being enjoyed in the Ontario District. An entry of particular interest states:

> December 11th and 12th our quarterly meeting for Ontario circuit was held in Ontario. It was attended with showers of blessings, and

we have reason to believe that much good was done. Here I found that the work which had for some time been going on in Palmyra, had broken out from the village like a mighty flame, and was spreading in every direction. When I left the place, December 22nd, there had, in the village and its vicinity, upward of one hundred and fifty joined the society, besides a number that had joined other churches, and many that had joined no church.[68]

From the foregoing evidence, it is easy to see that Joseph Smith could have had contact with Lane at a number of points during this extended period. If such an acquaintance existed, when would it have been? Oliver Cowdery, in December 1834, undertook to enlighten the readers of the *Messenger and Advocate* on the circumstances shaping the earliest foundations of the Church. As he prepared to recount the events of Joseph's "15th year" (1820), he prefaced his remarks with this statement:

> It is necessary to premise this account by relating the situation of the public mind relative to religion, at this time:
>
> One Mr. Lane, a presiding Elder of the Methodist church, visited Palmyra and vicinity. Elder Lane was a tallented man possessing a good share of literary endowments, and apparent humility. There was a great awakening, or excitement raised on the subject of religion, and much inquiry for the word of life. Large additions were made to the Methodist, Presbyterian, and Baptist churches.—Mr. Lane's manner of communication was perculiarly calculated to awaken the intellect of the hearer, and arouse the sinner to look about him for safety—much good instruction was always drawn from his discourses on the scriptures, and in common with others, our brother's mind became awakened.[69]

Cowdery's account at this juncture is in harmony with Joseph Smith's account relative to the circumstances of 1820. However, in his next letter to the *Messenger and Advocate*, February 1835, he retracts his initial statement and says, "You

> ### Rev. Benajah Williams
>
> After this article was originally published in 1969, important evidence was discovered that identifies the route taken by Reverend Lane to Lundy's Lane, Upper Canada, in June 1820. Rev. Benajah Williams of Mendon, Monroe County, New York, assigned to the Bloomfield circuit, was also on his way to the Annual Genesee Conference in Upper Canada. According to his journals, while en route to General Conference, Williams attended a two-day camp meeting, Saturday, June 15, and Sunday, June 16, at Squire Baker's in Richmond, Ontario County, New York. There he "found Br. Lane a Presiding Elder from Susquehanna District with five more preachers" on the 15th. On June 16, Williams recorded in his journal, "Br. Lane exhorted and spoke on Gods method in bringing about Reffermation his word was with as from the authority of God." Richmond Township, Ontario County, is located fourteen miles west of Canandaigua, Ontario County. Richmond Center is situated approximately twenty-five miles straight-line distance to the southwest of the Joseph Smith Sr. log home in what was then Palmyra Township, Ontario (later Wayne) County, New York. Benajah Williams Journal, June 15–16, 1820, vol. 1, 1818–24. These important journal entries were brought to my attention in 1999 by the late Steven Sorenson, former director of the LDS Church Historical Department. They were then housed at the Ambrose Swasey Library, Colgate Rochester Crozer Divinity School, Rochester, New York. The rarely used Williams journals were later withdrawn from their accession list and acquired by a document dealer in Philadelphia, Pennsylvania. (Larry C. Porter, interview by Samuel Alonzo Dodge, July 30, 2009, Provo, UT)

will recollect that I mentioned the time of a religious excitement, in Palmyra and vicinity to have been in the 15th year of our brother J. Smith Jr's age—that was an error in the type—it should have been in the 17th.—You will please remember this correction, as it will be necessary for the full understanding of what will follow in time. This would bring the date down to the year 1823."[70]

Cowdery thus circumvents the happenings of 1820 by omitting any entry relative to the First Vision. Instead, he suddenly moves ahead three years, identifies the religious fervor, and begins the account with the visit of the angel on the evening of

September 21, 1823. However, by including an account of the appearance of the Father and Son in his 1838 account and by identifying the time as "early in the spring of eighteen hundred and twenty," Joseph Smith filled in the omissions in Cowdery's letter and then continued to narrate the events of his life up until the time and events that Cowdery noted found their sequence.[71]

Years later, in 1883, William Smith, Joseph's younger brother, gave his reminiscences of Lane on the scene: "In 1822 and 1823, the people in our neighborhood were very much stirred up with regard to religious matters by the preaching of a Mr. Lane, an Elder of the Methodist Church, and celebrated throughout the country as a 'great revival preacher.'"[72]

Again, in 1893, just prior to his death, William further identified Lane as one who was directly responsible for Joseph's prayerful inquiry: "Rev. Mr. Lane of the Methodists preached a sermon on 'What church shall I join?' And the burden of his discourse was to ask God, using as a text, 'If any man lack wisdom let him ask of God who giveth to all men liberally.' And of course when Joseph went home and was looking over the text he was impressed to do just what the preacher had said, and going out in the woods with child like, simple trusting faith believing that God meant just what He said, kneeled down and prayed."[73]

What were the recollections of Joseph himself relative to an association with Lane? Nowhere in the Prophet's personal writings does he appear to have mentioned George Lane by name.[74] He does speak of a certain Methodist minister who was active in the revival sequence, and in whom he confided the aspects of his vision, but he did not identify that man further.[75] Lucy Mack Smith, another principal in those eventful days, similarly makes no mention of him by name.[76] However, both Oliver Cowdery and Joseph's younger brother William specifically name Lane as a key figure in awakening Joseph to the possibility of asking

God for wisdom. Oliver attributed his knowledge to Joseph, and William presumably spoke from the same source or from personal memory.[77]

What of Rev. George Lane's own expressions relative to Joseph Smith or Mormonism? The writer has thus far been unable to find any account, public or private, which would indicate Lane's personal reactions either to the Prophet or to the Mormon sect. However, there were certain circumstances, outside of the Ontario scene, which may well have prompted Lane to make some comment on Mormonism. Irene, an older sister of Lane, lived among the Mormons and became a member of the Church near the end of her life. She married David Foote at Windsor, Broome County, New York, in 1791, and in the fall of 1798 they moved to Dryden, Cayuga (now Tompkins) County, New York. During the spring of 1830, David borrowed a copy of the Book of Mormon from a neighbor and after reading it testified that it was a true book. In November 1833, he journeyed to Genesee, Livingston County, New York, to investigate the new religion. While there, he was baptized by Elder John Murdock. As a result of his conversion, David's daughter Betsey, another daughter, and a son, Warren, linked their fortunes to the Mormon faith. Irene died at Montebello, Illinois, March 5, 1846, and was buried in the Nauvoo cemetery.[78]

Rev. George Lane's wife, Sarah, in ill health, had not accompanied her husband to his 1824 appointment as presiding elder of the Ontario District but rather had remained in Wilkes-Barre. As Sarah's health continued to fail, Lane elected to "locate" in 1825. For nine years, 1825–34, he was engaged as a merchant in Berwick, Pennsylvania. "But these were not years of idleness; he had his regular appointments for twenty miles around Berwick, and many in that region will arise and call him blessed."[79]

Sarah Harvey Lane died on October 11, 1832, in Kingston, Pennsylvania, while visiting at the home of the Pierce Butler family.⁸⁰ Reverend Lane continued his mercantile business for a season, but again unable to stay away from the itinerant ministry, he sold his interest in the store and was admitted into the Oneida Conference in 1834 (the Oneida Conference had been formed in 1829 by a division of the old Genesee Conference). He was once more appointed as presiding elder of the Susquehanna District, making his residence at Wilkes-Barre in his house on the public square.⁸¹

The general conference of the Methodist Church elected George Lane assistant book agent in 1836. He removed to New York City and transferred his relations to the New York Conference. In September 1840, he became book agent. In all, he served the Methodist Book Concern for a total of sixteen years. During twelve of those years, he held the office of treasurer of the missionary society.⁸²

In New York, Lane met Miss Lydia Bunting. They were married January 24, 1837.⁸³ Two children were born to the couple, Sarah Georgiana and Lydia.⁸⁴ In 1852, Lane received a superannuated relation, and at the age of sixty-eight, Lane and his wife retired to Mount Holly, New Jersey. With Lane's health declining, it was thought best to return him to more familiar surroundings amidst family and friends in Wilkes-Barre, Pennsylvania. Rev. George Lane died there on May 6, 1859, at age seventy-five, at the home of his son, Charles A. Lane.⁸⁵ He was buried beside his first wife, Sarah Harvey Lane, in the Hollenback cemetery at Wilkes-Barre.

In passing, he was memorialized by his lifelong friend, Rev. George Peck:

> After a most intimate acquaintance with the Rev. George Lane, of more than forty years, observing him under a great variety of circumstances, and some of them exceedingly difficult and trying, we can say what we can say of only a few individuals, that we never saw in him anything to reprove, or anything which, all things considered,

deserves to be characterized as a fault. We love to contemplate the history, both the inward and the outward life, of this holy man and eminent servant of Jesus Christ. He has a high seat in heaven. He "turned many to righteousness," and he "shall shine as the brightness of the firmament, and as the stars for ever and ever." He was in deed and in truth, our friend for many long years, and we loved him. May God give us more of his excellent spirit; and now that he has gone to heaven in a chariot of fire, may his mantle fall upon his sons in the Gospel.[86]

Having examined in detail the life of the Christian gentleman, Rev. George Lane, the writer affirms the epitaph inscribed to the itinerants of the old Genesee Conference: "a ministry of good 'Gifts,' much 'Grace,' and marked 'Usefulness.'"[87]

Notes

1. *Minutes of the Annual Conferences of the Methodist Episcopal Church*, 1860, 40.

2. *The Christian Advocate and Journal* (New York), June 23, 1859, 1.

3. Oscar Jewell Harvey, *The Harvey Book* (Wilkes-Barre, PA: E.B. Yordy, 1899), 128.

4. James Hill Fitts, *Lane Genealogies* (Exeter, NH: News-Letter Press, 1897), 2:49.

5. George Peck, *Early Methodism Within the Bounds of the Old Genesee* (New York: Carlton and Porter, 1860), 492.

6. Marjory B. Hinman and Bernard W. Osborne, comps., *The White Man Settles Old Onaquaga* (Onaquaga, NY: Old Onaquaga Historical Society, 1968), 15, 17.

7. *Christian Advocate and Journal*, June 23, 1859, 1.

8. Harvey, *Harvey Book*, 129.

9. Peck, *Early Methodism*, 447–49.

10. Peck, *Early Methodism*, 492.

11. *Christian Advocate and Journal*, June 23, 1859, 1.

12. *Minutes of the Annual Conferences*, 1860, 40.
13. *Christian Advocate and Journal*, June 23, 1859, 1.
14. *Christian Advocate and Journal*, June 23, 1859, 1.
15. *Minutes of the Annual Conferences*, 1860, 40.
16. *Christian Advocate and Journal*, June 23, 1859, 1.
17. *Minutes of the Annual Conferences*, 1860, 40.
18. *Christian Advocate and Journal*, June 23, 1859, 1.
19. *Minutes of the Annual Conferences*, 1860, 40.
20. Peck, *Early Methodism*, 234–35.
21. Peck, *Early Methodism*, 235–38.
22. *Minutes of the Annual Conferences*, 1860, 40.
23. Stewart Pearce, *Annals of Luzerne County* (Philadelphia: J. B. Lippincott, 1860), 294.
24. *Journal of the Genesee Conference*, 1810–28, 1:1, 5. This is a transcribed copy of the original journal, prepared at the instigation of the Wyoming Conference in 1860. It contains volumes 1 and 2 under a single cover. This transcript is in the Wyoming Seminary, Kingston, PA.

To "locate" is to leave the itinerancy and to either become a local minister or assist in ministerial duties when requested.

25. *Minutes of the Annual Conferences*, 1860, 40–41.
26. *Stewards' Book for Wioming Surket* [sic], 1804–10. The original *Stewards' Book* is at the Wyoming Seminary, Kingston, PA.
27. Peck, *Early Methodism*, 166.
28. Harvey, *Harvey Book*, 132–34.
29. F. C. Johnson, *The Historical Record* (Wilkes-Barre: Wilkes-Barre Record, 1888), 2:191.
30. William B. Sprague, *Annals of the American Methodist Pulpit* (New York: Robert Carter & Brothers, 1861), 811.
31. Harvey, *Harvey Book*, 134.
32. Harvey, *Harvey Book*, 129–30.
33. Harvey, *Harvey Book*, 130. See *Susquehanna Democrat* (Wilkes-Barre), October 21, 1814, for announcement of the opening of the new store in Wilkes-Barre.
34. Harvey, *Harvey Book*, 130.

35. Luke A. Sarsfield, letter to Larry C. Porter, October 22, 1968. Certain primary documents of the Wilkes-Barre Bridge Company are located in the Wyoming Historical and Geological Society, Wilkes-Barre, PA.

36. George Peck, *The Life and Times of Rev. George Peck* (New York: Nelson and Phillips, 1874), 97.

37. Peck, *Early Methodism*, 311–13.

38. Peck, *Early Methodism*, 313.

39. Harvey, *Harvey Book*, 130.

40. *Journal of the Genesee Conference*, 1810–28, 77.

41. Abel Stevens, *The Centenary of American Methodism: A Sketch of Its History, Theology, Practical System, and Success* (New York: Carlton and Porter, 1865), 112.

42. *Minutes of the Annual Conferences*, 1819, 50–52.

43. Pomeroy Tucker, *Origin, Rise, and Progress of Mormonism* (New York: D. Appleton, 1867), 12.

44. Stevens, *Centenary of American Methodism*, 111.

45. *Minutes of the Annual Conferences*, 1819, 51–52.

46. *Minutes of the Annual Conferences*, 44.

47. Albert Clarke, *Methodist Episcopal Church, Lanesboro, Pennsylvania* (Lanesboro, PA: n.p., 1912), 11.

48. Peck, *Life and Times of Rev. George Peck*, 68.

49. George Peck, "Mormonism and the Mormons," *Methodist Quarterly Review*, January 1843, 112.

50. Clarke, *Methodist Episcopal Church*, 9.

51. Clarke, *Methodist Episcopal Church*, 11–12.

52. Clarke, *Methodist Episcopal Church*, 12. See *Early Methodism*, 332–33.

53. Peck, *Life and Times of Rev. George Peck*, 108–9.

54. *Journal of the Genesee Conference*, 1810–28, 85, 92. Reference is to the annual examination of each itinerant to approve him for continued service.

55. *Journal of the Genesee Conference*, 1810–28, 85.

56. *Journal of the Genesee Conference*, 1810–28, 101–2.

57. *Journal of the Genesee Conference*, 1810–28, 90.

58. Oscar Jewell Harvey, *A History of Lodge No. 61, F. and A.M., Wilkesbarré, Pa.* (Wilkes-Barre: E. B. Yordy, 1897), 63.

59. George Lane to the members of the Free Mason Lodge in Wilkes-Barre, n.d. A copy of the original letter is located at the Wyoming Historical and Geological Society, Wilkes-Barre, PA. See also, *A History of Lodge No. 61 F. and A. M., Wilkesbarré, Pa.*, 63–65.

60. *Times and Seasons*, April 1, 1842, 748.

61. *Times and Seasons*, January 1, 1841, 5.

62. *Journal of the Genesee Conference*, 1810–28, 76–84.

63. *Journal of the Genesee Conference*, 1810–28, 85–104.

64. Peck, *Life and Times of Rev. George Peck*, 114–17.

65. *Journal of the Genesee Conference*, 1810–28, 119–40.

66. *Minutes of the Annual Conferences*, 1823, 50.

67. *Minutes of the Annual Conferences*, 1824, 52.

68. Rev. George Lane, "Revival of Religion on Ontario District," *Methodist Magazine* 8 (1825): 160.

69. *Latter Day Saints' Messenger and Advocate*, December 1834, 42.

70. *Latter Day Saints' Messenger and Advocate*, February 1835, 78.

71. Joseph Smith, Documentary History of the Church, Journal History of the Church (MSS, in LDS Church Historian's Office), Book A-1, 1–3 (hereafter cited as DHC). See also *History of the Church of Jesus Christ of Latter-day Saints*, ed. B. H. Roberts (Salt Lake City, 1902), 1:2–6.

72. William Smith, *William Smith on Mormonism* (Lamoni, IA: Herald Steam Book and Job Office, 1883), 6.

73. *Deseret Evening News*, January 20, 1894, 11.

74. In retrospect, Joseph himself would have instructed Oliver in identifying Reverend Lane by name as the person through whom, "in common with others, our brother's mind became awakened." When Oliver first talks about giving the readers of the *Messenger and Advocate* "a full history of the rise of the church," he declared: "That our narrative may be correct, and particularly the introduction, it is proper to inform our patrons, that our brother J. Smith Jr. has offered to assist us. Indeed, there are many items connected

with the fore part of this subject that render his labor indispensible. With his labor and with authentic documents now in our possession, we hope to render this a pleasing and agreeable narrative, well worth the examination and perusal of the Saints." *Messenger and Advocate*, October 1834, 13. Oliver is obviously getting his description of Reverend Lane from the Prophet as given on page 11, herein.

75. Joseph Smith, Journal History (MS in LDS Historian's Library), Book A-1, 3. See also DHC, 1:6.

76. Amidst the profusion of dates ascribed to Joseph's vision, Lucy Mack Smith confirms Joseph's dating of that experience as the spring of 1820. Lucy Smith, *Biographical Sketches of Joseph Smith the Prophet and his Progenitors for Many Generations* (Liverpool: S. W. Richards, 1853), 74, 76.

77. See Oliver Cowdery's account in *Messenger and Advocate*, October 1834, 13, and December 1834, 42; William Smith, *William Smith on Mormonism* (Lamoni, IA: Harold Steam Book, 1883), 6.

78. Warren Foote, "Autobiography of Warren Foote, 1817–1879," an unpublished journal. The special circumstances of her baptism on February 28, 1846, are stated on page 86. For information of her husband and of her burial, see also Andrew Jenson, *Latter-day Saint Biographical Encyclopedia* (Salt Lake City: Andrew Jenson History Company, 1901), 1:374–75.

79. *Minutes of the Annual Conferences*, 1860, 41.

80. Harvey, *Harvey Book*, 132.

81. *Christian Advocate and Journal*, June 23, 1859, 1.

82. *Minutes of the Annual Conferences*, 1860, 41. See H. C. Jennings, *The Methodist Book Concern: A Romance of History* (New York: Cincinnati, 1924), 82–83, for additional information on Lane's activity in the book concern.

83. Harvey, *Harvey Book*, 132.

84. *Lane Genealogies*, 2:69.

85. Harvey, *Harvey Book*, 132.

86. *Christian Advocate and Journal*, June 23, 1859, 1.

87. F. W. Conable, *History of the Genesee Annual Conference* (New York: Phillips and Hunt, 1885), 21.

Emergence of a Fundamental: The Expanding Role of Joseph Smith's First Vision in Mormon Religious Thought

James B. Allen

This essay was originally published in the Journal of Mormon History *7 (1980): 43–61. This paper was originally presented before the annual meeting of the Mormon History Association in Canandaigua, New York, May 1, 1980.*

One of the barriers to understanding history is the tendency many of us have to superimpose upon past generations our own patterns of thought and perceptions of reality. This is partly the result of giving too little thought to the historical development of ideas. In Mormon history, for example, we are well aware of the many changes that have taken place in Church organization and practices in the past 150 years, but we are tempted to assume that ideas and perceptions have remained relatively unchanged, especially since the death of Joseph Smith. Only recently have Mormon historians begun to study in detail the historical development of ideas within the Church, but such a study, if complete, could provide valuable insight into why some concepts have changed from generation to generation while others have remained constant as pillars of the faith. It would also demonstrate the relationship of ideas to each other, and the changing role of basic concepts in such important functional activities as testimony building, missionary work, and the development of teaching programs. This paper explores one example of changing perceptions within the Mormon community: its growing awareness and changing use of Joseph Smith's First Vision.

Next to the Resurrection of Christ, nothing holds a more central place in modern Mormon thought than that sacred event of 1820. It is celebrated in poetry, song, drama, and nearly all the visual arts; it forms the basis for the first missionary discussion; no Latter-day Saint publication that touches on early Church history leaves it out; sermons and lessons expounding upon the doctrine of God almost invariably use the vision to illustrate several aspects of that doctrine. Because it is the most sacred event in Church history, a belief in its literal reality is fundamental to belief in Mormonism itself. But the First Vision was not always so well known or frequently used by the general membership of the Church. Only in 1838 did Joseph Smith prepare an account of it for official publication; not until 1840 did any account appear in print; and not for another half century was it publicly discussed with great regularity or used for the wide variety of purposes to which it lends itself today.

Let me clarify at the outset that when I use the term "First Vision" here, I am referring to detailed *accounts* of the vision— accounts that specifically call attention to Joseph Smith's initial religious quest, his prayer in the grove, and the grand theophany he experienced there. References to a common understanding that Joseph had received instructions from God, or had even experienced his presence, do not demonstrate that the details of the vision were fully known. It is the detailed accounts that concern us here, and the question is when and why the vision as a descriptive report began to assume its present role in Mormon thought.[1]

The First Vision occurred in 1820—a historic reality. But it did not become a *perceived* reality by the general Mormon community until that community heard about it and understood it. Clearly, we have no way of knowing what every Mormon knew or believed at any given moment, for contemporary journals simply are not that complete on this issue. Nor do we know all that Joseph Smith was publicly teaching, for so many of his sermons went unrecorded. But to the degree that printed sources reveal what Mormons generally understood, we can at least begin to appreciate how and why their awareness of the First Vision went through a significant metamorphosis in the first century of Latter-day Saint history.[2]

In the 1830s, long before historical accounts of the vision were circulated generally among the Saints, it was a common understanding among them that Joseph Smith had received direct and personal communication from God. References to this appeared often, but in the context of the times, they did not necessarily imply to the Saints the details of the vision as they are known today. Only later, with the benefit of the published accounts, could these early statements be seen as clear allusions to that specific event of 1820. A basic revelation in 1830, for example, declared of Joseph Smith: "For, after that it truly was manifested unto this first elder, that he had received a remission of his sins, he was entangled again in the vanities of the world; but after truly repenting, God ministered unto him by an holy angel."[3] This certainly was no description of the vision, but the allusion to receiving a remission of his sins conformed exactly with Joseph Smith's later detailed accounts. There are many such oblique references in contemporary sources, including an anti-Mormon statement in the

Palmyra Reflector in 1831 that Joseph Smith "had seen God frequently and personally."[4]

It is significant that early anti-Mormon literature did not attack Joseph Smith on the basis of his recitals of the First Vision, notwithstanding the abundance of Mormon statements originating a half century later to the effect that bearing testimony of it was what caused his greatest trouble.[5] Though he was criticized for telling the story when it first occurred, in later years, the persecution heaped upon the Mormon prophet was associated with other things, and the vision was of little or no significance in the minds of those who were the persecutors.[6]

Beyond the possibility that Joseph Smith wanted to keep the details of his great theophany private because they were so sacred, there were at least two factors within the Mormon community of the 1830s that helped make it unnecessary or even inappropriate to lay out the vision as precisely as became the practice in the 1840s and thereafter or to use it for the didactic purposes that are common today. One was a conscious effort among Mormon founders to avoid creeds and dogma.[7] To the degree that the First Vision could lend itself to creating or supporting even a loose creedal statement about the personal characteristics of God, it simply would not have fit the rather open attitude toward doctrine that characterized the early years of the Church. When the first edition of the Doctrine and Covenants was being prepared for publication, some Church members objected on the grounds that it could become too much like a creed.[8] Joseph Smith nevertheless apparently felt it important to make certain carefully selected revelations generally available, though even in doing so he implied that everything in the publication was not necessarily binding on the conscience of the whole Mormon community. The preface stated, "We have, therefore, endeavored to present, though a few words, *our* belief, and when we say this, humbly trust, the faith and principles of this society as a body." Nothing in the 1835 Doctrine and Covenants could be construed as a creedal statement about the nature of God, though certainly the "Lectures on Faith," bound in the same volume, came close. Even they, however, were not confessions or articles of faith—only transcriptions of lectures delivered before a theological class in Kirtland. Joseph Smith, moreover, continued to oppose the idea of rigid confessions of faith, even after he had allowed the First Vision to be published and had written his own "Articles of Faith." As he told Josiah Butterfield in 1843, "The most prominent difference in sentiment between the Latter-day Saints and sectarians was, that the latter were all circumscribed by some peculiar creed, which deprived its members of the privilege of believing anything not contained therein, whereas the Latter-day Saints have no creed, but are ready to believe all true principles that exist, as they are made manifest from time to time."[9]

Later, he even criticized the high council in Nauvoo for trying Pelatiah Brown simply for making a doctrinal error.[10]

When this lack of emphasis on creeds is coupled with a second factor in the early Mormon community, then the inappropriateness of using the First Vision as a device for teaching the nature of God seems apparent. That factor was the general perception of God which, in the 1830s at least, was different in several respects from the doctrines advanced by Joseph Smith in the 1840s and built upon in later years by other Church leaders. We don't pretend to know when Joseph Smith formulated the advanced doctrines he taught in the 1840s or when he became convinced that the need to know God meant also the need to know of his finite, corporeal nature. We know only that he allowed other ideas to be circulated and saw no need publicly to contradict them until the 1840s.

What *did* the Mormons believe about the nature and character of God in the 1830s? Professor Thomas G. Alexander deals significantly with this subject in another context,[11] but we must say enough about it here to illustrate why a detailed account of the First Vision, as Mormons think of and use it today, would have been unnecessary in the belief system of the Mormon community of the 1830s, and may even have been disturbing to some of the newly converted Saints. It is not beyond possibility, of course, that Joseph Smith deliberately kept it from public circulation partly for this reason.

Perhaps the most significant observation to be made about the pre-Nauvoo concept of God held by ordinary Mormons is that it was not radically different from some other Christian perceptions, and that newly converted Saints probably did not need to change their image of God very much just because they had become Mormons. There may, in fact, have been several concepts of God within the popular Mormon community.

The traditional Christian view, still held by mainline Protestant theologians, was Trinitarian—that is, belief in the Father, Son, and Holy Spirit as one God, indivisible in substance yet manifesting himself three different ways. By the time Mormonism arose, however, some liberal Protestant thinkers had already departed from Trinitarianism, taking the ancient Arian position that Christ was distinctly separate from God. He was less than God, but more than man—he was a preexistent divine being.[12] William Ellery Channing declared in 1815 that "there is only one person possessing supreme Divinity, even the Father," and that the Son was sent by the Father.[13] In 1819, in a famous ordination sermon, he made the distinction between the two persons even more clear.[14] His definition of the nature of the Father bore no resemblance to the God Joseph Smith preached about in Nauvoo, but at least Channing and other liberal Protestants separated the persons of the Father and the Son. So also, apparently, did a few evangelical Protestants of Joseph Smith's day.[15] One suspects that whatever creeds or dogmas remained, they were not highly emphasized to the popular audiences. Many ordinary Christians, caring little for the niceties of theology, probably thought of God and Christ as separate entities, though they may not have thought of the Father as having corporeal existence (i.e., a tangible body of flesh). Some, at least, emphasized the idea that God was a *person*, though in the mind of the distinguished Henry Ware this did not imply physical shape, form, or place. Rather, preached Ware, "consciousness, and the power of will and action constitute him a person."[16]

Converts to Mormonism in the early and mid-1830s would find little, if any, discomfort with the concept of God set forth in the teachings of their new religion, no matter which Christian tradition they came from. The lack of a creedal definition left them somewhat free to retain traditional views, and Mormon writings were not drastically different in tone on this issue than the teachings of other groups. Several passages in the 1830 edition of the Book of Mormon, for instance, could be interpreted as supporting the traditional view that God and Christ were the same entity: "And he said unto me, Behold the virgin which thou seest, is the mother of God, after the manner of the flesh";[17] "Behold the Lamb of God, yea, even the Eternal Father";[18] "Yea, the Everlasting God was judged of the world";[19] "The Lamb of God is the Eternal Father and the Savior of the World."[20] These passages were modified in the 1837 edition of the Book of Mormon so that they no longer seemed Trinitarian, but enough remained unmodified that, without the benefit of Joseph Smith's Nauvoo teachings or the exposition on the Father and the Son published by the First Presidency in 1916, the convert from a Trinitarian tradition could find a familiar idea. Consider, for example, this passage from Mosiah: "I would that ye should understand that God himself shall come down among the children of men, and shall redeem his people. And because he dwelleth in flesh he shall be called the Son of God, and having subjected the flesh to the will of the Father, being the Father and the Son—the Father, because he was conceived by the power of God; and the Son, because of the flesh; thus becoming the Father and the Son—and they are one God, yea, the very Eternal Father of heaven and of earth" (Mosiah 15:1–4; see also Alma 11:38–39, 44).

This and other passages were capable of causing doctrinal difficulties in later years and had to be reconciled with the Mormon doctrine of God by later Church members, but at least in the mid-1830s they were not likely to form a stumbling block for converts from traditional Christianity.

At the same time, Mormon writings also lent themselves to comfortable interpretation by those who saw the Father and the Son as distinct and separate identities with a oneness of will and purpose: "And behold, the third time they did understand the voice which they heard; and it said unto them: behold my Beloved Son, in whom I am well pleased, in whom I have glorified my name—hear ye him" (3 Nephi 11:6–7; see also vv. 10–11).

Many such passages are found in the Book of Mormon, the Doctrine and Covenants, and the Book of Moses, parts of which were published as early as 1831–32. But even when they separate the persons of the Father and the Son, they do not necessarily imply that the Father is the corporeal being revealed in the story of the First Vision—or, at least, in the standard interpretations of that story. This was true also of the "Lectures on Faith," which were not removed from the Doctrine and Covenants until 1921. The fifth lecture specifically separated the persons of the Father and the Son, though in terms that did not impute corporeality to the Father. The lecture, in fact, implied quite the opposite:

> There are two personages who constitute the great, matchless, governing and supreme power over all things. . . . They are the Father and the Son; The Father being a personage of spirit, glory and power: possessing all perfection and fulness: The Son, who was in

the bosom of the Father, a personage of tabernacle, made, or fashioned like unto man. . . . And he being the only begotten of the Father, full of grace and truth, and having overcome, received a fulness of the glory of the Father—possessing the same mind with the Father, which mind is the Holy Spirit.[21]

The distinction between the Father as a "personage of spirit, glory and power" and the Son as a "personage of tabernacle" certainly suggests that the Father was not thought of as having a physical, material body. The concept of God thus presented in these lectures was not drastically different from the ideas new converts brought with them and clearly did not lend itself to illustration by use of the First Vision. But the Mormons were being prepared for a radically unorthodox view of God that would, eventually, open the way for the First Vision to be employed as evidence.

This does not mean that some Mormons did not believe in a corporeal God—only that there was still no creedal statement to that effect and that there was room for diversity of belief. It is likely that many Mormons held an anthropomorphic view, and one anti-Mormon writer even included in his 1836 denunciation of the Saints in Kirtland a statement that they believed that "the true God is a material being, composed of body and parts."[22] But this and other ideas about God had not yet found their way into the Mormon press, and their profound significance was certainly not a part of the general Mormon consciousness.

One important step came in 1838, when Parley P. Pratt published one of his early defenses of Mormon doctrine. This interesting document included the first printed description in Mormon sources of an anthropomorphic, corporeal God. "We worship a God," wrote Pratt, "who has both body and parts: who has eyes, mouth and ears, and who speaks when he pleases, to whom he pleases, and sends them where he pleases."[23] This was quickly followed by other such statements. Samuel Bennett's

1840 defense of Mormonism decried the notion that God could not be seen by man and declared that "he hath in a multitude of instances shown himself to the children of men (chosen witnesses), in different ages of the world, and especially in these last days hath his bodily presence been manifested, and his voice hath sounded in the ear of mortal man, without consuming him.... To say that it was the *similitude—figurative, metaphorical*, etc., is nothing but an evasion."[24]

The idea that God showed himself to certain chosen witnesses foreshadowed frequent Mormon statements in later years that the purpose of the First Vision was to establish a testator for his existence and nature. That same year, Orson Pratt published the first printed account of the vision of Scotland, and two years later, three more accounts, including Joseph Smith's, appeared in print. In 1843 Joseph Smith declared unequivocally that "the Father has a body of flesh and bones as tangible as man's; the Son also" (D&C 130:22), and a year later he preached his most famous sermon on the doctrine of God that said, in part, "It is the first principle of the gospel to know for a certainty the character of God, and to know that we may converse with Him as one man converses with another, and that He was once a man like us; yea, that God himself, the Father of us all dwelt on an earth, the same as Jesus Christ Himself did."[25]

The revolutionary implications of that statement for Mormon doctrine were tremendous, and it helped provide the framework for many additional doctrinal innovations. The 1835 teachings about God did not make such knowledge a necessity of faith, but in the 1840s it became fundamental to the faith.

None of this provides any conclusive reason why Joseph Smith withheld the vision from the public eye until 1840, though another bit of curious circumstantial evidence suggests that withholding the account was so deliberate by Joseph Smith that in 1834 he actually intervened to prevent it from being printed.

The first published history of the Church was in a series of letters by Oliver Cowdery printed in the *Messenger and Advocate* in 1834–35. In the third letter, Cowdery told of Joseph Smith's initial quest for religious truth, including the religious revival and the young man's desire to know which church was right. The story was told in terms strikingly similar to those used by Joseph Smith in his accounts of the First Vision. Cowdery even said that it took place in the thirteenth year of Joseph's life. (In Joseph Smith's 1832 account, he said his quest began when he was twelve and continued until he was fifteen, while in the 1838 account he said he was in his "fifteenth year" when the vision occurred.) Elements of both the 1832 and 1838 accounts of religious turmoil before the vision can be seen in Cowdery's letter, and he promised to continue the history in the next letter.

When the next letter was printed, however, Cowdery did not proceed with the vision story but rather made an amazing self-correction by asserting that he had made a mistake on the date of the revival. It should have been the seventeenth year of Joseph's life, he said, "which would bring the date down to the year 1823." Then, without further reference to the religious excitement, he proceeded with the account of the visitation of Moroni. One of two things had happened. Either Oliver Cowdery had made an honest mistake in dating or, upon reflection or instruction, he had decided it inappropriate to tell the story of the vision and simply used this device to get on to the next important episode. What argues convincingly for the possibility that he originally intended to recount the vision is that the third letter contains material remarkably similar to Joseph Smith's own written introductions to that sacred event. Could it be that Joseph had his personal reasons for not wanting the story circulated at the time and so simply instructed Oliver Cowdery not to print it? We will never know, but in light of what has been said earlier, such a conclusion seems logical.[26] Joseph

Oliver Cowdery published the first history of the Church in a series of letters in the Messenger and Advocate *in 1834–35. (Oliver Cowdery portrait, Lewis A. Ramsey, Courtesy of Church History Museum)*

finally decided to publish it himself, he wrote in 1838, in order to "disabuse the public mind, and put all inquirers after truth in possession of the facts."[27]

It is worth noting that Joseph Smith himself never used the First Vision to illustrate his own expanded teachings about God. It appears, in fact, that he seldom referred to it at all, except in private conversation, even after it was published. But the fact that it *was* published provided a ready tool that his followers would later use in every conceivable way to teach about the God that he defined for them in Nauvoo. With the opportunity finally there, it may seem surprising that more Mormon writers did not rush in with enthusiasm between 1840 and 1880 to use the vision as a proof text for Mormon doctrine. But they did not. Only a few, in fact, referred to it at all during those forty years.

One reason for not using the First Vision then may have been that the first generation of Mormon theologians placed so much emphasis on the idea that the Restoration of the gospel began when the angel Moroni delivered the Book of Mormon. This event, after all, was depicted from the beginning as fulfilling the prophecy in Revelation 14:6, where John declared: "And I saw another angel fly in the midst of heaven, having the everlasting gospel to preach unto them that dwell on the earth." Even Orson Pratt, who first published the vision in 1840 and was one of the most meticulous of the early Church leaders in his effort to systematize doctrine, continued to emphasize the idea that the Restoration was inaugurated by the *angel*. In an 1848 tract, he asked the question "In what manner does Joseph Smith declare that a dispensation of the gospel was committed unto him?" His answer was that Joseph Smith testified of the visit of an angel of God and that this claim was in fulfillment of biblical prophecy: "Though Mr. Smith had taught a perfect doctrine, yet if he had testified that this doctrine was not restored by an angel, all would at once have known him to be an imposter. . . . John testifies that when the everlasting gospel is restored to the earth it shall be by an *angel*. Mr. Smith testifies that it was restored by an *angel*, and in no other way. *This is another presumptive evidence that he was sent of God.*"[28] Since much, if not most, of this early doctrinal material was published in works intended for non-Mormon consumption, it may be that the emphasis continued to be placed on the angel and the Book of Mormon because they fulfilled biblical prophecy, while the First Vision took a backseat in the literature only because it did not fulfill the prophecy.

There were exceptions to this pattern of emphasis, but they were in literature designed more specifically for the Saints. In 1849, Orson Pratt referred briefly to the vision in a *Millennial Star* article to demonstrate that the Father and the Son were two distinct persons—the first such doctrinal use of the First Vision we have discovered so far.[29] Then in 1851, Willard Richards published the Pearl of Great Price that contained, as he said, several items that had been published earlier but, due to limited circulation of Church journals, were "comparatively unknown at present." Among these was Joseph Smith's 1838 account of the First Vision, and it is significant that the publication was intended specifically for believers and not, the editor said, "as a pioneer of faith among unbelievers." But though the vision was becoming more widely known among the Saints, its use would still be limited. Even *Key to the Science of Theology*, published by Orson Pratt's brother Parley in 1855, completely ignored the vision in its extensive treatment of the Godhead. When Willard Richards published his *Compendium of the Faith and Doctrines of the Church of Jesus Christ of Latter-day Saints* in 1857, he also failed to use the vision as a proof text for the nature of God. He used it only as an illustration in his section on the "Names, Titles and Characters" given to Jesus.

The major use made of the vision over the next several years was simply to illustrate, for the benefit of the Saints, the initial historic authority and calling of Joseph Smith. This is the way the founding prophet himself used his theophany, and this was the use that continued until after the death of Brigham Young.[30] Orson Pratt was the major purveyor of the story, but even he did not enlarge upon it for any great doctrinal purposes.[31]

Then in the 1880s appeared a second generation of Church writers and theologians. When Orson Pratt died in 1881, only two General Authorities remained alive and in the Church who had been ordained to office during the lifetime of Joseph Smith: John Taylor and Wilford Woodruff. Many Saints remained alive who had known the Prophet, but there were more in the Church who had never seen him, including many second- and third-generation Mormons. These people, moreover, were going through a period of intensive religious crisis, as new federal laws stepped up antipolygamy prosecution and seemed to challenge the very existence of the Church. The time was ready-made for the outpouring of a new identity with the founding prophet—new reminders to the Saints of what their heritage really was and of what Joseph Smith's testimony really meant to them personally. The First Vision was a natural tool for such a purpose, and a new generation of writers could hardly fail to use it.

Beautifully symbolic of this new direction was the fact that it seemed to begin with art and music—certainly among the most effective means of popularizing an idea. In 1869, C. C. A. Christensen, a Danish convert and immigrant to Utah, began to paint significant incidents from Mormon history onto large canvases. In 1878, he sewed together the first group of eight paintings, rolled them on a long wooden pole, and began touring Utah, giving illustrated lectures on the history of the Church.[32] Among these was a painting of the First Vision, and among those who listened to the artist was young George Manwaring, who eventually became the author of several well-known Mormon hymns. Manwaring was inspired by the painting, and it was not long before he wrote "Joseph Smith's First Prayer." Set to music composed by Adam Craik Smyth, it appeared in the *Deseret Sunday School Union Music Book* in 1884 and ever since has been one of Mormonism's most well-loved hymns.[33] The title was later changed to "Oh, How Lovely Was the Morning." It was thus four decades after the organization of the Church that the vision found its way into artistic media, but it was largely through these media that it eventually found its way into the hearts and minds of the Saints.

The printed word and public sermons, meanwhile, began to play an increasingly significant role. George Q. Cannon was a sort of transition figure between first- and second-generation Mormon writers, and as early as 1880, he suggested that the vision could be used to teach children about the nature of their

Creator.[34] In 1883, he gave one of the first sermons to expand upon the vision by using it to demonstrate the need to restore a true knowledge of God. This, his sermon implied, was in fact the major purpose for the vision, and therein Cannon formulated the essential approach to the meaning of the vision that would be used in the Church for at least the next one hundred years. "The first that we knew concerning God," he said, "was through the testimony of the Prophet Joseph. Even the personality of God was doubted." He then stated what has become a standard Mormon perception of the world's view of God, "that His center was nowhere, and His circumference was everywhere. . . . Even ministers of religion could not conceive of the true idea." This led to his announcement of the grand purpose of the vision:

> But all this was swept away in one moment by the appearance of the Almighty Himself—by the appearance of God, the Father, and His Son Jesus Christ, to the boy Joseph. . . . In one moment all this darkness disappeared, and once more there was a man found on the earth, embodied in the flesh, who had seen God, who had seen Jesus, and who could describe the personality of both. Faith was again restored to the earth, the true faith and the true knowledge concerning our Creator. . . . This revelation dissipated all misconceptions and all false ideas, and removed the uncertainty that had existed respecting these matters. The Father came accompanied by the Son, thus showing that there were two personages of the Godhead, two presiding personages whom we worship and to whom we look, the one the Father, and the other the Son. Joseph saw that the Father had a form; that He had a head; that He had arms; that He had limbs; that He had feet; that He had a face and a tongue with which to express His thoughts; for He said unto Joseph: "This is my beloved Son"—pointing to the Son—"hear Him."
>
> Now, it was meant that this knowledge should be restored first of all. It seems so, at least, from the fact that God Himself came; it seems that the knowledge had to be restored as the basis for all true

faith to be built upon. There can be no faith that is not built upon a true conception of God our Father. Therefore, before even angels came, He came himself, accompanied by His Son, and revealed Himself once more to man upon the earth.[35]

The metamorphosis was complete: from the vision experience itself in 1820, to Joseph Smith's decision not to publicize it, through the 1830s when the Saints knew little or nothing about it, through the 1840s when the vision was told and Joseph Smith's expanded concept of God was made known to the Saints, through a generation when it was used primarily to establish Joseph Smith's prophetic authority, to the beginning of a period in which both the new concept of God and the vision would be considered central to the faith.

In a way, George Q. Cannon was a logical person to complete that metamorphosis. Converted in England in 1840, he migrated to Nauvoo in 1843 and was therefore acquainted with Joseph Smith for only a year before the Prophet's death. The First Vision had just become a part of Mormon literature when Cannon was converted, and he probably was not fully sensitive to the fact that Saints for at least a decade had exercised faith without knowing of either the new definition of Deity or the vision that illustrated it. He became an Apostle, a member of the First Presidency of the Church, superintendent of the Sunday School, and editor of the *Juvenile Instructor*, all of which put him in a position of authority capable of exercising important influence on Mormon thought.

Cannon and others continued to use the First Vision for its new didactic purposes, and this seemed to open the door for seeing in its proofs or demonstrations of multitudinous other ideas. Cannon even saw it as proof that Darwin was wrong. Every Latter-day Saint, he said, must believe the concept of God taught by Joseph's vision and "if this is so, where is there room found for believing in Darwin's theory?"[36]

From there, the story of the First Vision as a fundamental theme in the presentation of Mormon doctrine only expanded upon the pattern established by the artists, preachers, and writers of the 1880s. Brigham H. Roberts, the first important systematizer of Mormon thought after the death of the Pratts, helped standardize the approach in print by augmenting what Cannon had begun. In his *Outlines of Ecclesiastical History* (1893), Roberts listed five reasons why the vision was of "vast importance": (1) it revealed that God had "both body and parts, that he was in the form of a man, or, rather, that man had been made in his image"; (2) it proved that the Father and the Son are distinct persons and that the oneness of the Godhead spoken of in the scriptures is a oneness of purpose; (3) "it swept away the rubbish of human dogma and tradition" by announcing that none of the churches of Joseph's day were acknowledged by God; (4) it showed, contrary to the claims of the Christian world, that revelation had not ceased; and (5) it created a witness for God on the earth, thus laying the foundation for faith.[37] These themes were repeated in later writings by Roberts[38] and eventually became the standard for Church lesson manuals and other publications. "There is nothing in our doctrine of Deity today—but what was germinally present in that first great revelation," Roberts declared in 1903,[39] and the new way of using the vision would amply demonstrate this.

The vision and its attendant uses quickly began to appear in lesson manuals, augmenting the Mormon awareness of its transcendent importance. In 1899, the Young Men's Mutual Improvement Association used it to demonstrate that it had ushered in the "Dispensation of the Fulness of Times."[40] The vision was thus replacing the angel in Mormon thought as the implementing factor in the Restoration. Nephi Anderson's history of the Church for young people (1900) used the vision in exactly the same way as Roberts's *Ecclesiastical History*.[41] When the first priesthood manuals were printed in 1909, the priests, elders, and high priests all had lessons on the vision. In these and other manuals, it was used specifically to teach certain doctrinal concepts of God as well as give the Saints important spiritual direction. A history written by John Henry Evans in 1905 and used extensively by the Sunday School declared that the vision "will some day be generally regarded as the most important event in the history of the world, excepting only the revelation of Godhood in the person of our Lord Jesus Christ."[42] The vision was thus formulating not only historical perceptions but prophetic images as well.

At the beginning of the twentieth century, the First Vision also took a permanent place in the missionary literature of the Church. It had been there before, beginning with Orson Pratt's *Remarkable Visions* in 1840, but somewhere around 1910, the pamphlet "Joseph Smith Tells His Own Story" was published as a separate tract, and it has remained in print ever since as one of the Church's major missionary tools.

There were other things happening that would enhance the vision in the Mormon mind. More artistic representations, as Richard Oman has shown,[43] were emerging. The Sacred Grove was acquired by the Church in this period, and pilgrimages to the grove became sacred experiences for many Mormons. No one knew the spot where the vision occurred—or even if the trees left standing when the grove was purchased were in the same part of the original grove where Joseph went to pray—but none of that was really important. The grove became the visible symbol of the theophany that inaugurated the Restoration of all things, and from it the visiting Saints would gain spiritual sustenance and greater faith in the reality of the vision itself.[44]

In 1920, the centennial anniversary of the vision, the celebration was a far cry from the almost total lack of reference to it just fifty years earlier. The Mutual Improvement Associations issued a special commemorative pamphlet,[45] the vision was memorialized in music, verse, and dramatic representations, and the Church's official publication, the *Improvement Era*, devoted almost the entire April issue to that event. The new emphasis was a fitting symbol of what had happened.

By the beginning of the twentieth century, belief in the First Vision was fundamental to the faith of the Latter-day Saints. J. Reuben Clark Jr., a member of the First Presidency, probably captured best its expanded meaning for the Saints when he told religious educators in 1938 that the second of two essentials to which Mormon teachers must "give full faith" was "that the Father and the Son actually and in truth and very deed appeared to the Prophet Joseph in a vision in the woods," together with all that this and the other visions and revelations Joseph Smith received implied. The reality of the vision was at the center of the whole concept of the Restoration, and, declared President Clark, "no teacher who does not have a real testimony . . . of the divine mission of Joseph Smith—including in all its reality the First Vision—has any place in the Church school system."[46] When another General Authority declared in 1973 that "the First Vision is the very foundation of this Church, and it is my conviction that each member of this Church performs his duty in direct relation to his personal testimony and faith in the First Vision,"[47] he was only reflecting the culmination of the emergence of the vision as a Mormon fundamental.

As they began to use Joseph Smith's first religious experience for various instructional purposes, Mormon teachers and writers were also creating certain secondary but highly significant historical perceptions in the minds of the Latter-day Saints. There was no intent to distort or mislead, but what happened was only one example of a very natural intellectual process that helps explain the emergence of at least some basic community perceptions. It seems to be a truism that whenever great events take place, second- and third-generation expounders tend to build a kind of mythology around them by presuming corollary historical interpretations that often have little basis in fact. In this case, the deepening awareness of the vision, along with a growing community sensitivity for how essential it was to Mormon faith and doctrine, created an atmosphere in which other historical inferences could easily be drawn. These included the ideas that (1) over the centuries, considerable "rubbish concerning religion" had accumulated that only revelation could correct; (2) most, if not all, Christians believed in the traditional Trinitarian concept of God; (3) the Christian world denied the concept of continuing revelation; (4) Joseph Smith told the story of his vision widely; and (5) he continued to be persecuted or publicly ridiculed for it, even to the time of his death. Such historical interpretation, much of it misleading, soon dominated popular Mormon thought. The challenge for individual believers, including Mormon historians, would be to separate the essential truths of the vision experience from corollaries that may not be so essential to the faith.

Once the vision assumed its predominant place in Mormon writing and preaching, it became much more than Joseph Smith's personal experience—it became a shared community experience. Every Mormon and every prospective convert was urged to pray for his or her own testimony of its reality—in effect, to seek a personal theophany by becoming one with Joseph in the grove. Latter-day Saints did not forget the importance of the angel Moroni, but gradually the First Vision took precedence over the visit of the angel as the event that ushered in the Restoration of the gospel. It was only a short step from there to the expanded use of the vision as a teaching device whenever the doctrine of God or the principle of revelation played any part in the discussion. As the years passed, the list of lessons, truths, principles, and historical interpretations taught or illustrated by the vision grew longer. Each writer or preacher saw it as fundamental, but each also had his or her own private insight into what it could illustrate or portray. A partial list of what people have said since 1880 about what the First Vision teaches, how it may be used, or why it is significant would include at least the following:

1. The Father and the Son are two distinct "personages alike in form, substance, and glory," God the Father has a physical body with all the parts possessed by man, and the Father and the Son look exactly alike.[48]

2. Joseph Smith had priesthood authority when he had his vision, for no man can see the face of the Father and live unless he has the priesthood. He had received this priesthood before the world was made.[49]

3. The traditions of men respecting God were false, but "all this was swept away in one moment" by the appearance of the Father and the Son, and "faith was again restored to the earth, the true faith and the true knowledge concerning our Creator." The world has thus profited as vagueness, doubt, and uncertainty have been eliminated.[50]

4. Joseph Smith "startled the world. It stood aghast at the statement which he made, and the testimony which he bore" of having seen God.[51]

5. Since a true knowledge of God did not exist in 1820, the purpose of the vision was so that God "might have a testator upon the earth."[52]

6. Through the testimony of the testator, people would be educated in a correct manner so that they would "cease to worship the bodiless, immaterial, unnatural, nonentity, and be turned to the worship of the living—and true God."[53]

7. Revelation had not ceased, or, as some writers put it, "the Heavens were no longer brass."[54]

8. The vision is evidence of God's existence, not just proof of his personality.[55]

9. The vision ushered in the "Dispensation of the Fulness of Times."[56]

10. The vision impeded the progress of Satan.[57]

11. Joseph Smith learned that God and Christ sympathized with him and loved him.[58] By implication, this meant they loved all the rest of God's children, too.

12. The vision was the greatest declaration Joseph Smith ever made to the world.[59]

13. As a result of the vision, there lived in 1820 "one person who knew that the word of the Creator, 'Let us make man in our own image, after our likeliness,' had a meaning more than in metaphor."[60]

14. "It shows that the Son is appointed by the Father to direct in the affairs of this world."[61]

15. It shows that God grants blessings to those who seek.[62]

16. God answers prayers in ways often unlooked for.[63]

17. The vision opened the way for the dead as well as the living to hear the gospel.[64]

18. The fact of the Great Apostasy was first announced in this vision.[65]

19. It established "the fact that God can and will speak to man, whenever He chooses so to do, in any age."[66]

20. Satan is always ready to stop the Lord's work.[67]

21. God has almost invariably selected young boys for his special messengers, and the vision holds true to this pattern.[68]

22. Joseph Smith's prayer in the grove was "the first real faith cry that had gone up from this cold, superstitious world since the dense darkness of the middle ages had driven truth from the altar and living belief from the human heart. It marked the beginning of an epoch. It was the beginning of the real modern spiritual renaissance."[69]

23. "When this boy walked out of that sacred grove, that day, he was greater than the most learned theologians and profoundest philosophers."[70]

24. The vision was at once the most complete revelation of the powers of both heaven and hell.[71]

25. The vision is evidence of Joseph Smith's divine mission.[72]

26. The Church is a necessary result of the vision.[73]

27. The vision is evidence for the Resurrection.[74]

28. Knowledge gained from the vision is saving knowledge for mankind.[75]

In 1980, the children of the Primary organization presented a special sesquicentennial program in every ward and branch of the Church. Here was a perfect example of how deeply the First Vision had become rooted in the conscience of the Mormon community. The theme of the presentation was "If any of you lack wisdom, let him ask of God"—the quotation from James 1:5 that led Joseph Smith to the grove 160 years before. The program portrayed a father and a mother talking to their children about the Restoration of the gospel, and the first event discussed was Joseph Smith's First Vision. As the mother told of Joseph going into the grove, a children's chorus sang "Oh, How Lovely was the Morning." As the story progressed, the father asked, "What great truths about our Heavenly Father and Jesus Christ did Joseph Smith learn from this divine appearance?" The answers, coming from three different children, were "He learned that God the Father and his Son, Jesus Christ, are two separate beings"; "Joseph got to see what Heavenly Father and Jesus really looked like"; and "Joseph learned that our heavenly Father hears and answers our prayers."[76]

George Q. Cannon's merest suggestion in 1880 that the vision could be used to teach certain truths to children was more than fulfilled in the next hundred years. The vision was no longer just Joseph Smith's personal experience, nor was it rehearsed simply to establish the initial prophetic authority of the founder of the Church. In the twentieth century, it became a shared community experience—one that every Mormon must respond to personally, and one that every teacher could use appropriately to verify a multitude of doctrines and historical concepts. It was indeed not just Joseph Smith's theophany, but the great Mormon theophany.

Notes

The author expresses appreciation for the research assistance of Leonard Grover.

1. I asked this question, along with others, in an article printed over forty years ago. See James B. Allen, "The Significance of Joseph Smith's First Vision in Mormon Thought," *Dialogue: A Journal of Mormon Thought* 1 (Autumn 1966): 28–45. The other questions raised there have been answered rather fully by me and other students, but this one was treated only briefly and perfunctorily. It has continued to intrigue me, and this essay is an attempt to put the issue in a more complete and interpretive framework than I had time to do or was capable of doing then. See also Milton V. Backman Jr., *Joseph Smith's First Vision: The First Vision in Historical Context* (Salt Lake City: Bookcraft, 1971); Dean C. Jessee, "The Early Accounts of Joseph Smith's First Vision," *BYU Studies* 9, no. 3 (Spring 1969): 275–94; Richard Lloyd Anderson, "Circumstantial Confirmation of the First Vision through Reminiscences," *BYU Studies* 9, no. 3 (Spring 1969): 373–404; James B. Allen, "Eight Contemporary Accounts of Joseph Smith's First Vision: What Do We Learn from Them?," *Improvement Era*, April 1970, 4–13; Wesley P. Walters, "New Light on Mormon Origins from the Palmyra Revival," *Dialogue: A Journal of Mormon Thought* 4, no. 1 (Spring 1969): 60–81; Richard L. Bushman, "The First Vision Story Revived," *Dialogue: A Journal of Mormon Thought* 4, no. 1 (Spring 1969): 82–93.

2. This paper is based on a study of *contemporary* sources rather than reminiscences, which could have been affected by the tendency of the writers to read their current understanding into past experiences. There are a few reminiscences, written many years after the events discussed here, that, if accurate, would at least partially negate some of the ideas presented here. The reminiscences of Edward Stevenson, for example, suggest that Joseph Smith was publicly telling the story of his First Vision in great detail in the early 1830s. The reminiscence was written, however, some fifty years later, and on this issue it runs directly counter to all the available contemporary evidence. No one questions the personal integrity of Stevenson, but it is likely that after fifty years, his memory played tricks on him by combining things he heard in one period with things he heard at other times. Another possibility is that he heard Joseph relate the account privately, to a select group, even

though he was not proclaiming it publicly. See Edward Stevenson, *Reminiscences of Joseph, the Prophet, and the Coming Forth of the Book of Mormon* (Salt Lake City: printed by author, 1893), 4.

3. *A Book of Commandments for the Governance of the Church of Christ* (Zion [Independence, MO]: W. W. Phelps, 1833), 24:6–7. Cf. D&C 20:5–8. See also D&C 1:17.

4. *Palmyra Reflector*, February 14, 1831.

5. Such statements leave the impression that all of the Prophet's persecution was based largely on his telling of the vision. In 1906, for example, one Church leader even attributed Joseph Smith's death to his testimony of the vision: "The greatest crime that Joseph Smith was guilty of was the crime of confessing the great fact that he had heard the voice of God and the voice of His Son Jesus Christ, speaking to him in his childhood; that he saw those Heavenly Beings standing above him in the air of the woods where he went out to pray. That is the worst crime he committed, and the world has held it against him. . . . Joseph Smith declared that it was true. He suffered persecution all the days of his life on earth because he declared it was true. He carried his life in his hands, so to speak, every moment of his life until he finally sacrificed it in Carthage jail for the testimony that he bore." Joseph F. Smith, "Two Sermons by President Joseph F. Smith," Sermon Tract No. 1 (published by the Southern States Mission, Chattanooga, TN, 1906).

6. See Kenneth W. Godfrey, "Causes of Mormon Non-Mormon Conflict in Hancock County, Illinois, 1839–1846" (PhD diss., Brigham Young University, 1967), for a discussion of causes for persecution. See also Dallin H. Oaks and Marvin S. Hill, *Carthage Conspiracy: The Trial of the Accused Assassins of Joseph Smith* (Urbana: University of Illinois Press, 1975). Even Joseph Smith's own account of persecution related to the vision refers specifically to the period immediately after it happened—that is, around 1820. Neither that nor his extended history, edited in collaboration with some of his closest associates, suggests any later criticism specifically because of the vision story. See Joseph Smith—History 1:22–26. The extended history became *History of the Church of Jesus Christ of Latter-day Saints, Period 1: Joseph Smith*, ed. B. H.

Roberts, 6 vols. (Salt Lake City: Deseret News, 1902–12). For details regarding the authenticity of this history, see Dean C. Jessee, "The Reliability of Joseph Smith's History," *Journal of Mormon History* 3 (1976): 23–46; and "The Writing of Joseph Smith's History," *BYU Studies* 9 (Spring 1971): 439–73.

7. Professor Peter L. Crawley has developed this idea fully in an unpublished manuscript currently under revision. Copy in possession of author.

8. This led the editors (Joseph Smith, Oliver Cowdery, Sidney Rigdon, and Frederick G. Williams) to write in the preface: "There may be an aversion in the minds of some against receiving anything purporting to be articles of religious faith, in consequence of there being so many now extant; but if men believe a system, and profess that it was given by inspiration, certainly the more intelligibly they can present it, the better. It does not make a principle untrue to *print* it, neither does it make it true not to print it." *Doctrine and Covenants of the Church of the Latter-day Saints* (Kirtland, OH: F. G. Williams, 1835), 111.

9. *History of the Church*, 5:215.

10. "I did not like the old man being called up for erring in doctrine. It looks too much like the Methodist, and not like the Latter-day Saints. Methodists have creeds which a man must believe or be asked out of their church. I want the liberty of thinking and believing as I please. It feels so good not to be trammelled. It does not prove that a man is not a good man because he errs in doctrine." *History of the Church*, 5:340.

11. Thomas G. Alexander, "The Reconstruction of Mormon Doctrine: From Joseph Smith to Progressive Theology," *Sunstone* 22 (July–August 1980): 24–33. See also James B. Allen, "Line Upon Line," *Ensign*, July 1979, 32–39.

12. Sidney Ahlstrom, *A Religious History of the American People* (New York: Image Books, 1975), 1:476.

13. As quoted in Ahlstrom, *Religious History*, 479–80.

14. The sermon is reproduced in H. Shelton Smith, Robert T. Handy, and Lefferts A. Loetscher, eds., *American Christianity: An*

Historical Interpretation, with Representative Documents (New York: Charles Scribner's Sons, 1960), 1:493–502; see especially 496.

15. The sermons of Charles G. Finney, for example, show no particular concern with defining the nature of God, but his emphasis on the *sonship* of Christ clearly suggests that he thought of the Son as distinct from the Father. See Charles G. Finney, *Sermons on Gospel Themes* (New York: Dodd Mead, 1876).

16. Henry Ware Jr., *The Personality of Deity* (Boston: James Munroe, 1838), 7. This is a printed version of a sermon preached in the chapel of Harvard University, September 23, 1838.

17. Book of Mormon, 1830 ed., 25, line 3. Cf. with present 1 Nephi 11:18.

18. Book of Mormon, 1830 ed., 25, line 10. Cf. with present 1 Nephi 11:21.

19. Book of Mormon, 1830 ed., 26, line 9. Cf. with present 1 Nephi 11:32.

20. Book of Mormon, 1830 ed., 32, line 10. Cf. with present 1 Nephi 13:40.

21. "Lectures on Faith," bound with 1835 edition of the Doctrine and Covenants, 52–53.

22. Truman Coe, "Mormonism," letter in the *Ohio Observer*, August 11, 1836, as reproduced by Milton V. Backman Jr., "Truman Coe's 1836 Description of Mormonism," *BYU Studies* 17, no. 3 (Spring 1977): 347–55. It is important to note that just because an anti-Mormon charged in derision that the Mormons believed in this kind of God does not prove that this is what they really believed. Coe and other anti-Mormon writers frequently made charges that were either distorted or downright untrue.

23. Parley P. Pratt, *Mormonism Unveiled: Zion's Watchman Unmasked, and its Editor, Mr. L. R. Sunderland, Exposed: Truth Vindicated: The Devil and Priestcraft in Danger!* (New York: Parley P. Pratt, 1838), 29.

24. Samuel Bennett, *A Few Remarks By Way of Reply to an Anonymous Scribbler, Calling Himself a Philanthropist: Disabusing the Church of Jesus Christ of Latter-day Saints of the Slanders and*

Falsehoods Which he has Attempted to Fasten Upon It (Philadelphia: Brown, Bicking & Guilpert, 1840), 11.

25. From the famous King Follett funeral discourse, available in several places with minor variations but most readily available in *History of the Church*, 6:305. We can only speculate what impact either this new doctrine of God or the First Vision would have had if they had been publicly announced in the 1830s. I suspect they would have had little, if any, effect so far as conversions and loyalty to the Church are concerned. When they were finally announced, most Saints were prepared to accept them along with everything else the Prophet taught—their confidence in Joseph Smith simply made it natural for them to accept whatever claims he made. When one English convert first read the vision in 1840, he simply remarked in his diary that he "felt it good." See James B. Allen and Thomas G. Alexander, eds., *Manchester Mormons: The Journal of William Clayton, 1840 to 1842* (Salt Lake City: Peregrine Smith, 1974), 158.

26. Cowdery letters, published in *Messenger and Advocate*, December 1834 and February 1835. There are some additional problems in these accounts that could provide different kinds of speculation. In the first printing of the December 1834 issue, the dating we have identified above as thirteenth year was actually obscured in printing. It was set in roman numerals, but the "13" cannot clearly be made out. When the paper was reprinted in 1840, however, it was spelled out as "thirteenth." However, in the next letter Cowdery said that he identified the time as the 15th year of Joseph's age, and it should have been 17th. Another problem lies in the identifying of the religious reformation with the visit of a certain Reverend Lane in the area. The evidence for when this minister actually visited that vicinity is obscure. Richard L. Anderson discusses the problem of these letters in detail in his "Circumstantial Confirmation of the First Vision."

27. Joseph Smith—History 1:1.

28. Orson Pratt, *Divine Authority or the Question, Was Joseph Smith Sent of God?* (Liverpool: R. James, 1848), 4.

29. *Millennial Star*, October 15, 1849, 310.

30. Few books were published for the benefit of the Saints during this time, so the *Journal of Discourses* becomes our major guide to the period. At least one small book compiled for non-Mormons reproduced the Wentworth letter, which told of the vision. See George A. Smith, *The Rise, Progress and Travels of the Church of Jesus Christ of Latter-day Saints* (Salt Lake City: Deseret News Office, 1869).

31. In one case, he told the story and then used it to demonstrate the idea that God imparts knowledge only according to individual readiness and capacity, and in another he used it as proof of Joseph Smith's honesty, but there was no doctrinal elaboration of the kind seen so frequently in the Church today. Orson Pratt, in *Journal of Discourses*, 12:354–55, 14:261–62.

32. See Carl Carmer, "A Panorama of Mormon Life," *Art in America*, May–June 1970, for details of the C. C. A. Christensen story.

33. See George D. Pyper, *Stories of Latter-day Saint Hymns: Their Authors and Composers* (Salt Lake City: Deseret News Press, 1939), 33–38.

34. Editorial, in *Juvenile Instructor*, July 15, 1880, 162.

35. George Q. Cannon, in *Journal of Discourses*, 24:371–72.

36. *Juvenile Instructor*, June 15, 1883, 191.

37. B. H. Roberts, *Outlines of Ecclesiastical History* (Salt Lake City: George Q. Cannon & Sons, 1893), 307–8. In a footnote on page 307, Roberts seemed to anticipate the objection that even though Joseph said he saw two persons, he did not necessarily describe God in the way Mormons do and that therefore, the vision is not proof that God is like man. Roberts argued: "While the Prophet Joseph in describing this first great vision refers to the Lord and His Son Jesus Christ as two glorious personages without giving at that time any particular description of their persons, it is clear that they were in the form of men." Roberts then quoted the King Follett funeral discourse to prove the doctrine further.

38. See, for example, B. H. Roberts, *A New Witness for God* (Salt Lake City: George Q. Cannon & Sons, 1895), 171–74.

39. B. H. Roberts, *Mormon Doctrine of Deity* (Salt Lake City: Deseret News, 1903), viii.

40. General Board of the Young Men's Mutual Improvement Associations, *Dispensation of the Fullness of Times* (Salt Lake City: Deseret News, 1899), 23.

41. Nephi Anderson, *A Young Folks' History of the Church of Jesus Christ of Latter-day Saints* (Salt Lake City: George Q. Cannon & Sons, 1900), 16–17. Other histories for young people used the First Vision in a similar manner.

42. John Henry Evans, *One Hundred Years of Mormonism* (Salt Lake City: Deseret News, 1905), 18.

43. Richard Oman is an art historian in the Arts and Sites Division of the Historical Department of The Church of Jesus Christ of Latter-day Saints, in Salt Lake City. He has put together an impressive collection of slides showing various artistic representations of Joseph Smith's visions.

44. For some interesting comments on the Sacred Grove, see T. Edgar Lyon, "How Authentic are Mormon Historic Sites in Vermont and New York?," *BYU Studies* 9, no. 3 (Spring 1969): 343–45.

45. General Boards of the Mutual Improvement Associations of The Church of Jesus Christ of Latter-day Saints, *In Commemoration of the Divine Ushering in of the Dispensation of the Fulness of Times through Joseph Smith, the Prophet, In the Spring of 1820* (1920).

46. J. Reuben Clark Jr., *The Charted Course of the Church in Education* (address delivered at Brigham Young University Summer School, Aspen Grove, UT, August 8, 1938), 3, 7. The first of the two essential principles concerned the Atonement of Christ and all its implications.

47. Elder Robert L. Simpson, in *Conference Report*, October 1973, 102.

48. George Q. Cannon, in *Juvenile Instructor*, July 15, 1880, 162; and in *Journal of Discourses*, 24:372, 341.

49. Orson Pratt, in *Journal of Discourses*, 22:29.

50. George Q. Cannon, in *Journal of Discourses*, 24:371, 372.

51. George Q. Cannon, in *Journal of Discourses*, 24:341. See also Bruce R. McConkie, *Mormon Doctrine*, 2nd ed. (Salt Lake City: Bookcraft, 1966), 286, in which Elder McConkie states that Joseph's

account of the vision rocked "the whole religious foundation of the Christian world."

52. George Teasdale, in *Journal of Discourses*, 25:18.

53. *Juvenile Instructor*, November 1, 1884, 330.

54. George Q. Cannon, *The Life of Joseph Smith the Prophet* (Salt Lake City: Juvenile Instructor Office, 1888), 37. This phrase was picked up by Joseph Fielding Smith in *Essentials in Church History* (Salt Lake City: Deseret News Press, 1922), 41.

55. William Morton, *The Gospel Primer* (Salt Lake City: Juvenile Instructor Office, 1897), 19.

56. See note 40. One orator grew highly elaborate on this point: "The vision was indeed the earthquake which dried up the rivers of unbelief, which started the fountains of truth and which shook the mountain from whose side the little stone rolled forth to accomplish its destiny of filling the whole earth with the Gospel of purity." Alma O. Taylor, "The First Vision: An Address Delivered at the Speakers' Contest, Y.M.M.I.A., Salt Lake Stake of Zion," *Improvement Era*, July 1900, 686.

57. Taylor, "First Vision," 686.

58. George Q. Cannon, *The Latter-day Prophet: History of Joseph Smith Written for Young People* (Salt Lake City: Juvenile Instructor Office, 1900), 16.

59. Angus J. Cannon, *A Latter-day Prophet* (Independence, MO: Zion's Printing and Publishing, n. d.), 5.

60. James E. Talmage, *The Story of Mormonism* (Liverpool: Millennial Star Office, 1907), 9.

61. General Authorities of the Church, *Priest's Quorum Course of Study* (Salt Lake City: The Church of Jesus Christ of Latter-day Saints, 1909), 27.

62. General Authorities of the Church, *High Priest Course of Study* (Salt Lake City: The Church of Jesus Christ of Latter-day Saints, 1909), 45.

63. General Authorities of the Church, *History of the Gospel: High Priests Course of Study, 1910* (Salt Lake City: The Church of Jesus Christ of Latter-day Saints, 1910), 87.

64. General Authorities of the Church, *Divine Mission of the*

Savior, Priest's Quorum Course of Study for 1910 (Salt Lake City: The Church of Jesus Christ of Latter-day Saints, 1910), 90.

65. Osborne J. P. Widtsoe, *The Restoration* (Salt Lake City: The Deseret News, 1912), 18. Here, incidentally, is another case where enthusiasm for the messages of the vision created at least some historical misperceptions. The idea that there had been an apostasy from the ancient church of Christ was very prevalent in Joseph Smith's day, even before the vision.

66. Widtsoe, *Restoration*, 18.

67. General Authorities of the Church, *The Latter-day Prophet*, Course of Study for Deacons, 1918 (Salt Lake City: The Church of Jesus Christ of Latter-day Saints, 1918), 16.

68. J. M. Sjodahl, "Account of Joseph's First Vision Compared with Biblical Records of Divine Manifestations," *Improvement Era*, April 1920, 488–89.

69. Nephi Jensen, "Joseph Smith: An Oration," *Improvement Era*, April 1920, 556.

70. Jensen, "Joseph Smith," 556.

71. Melvin J. Ballard, "One Hundred Years Ago," *Improvement Era*, June 1920, 693.

72. John A. Widtsoe, *The Divine Mission of Joseph Smith* (Independence, MO: Zion's Printing and Publishing, 1926), 9.

73. Joseph F. Merrill, "Why the Mormon Church?" (address delivered over Radio Station KSL, May 22, 1927, printed broadside).

74. Heber C. Iverson, "The Soul's Reality and Resurrection," (address delivered over Radio Station KSL, April 22, 1928, broadside reprinted from *Deseret News*, April 28, 1928).

75. James E. Talmage, "The Unknown God" (address delivered over Radio Station KSL, January 27, 1929, printed in pamphlet form), 7.

76. *If Any of You Lack Wisdom, Let Him Ask of God*, 1980 Children's Sacrament Meeting Presentation (Salt Lake City: The Church of Jesus Christ of Latter-day Saints, 1978), 4–6.

The First Vision Story Revived

Richard Lyman Bushman

This essay was originally published in Dialogue: A Journal of Mormon Thought *4, no. 1 (Spring 1969): 82–93, as part of a roundtable that featured the Reverend Wesley Walters and Professor Bushman.*

The Reverend Mr. Walters's article on the First Vision raised quite a stir among Mormon scholars when an early version circulated about a year and a half ago. The essay was clearly another piece of anti-Mormon writing, a genre familiar enough to Mormon scholars. Mr. Walters's purpose, like that of many of his predecessors, was to discredit Joseph Smith's account of the First Vision and all that depended on it. But the style of his attack was both refreshing and disconcerting. In the first place, it was free of the obvious rancor characteristic of anti-Mormon writers from E. D. Howe to Fawn Brodie. However fervent their claims to objectivity and mere scholarly curiosity, sooner or later anti-Mormon authors disclose their antipathy. They cannot resist twisting the knife. Mr. Walters, by contrast, sticks to his facts. He forgoes the attacks on Joseph's character and the credibility or veracity of his followers. He candidly presents his argument and bluntly tells Mormons to reevaluate the foundations of their church. That kind of frankness is far more disarming than the more pretentious variety.

The article also set us back because Mr. Walters took an entirely new track and followed it with admirable care. Instead of hauling out the tiresome affidavits and reviving the money-digger stories, for the most part he passed over these and concentrated on a brand-new question: Were there revivals in 1819–20 in the vicinity of Palmyra as Joseph said? Everyone up until now had assumed that of course there were. Walters said no, and the sources of his answer were impressive. They stood apart from the biased materials on which most anti-Mormon work is based. They were contemporaneous with the event, and they were right to the point. Our consternation was a genuine compliment to the quality of Mr. Walters's work.

While Mr. Walters has put us on the spot for the moment, in the long run Mormon scholarship will benefit from his attack. Not only was there an immediate effort to answer the question of an 1819 revival, but Mormon historians asked themselves how many other questions about our early history remain unasked as well as unanswered. Not long after we saw his essay, a committee on "Mormon History in New York" sent a group of scholars east for special research. The results of the first year's efforts will soon be published in *Brigham Young University Studies*, and presumably like investigations will continue. Without wholly intending it, Mr. Walters may have done as much to advance the cause of Mormon history within the Church as anyone in recent years.

Meanwhile, of course, we have to assess the damage he has done to Joseph's story of the First Vision. Is it now impossible to hold that a revival occurred near Palmyra in 1819 or 1820 as

Mr. Walters would have us believe? In attempting to answer that question, it is wise to remember the difficulties in recovering a true account of past events, especially when the witnesses tell their stories many times, over many years. Behind the simplest event are complex motives and many factual threads conjoining that will receive varying emphasis in different retellings. In all accounts of his early religious experiences, for example, Joseph mentions the search for the true church and a desire for forgiveness. In some accounts he emphasizes one, in some the other. Similarly, in the earliest record of the First Vision, he attributes his question about the churches to personal study; in the familiar story written in 1838 or 1839, he credits the revival and the consequent disputes as raising the issue for him.[1] The reasons for reshaping the story usually have to do with changes in immediate circumstances. We know that Joseph suffered from attacks on his character around 1834. As he told Oliver Cowdery when the letters on Joseph's early experiences were about to be published, enemies had blown up his honest confession of guilt into an admission of outrageous crimes.[2] Small wonder that afterward he played down his prayer for forgiveness in accounts of the vision. Such changes do not evidence an uncertainty about the events, as Mr. Walters thinks, as if Joseph were manufacturing new parts year by year. It is folly to try to

---

Raising the Bar

Wesley Walters performed a service to the cause of Mormon history; he questioned things that Mormons had accepted as simple fact. He raised doubts, for example, about the revival in Joseph Smith's neighborhood around 1820. By questioning that accepted belief, Walters helped Mormon historians realize that we should not assume anything; everything has to be supported. Since his time, Mormon historians have plunged deeper and deeper into the sources. The editors of the Joseph Smith Papers Project, for one, take nothing for granted—partly because Wesley Walters raised the bar. (Richard Lyman Bushman, interview by Samuel Alonzo Dodge, July 31, 2009, Provo, UT)

explain every change as the result of Joseph's calculated efforts to fabricate a convincing account. One would expect variations in the simplest and truest story.

The audacity of Joseph's story complicates his narrative and our recovery of the truth. As a more mature and worldly-wise person would have expected, Joseph's boyish report of his vision met skepticism and reproof. The appearance of the Father and the Son to a fourteen-year-old was beyond the bounds of credibility and blasphemous as well. In the lexicon of the revivalists, it was an egregious form of enthusiasm, the belief that the divine visited you in special vision or with extraordinary power. Enthusiasm had been the bane of revivalists and other equivalents for centuries. Every camp meeting preacher was prepared to denounce it when it raised its ugly head. Not knowing what hit him, so to speak, Joseph marveled at the anger he aroused.

As his protracted meditations on the incident attest, the rebuff scarred him (see Joseph Smith—History 1:21–25); his reticence to tell the details of the story for some time afterward is perfectly understandable. The revelation received just prior to the organization of the Church in 1830 merely made passing reference to a manifestation of forgiveness before the visit of Moroni (see D&C 20:5, 6). Until 1838, in accounts for non-Church members he called the beings in the First Vision personages or angels, covering the fact that he claimed to see the Father and the Son. Only in the private narrations for his history written in 1831 and 1838 did he frankly say the Lord had come to him.[3] As Mr. Walters rightly points out, some Church members in the early years may have been unaware of the actual identity of the heavenly visitors.

With that much said by way of preface, what evidence does Mr. Walters present to discredit Joseph's story? The gist of his argument, as I understand it, is that Joseph held two events in his mind which he tried to bring together in his 1838 account. One was an actual event, the revival of 1824 when an unusual excitement occurred in Palmyra, and great multitudes, among them members of the Smith family, joined the churches. The other was a fictitious event, the First Vision, which was gradually forming in his imagination after 1830. In the process of combining his manufactured story with historical reality, Joseph found it convenient to set the vision in the time of the revival to help explain why he prayed. But it was necessary to move the story back to 1820 to leave room for the coming of Moroni and the reception of the plates. The falsity of the account shows up when we uncover the discrepancy in dates. The revival Joseph remembered occurred in 1824, not 1819 or 1820. Had the vision actually occurred in 1820, Joseph would not have put it in the wrong context. He would have told the story without contradiction. With that structure in mind, Mr. Walters sets out to prove that the revival Joseph had in mind must have been the revival of 1824, which fits his description exactly, while in 1819 and 1820 nothing came close.

The first evidence he offers is not Joseph's account but Oliver Cowdery's. In the first extended attempt to draw together the events of the early years, Oliver wrote a series of letters to the Church newspaper published in Kirtland, the *Messenger and Advocate*. The letters began in October 1834 and continued more or less regularly for a year. In December 1834, Oliver told of a revival during which Joseph had been awakened and in which Mr. Lane, a Methodist preacher, had played a part. Oliver connected this revival with the conversion of the Smith family and other events similar to the ones Joseph associated with the unusual excitement of his own, later account. Mr. Walters concludes that Joseph's revival and Oliver's were one and the same. The connection is important because the Lane who figures so prominently in Oliver's story was not assigned to the Palmyra area until 1824 and is known to have visited the region only briefly in 1819. Therefore, Oliver was not thinking of a revival in 1819. The one revival he had in mind was the 1824 awakening, when Lane was more likely to have made an impression. And Joseph presumably had the same episode in mind when he remembered a revival.

The argument falters in two spots. The first is in Oliver's trustworthiness as a witness to these events. He did not experience them himself. All of his evidence is hearsay, and the consequent flaws are evident. Mormons can object that Oliver mixes up the First Vision and the visit of Moroni because in his narrative the revival and Joseph's question about the churches led not to the grove but to his bedroom and the visit of Moroni. The First Vision itself is skipped entirely. Oliver seems to have scrambled the two events, putting together parts of two stories to make one. Even Mr. Walters must agree that Oliver errs on the dates. In one letter he says these events occurred in Joseph's fifteenth year. In the next, claiming a typographical error, Oliver places them in the seventeenth year, which would be from December 1821 to December 1822—at least two years before the 1824 revival which Mr. Walters claims Oliver meant to describe. Neither Mormons nor Mr. Walters can accept the validity of the account uncritically. Not that Oliver's veracity is in doubt. But remember that he is the first to prepare an account of the early years. He has bits of information from various sources: stories picked up at the Smiths' while living there, tales from the neighbors in Palmyra, and, as Oliver emphasizes, the assistance of Joseph. Probably the individual details are accurate enough; the whole narrative need not be discarded because of a few obvious flaws. But he misses on the chronology, sticking together pieces that do not belong. Mr. Lane did indeed leave his mark on Palmyra, as Oliver could have learned from the residents, but he was not necessarily the revival preacher who affected Joseph.

Joseph himself never mentions Lane. Oliver was the one to insert the name in the story.[4]

The possibility remains that Lane did take part in an awakening near Palmyra and that Oliver did not confuse the story quite as much as Mr. Walters thinks. In the summer of 1819, Lane was at a Methodist Conference next door to Palmyra in Phelps (Vienna Village). It is at least conceivable that his preaching started an "unusual excitement" and did touch Joseph in some way. Oliver says only that Mr. Lane "visited Palmyra and vicinity," which might have meant the quick visit of a minister attending the conference.[5] We must not exclude Mr. Lane entirely while the evidence is still so inconclusive.

The second flaw in the argument is Mr. Walters's belief that Oliver's confusion, however serious, was no greater than Joseph's—that Oliver's account is "virtually Joseph's own personal narrative." That is a large assumption to make when the only evidence is Oliver's claim that "Joseph Smith, Jr., has offered to assist us."[6] Oliver began the letters while he was in Missouri and Joseph in Kirtland, and close cooperation was impossible. Joseph said that he first learned that the narrative was to include his life as well as the rise of the Church from the *Messenger and Advocate*.[7] After he moved to Ohio, Oliver lived in Norton, in another county from Joseph. They could not have worked together very closely. Indeed, on one point in the story they were quite at odds: Oliver said Joseph's interest in religious questions began in his seventeenth year. In his 1831–32 narrative, Joseph said his interest began when he was between twelve and fifteen. In 1835, a year after the Cowdery letters were printed, Joseph said on two occasions that his First Vision took place when he was about fourteen. Had Joseph carefully edited Oliver's account, the error would not have passed.[8] The account was Oliver's, not Joseph's, and chronological discrepancies, such as the appearance of Lane, must be credited where they are due.

Rather than rely on Oliver's dubious report as the foundation of his case, Mr. Walters stresses that Joseph's own description in the official 1838 account does not fit the events of 1819 and 1820, while they accord perfectly with the revival of 1824. Joseph said that "there was in the place where he lived an unusual excitement on the subject of religion. It commenced with the Methodists, but soon became general among all the sects in that region of country. Indeed, the whole district of country seemed affected by it, and great multitudes united themselves to the different religious parties" (Joseph Smith—History 1:5). Walters concentrates on two points: the location of the revivals and their size. He admits there were revivals in 1819 and 1820, but they were not in Palmyra or nearby. And what activity did occur close to the Smith farm did not bring "great multitudes" into the churches. Only the 1824 revival fills the bill.

Reduction of the argument to essentials reveals the difficulties of the case. In effect Mr. Walters has to say how near is near and how big is big. When Joseph spoke of "the place where we lived," did he mean his own neighborhood, the village of Palmyra just two miles away, Manchester Village about five miles from the Smith farm, the ring of surrounding villages whose news neighbors would bring to the Smith house, or the western New York region? And of what did "great multitudes" consist for a young boy? Ten or twenty converts in three or four churches, fifty or sixty in ten, or hundreds in twenty or thirty? The uncertainty should be obvious. One cannot "conclusively test" Joseph's story as easily as might be thought.

It must be recalled that when Joseph spoke of "the place where we lived" in Illinois hundreds of miles from Palmyra, he may have referred only generally to a section of western New York, just as southern Californians from scores of little towns claim Los Angeles and its happenings as their own when at a distance. All the historian can do under the circumstances is to line up the places where revivals were reported in 1819 and 1820 and let the reader judge whether religious excitement occurred near enough to Joseph's house to meet the description.

I have not searched any of the records myself, but Mr. Walters names a number of places, and Professor Milton Backman of Brigham Young University, in an article shortly to appear in *Brigham Young University Studies*, locates others.[9] First, by way of comparison, notice the number of towns Mr. Walters mentions as having revivals in 1824 when the excitement was close enough in his judgment to fit Joseph's description. In addition to Palmyra, he lists Williamson, Ontario, Manchester, Sulphur Springs, Vienna, Lyons, and Macedon as nearby towns, a total of eight, and Mendon, Geneva, Gorham, and Clyde, another four, at a somewhat greater distance. For 1819 and 1820, Professor Backman and Mr. Walters together name Farmington, Penfield, Rochester, Lima, West Bloomfield, Junius, and Oaks Corners, a total of seven within twenty-five miles, and within forty-five miles, Cayuga, Geneva, Auburn, Aurora, Trumansburg, Ogden, East Riga, West Riga, Bergen, and Le Roy, with prospects of an awakening in Canandaigua and Waterloo, a total of twelve. That comes to eight nearby in 1824 and seven in 1819–20; and four more distant in 1824 and twelve in 1819–20. The 1819–20 season was really not so dull religiously as Mr. Walters says.

Mr. Walters's main argument is that no revival occurred in Palmyra itself. But even that fact cannot be established absolutely. It is a negative claim and depends on negative evidence, which is always tenuous. Mr. Walters relies on the absence of revival reports, but just because someone failed to write a report of an event does not mean it did not occur. In this case we even lack some of the records that would contain important traces. The Palmyra Presbyterian Church records are missing, and Methodist figures take in an entire circuit and fail to note changes in smaller locales. Furthermore, lots of things happen that are never recorded. "An unusual excitement on the subject of religion," all that Joseph claims for the place where he lived (the "great multitudes" were joining the churches in "the whole district of country"), might have been passed over in the national religious press covering as it did countless small towns. The news included in the Palmyra paper depended on the taste and inclinations of the editor. We know that he failed to report a Methodist camp meeting in June 1820 because a report of the death of a local citizen incidentally mentioned his attendance at a camp meeting the day before his death.[10] The point is that although we think a revival should have been recorded, there are many reasons why it could have been missed. We cannot know for sure that an event did not occur unless reliable witnesses on the scene say no, and thus far Mr. Walters has found none such to testify.

But apart from the possibility that some awakenings occurred right next door, as it were, the major question is whether or not seven revivals within twenty-five miles is enough to justify a statement eighteen years later and hundreds of miles away that there was an unusual excitement in the place where Joseph Smith lived. Perhaps the heart of the matter is the effective horizon of the Smith household. Was everything beyond Palmyra Village alien territory, news of which they did not associate with their own place? Or did their psychological environs extend farther? Remember that they sold cakes and beer at gatherings of various sorts and that the boys had to range about for work to supplement their scanty farm income. Joseph went to Pennsylvania for employment when he was in his early twenties. If the older sons followed a similar pattern, the Smith family would keep up with events over a rather broad territory. Fifteen or twenty miles would not take them into foreign parts. All this must be taken into account when judging dimensions of the district they called their own.

In assessing Mr. Walters's second line of reasoning, the inferior size of the 1819–20 revivals, two considerations must be kept in mind. The first is that the revivals of 1824 were not the standard for people in 1819. In his article, Mr. Walters tells us first of the hundreds converted in the later years and then goes back to 1819 to show how insipid it was by comparison. After reading about the carnage of the Civil War, we may think the War of 1812 no war at all. The important question, of course, is how it looked to the participants and, in this case, to a boy of fourteen. Without knowing anything greater, did the excitement of 1819 strike him as unusual? Did the reports of conversions in the surrounding area sound like great multitudes joining the churches? Remember that he was just developing personal religious concerns and, judging by the 1831–32 narrative of the First Vision, was sensitive to religious sincerity and hypocrisy. Would reports of awakenings and conversions, however modest by comparison to later revivals, have registered with this sensitized young man as unusual and great?

The second consideration is that admissions to membership do not necessarily measure the intensity of a revival. The first stage in the conversion process was awakening or conviction, when the preacher aroused fears in the prospective convert. At this point, he began to realize his danger and to worry about pleasing God. This was the most violent period. An awakened person was filled with anguish and might faint under moving preaching. The intense concern could continue for a few days or a few years. Sometimes it simply faded away and never reached a climax in conversion. In Calvinist churches, which would include the Presbyterians and most Baptists, the person remained outside the church until he received grace and with it assurance of salvation. Some converts would pass through periods of awakening two or three times before they knew grace and joined a church. There might be an unusual excitement about a religion and only a few people actually qualify for admission. High admissions are a good sign of a revival; absence of admissions does not necessarily mean no religious excitement. Without being at the scene, one cannot accurately measure the intensity of religious excitement.

The point is important in the interpretation of Joseph's narrative, for all that he says went on in "the place where we lived" as "an unusual excitement on the subject of religion." The "great multitudes" joining churches occurred in "the whole district of country." The excitement may have been an awakening or a prospect of a revival, not a shower of grace itself with the resulting increase in memberships and reports in the national religious press.

But to get down to the facts, what indications are there of the size of the revivals in 1819 and 1820? Methodist figures are most elusive because, as mentioned before, they summed up membership for an entire circuit, and activity in one area could be lost. What we do know is that perhaps a hundred Methodist ministers met in the village of Vienna, next door to Palmyra, during the first week in July in 1819. It is likely that either during the conference or as it broke up, these ministers preached in nearby towns. A historian of Methodism in Phelps, where the village of Vienna was located, says that in the following year a "flaming spiritual advance" occurred in the area. A convert during this revival series spoke late in life of "a religious cyclone which swept over the whole region round about" at this time, when "the kingdom of darkness was terribly shaken."[11] As Mr. Walters says, the Ontario Methodist circuit shows no growth in these years, but there is evidence that the next circuit, which came very close to the Smith house, did. The figures may be a little uncertain, but the Lyons circuit minutes nonetheless show a jump from 374 to 654 in 1820, fully as many as Mr. Walters mentions in 1824 for Ontario Methodists.[12] Mr. Walters also cites a local Methodist who wrote about the years before 1823 that "for two or three years we saw no great awakenings." That certainly implies that two or three years earlier, right around 1820, there was an awakening. The significance of the comment is heightened when it is noted that the Methodists first advanced from a class meeting to a church the next year and the following year began chapel construction.[13] Orsamus Turner, a newspaperman in Palmyra who knew the Smiths personally, recalls that Joseph caught "a spark of Methodism in the camp meeting" somewhere along the road to Vienna, the place where the big Methodist conference was held. Since Turner left Palmyra in 1822, we can presume that the camp meeting and Joseph's awakening occurred before that date.[14] All told, there can be little doubt that the Methodists were up to something in 1819 and 1820.

The absence of the minutes of the Ontario Baptist Association for 1820, the association that included the area around Joseph's home, handicaps work on the Baptists. Mr. Walters gives loss and gain figures, which are deceptive because in a transient community the numbers moving out might outweigh a considerable number of converts. He does tell us in a footnote that six people were baptized in the Palmyra church between September 18, 1819, and September 23, 1820.[15] The Baptist church in Farmington (Manchester), just five miles away, baptized twenty-two in 1819, a sizable number in a congregation consisting of eighty-seven members in 1818.[16] Walters himself admits that must have been a revival. The Freewill Baptists in Junius, a town just east of Vienna, also reported a revival and added fifteen members in 1820.[17] Whether or not that counts as unusual depends, of course, on the standard one sets. But for these people, the additions were not commonplace. Palmyra's six converts in the year following September 1819 compared to one in 1821; Farmington's twenty-two in 1819, to none in 1821.[18]

Presbyterian figures for the Palmyra congregation itself are also missing for 1819 and 1820. The local church's own records are lost, and the congregation failed to report at the February 1820 meeting of the presbytery. Mr. Walters relies on the absence of reports in newspapers and general histories to reach his conclusion of no revivals. We do know that there was a substantial awakening at Geneva, within the same presbytery as Palmyra. From 1812 to 1819 the average increase in membership was nine; from July 1819 to July 1820, eighty joined, most of them in the fall of 1819.[19] Next door to Palmyra in Oaks Corners (located in the town of Phelps), the place where the Methodist Conference had met, the average admissions between 1806 and 1819 was five, with nine as the previous high. Thirty were admitted in 1820, the bulk of them in the winter and spring. The Presbyterians also reported "in gatherings" at five other churches within twenty-five miles of Palmyra.[20] When the Presbytery of Geneva, which included Palmyra, met in February 1820, sixteen churches reported two hundred new members. However we may judge the magnitude of the revival, the representatives felt that "during the past year more have been received into the communion of the Churches than perhaps in any former year."[21]

The question for us is whether or not the Smiths would have agreed with the judgment of the Geneva Presbytery. Did 1819 and 1820 seem like big years with "great multitudes" joining the churches in the "whole district of country"? Doubtless this was an important year for religion in New York as a whole and upstate particularly. All of the major denominations reported large increases. Methodist membership for 1820 in western New York increased by 2,256 members, the largest annual increase ever reported for the region to that time.[22] Presbyterian and Baptist growth was comparable. The Presbyterian annual report for 1819 said "the past has been a year of signal and almost unprecedented mercy" as far as "genuine religious revivals" went, and six of the eight areas of special grace were in New York.[23] Baptist numbers in western New York grew by more than 1,500 in 1819.[24] Some of this news filtered through to the Smiths via the *Palmyra Register*, which was publishing accounts with such extravagant statements as "the face of the country has been wonderfully changed of late" with reckonings of church admissions to back up the excitement.[25] Believing for a moment that four members of the Smith family had joined a church themselves that year as Joseph said, we can understand how reports like these would have registered and very possibly left the impression that great multitudes were uniting with various religious parties.

Doubtless the accounting will vary in succeeding years as some reports prove unfounded and evidence of additional revivals is discovered. The details of the picture are bound to change. As it now stands, however, I am satisfied myself that enough was going on in 1819 and 1820 to have impressed a religiously oriented young boy. Putting aside the possibility of revivals in Palmyra itself for the moment, there is hard evidence to prove activity in nearby Farmington and Phelps (Oaks Corners), both close to the Smith farm, and substantial revivals in the next circle of villages. Beyond that, western New York was very lively indeed. At best, critics of Joseph's story can claim that there was not enough excitement close enough to Palmyra to satisfy them. But again, that all depends on how near is near and big is big. I doubt very much that historical inquiry will ever settle that question to the satisfaction of all.

The weakest portion of Mr. Walters's essay is the attempt in the last pages to explain the various narratives of the First Vision and speculate if Joseph was making up the story as he went. As I suggested at the first, there are bound to be variations in the reports of any event, simply because the narrator emphasizes one portion or another of the story. Simple slips may account for other differences. In the 1831 story, for example, Joseph places the First Vision in his sixteenth year instead of his fifteenth, a mistake I for one can easily excuse, considering how I always have to stop to calculate just how old one is in his fifteenth year. Perhaps the only fundamental conflict in the facts is between the money-digging Joseph of the years before 1827 and the religious Joseph afterward who must have pious motives for everything he does. That conflict, of course, also coincides with the anti-Mormon accounts of Joseph's early life and the Prophet's own story. Mr. Walters assumes an impossible task when he tries to reconcile the stories of those who hated Joseph and wished to discredit him and the more sympathetic accounts. I think the evidence from the enemies of the Church and the evidence from Joseph's own mouth will always be contradictory. Bringing the two together as Walters does results in hopeless difficulties. He has Joseph concerned only with buried treasure and bearded spirits until 1827, when suddenly the need to mulct Martin Harris leads Joseph to introduce a religious note. From there on the money-digging precipitously disappears, and all we have is religion. The Book of Mormon, finished just two years later in 1829, is over five hundred pages of substantial religious narrative with only a few references that could be connected by any stretch of the imagination to the money-digging enterprises that presumably obsessed Joseph in 1827. That assumes a more drastic change in character than anything the revivals produced. It seems much easier to believe that Joseph had always been religious, as everything he and his mother say leads us to think. The money-digging side of his character was almost wholly the invidious creation of the neighbors, based on his employment for an individual or two who were seeking treasure. If we exclude this embittered gossip from the picture, the First

The Hermeneutics of Suspicion

Academics use the phrase "the hermeneutics of suspicion." Hermeneutics means interpretation, and the hermeneutics of suspicion means that you take nothing at face value. Beneath the surface of any writing or any action there's something else, probably something more base than appears on the surface.

I believe in the hermeneutics of trust. That is, you begin by trusting what people say. You may throw doubt on any assertion when the evidence requires it, but you begin by taking the subject seriously on his or her own terms.

Those who practice the hermeneutics of suspicion feel that to ferret out *the truth* you cannot trust appearances. Only by removing the masks that all of us present to the world do we arrive at reality. Moreover—and this is important—the critic can determine what that reality is. I, the critic, can judge what's really there.

The hermeneutics of trust begins with the position that we never can find out *the truth*, what really happened. Everything we know in this life is seen through someone's eyes. All a historian has to work with is the way this person saw it or that person saw it. There is no reality out there that isn't seen through human eyes. The purpose of history is not to find out what really happened but to collect the ways human observers have described what they think happened. We look at the world through others' eyes.

That viewpoint may disappoint us. We don't like to think we will never know the complete and final truth. But in another way it's lovely. It means we are introduced to the inner lives and the way of looking at the world of all these different people. My aim has been, when writing about Jonathan Edwards or Joseph Smith or Thomas Jefferson, to see the world as they saw it. That is the way I write history, and, frankly, I prefer to read that kind of history. I don't want the historian to reduce whatever happens to the modern, commonsense view of what the possibilities are. I want to know what Muhammad thought and what Buddha thought, not the beliefs of some modern writer. My aim as a historian is to explain what Joseph Smith understood was happening to him. (Richard Lyman Bushman, interview by Samuel Alonzo Dodge, July 31, 2009, Provo, UT)

Vision story, rather than being a late concoction, fits perfectly with the deep religious interests which Joseph says preoccupied him from age twelve and which show through in virtually everything we have from his own mouth from 1829 on.

If Mr. Walters has not undercut the First Vision story as he meant to, Mormons might profit nevertheless by inquiring what would happen to our faith if he had succeeded or what we would do if six eminent anthropologists presented "conclusive proof" that the Book of Mormon was fraudulent. The question I have in mind is, how much does our faith depend on supporting historical evidence? On the one hand, we make a great deal of it. Mormons delight in Hugh Nibley's arguments in behalf of the Book of Mormon. We all hope he will be equally successful in proving the authenticity of the Book of Abraham. On the other hand, we are prone to dismiss all this as irrelevant. I have heard Professor Nibley himself summarize a long argument for the Book of Mormon, to which his Mormon audience had listened raptly, by saying that, of course, none of this really matters. The important point for him was that God had revealed the truth to Joseph by the Holy Spirit; the historical case was mere trimmings, the game played for the sheer fun of it.

Looking on from the outside, an observer might think Mormons are hopelessly mixed up. If testimony is all that really matters, why worry about the historical evidence? Since an airtight case would fail to convince believing Mormons, they should forget about proofs for the Book of Mormon and replying to the Reverend Mr. Walters and concentrate on their religious experiences and the satisfactions of their group life.

For those blessed with it, spiritual experience is the most compelling data. Honesty requires that one remain true to it even in the face of other evidence to the contrary. Were a case made against the Book of Mormon, our sense of balance and personal integrity would compel Mormons to hold on to their beliefs. But I wager that we would search heaven and earth to break the case and prove the book true historically. Mormons are determined to have both material and spiritual evidence for their faith. The spiritual is the more important, but the material must have its place.

There is good reason for this combination. Mormons are committed to a God who acts in history. He led ancient Israel; he came to earth to redeem the world; he guides prophets in our time; and he helps individuals day by day with mundane problems. Our most basic commitment is to the power of God acting concretely in the lives of men. He comes and leaves footprints. To give up on historical proofs would be to relinquish in part our faith that God enters the here and now to lead and help and illuminate. Mormons feel divine power mainly in their spiritual experiences, but they believe traces of it can also be detected in the history of his people and his prophets. So long as we embrace that faith, we will, I think, search for proofs and evidences and reply to the likes of Mr. Walters when they try to confute us.

Notes

1. One of the articles in the special issue of *Brigham Young University Studies*, Dean C. Jessee's "The Early Accounts of Joseph Smith's First Vision," reprints three narrations by Joseph. *BYU Studies* 9, no. 3 (Spring 1969): 275–94.

2. See his letter to Oliver Cowdery in the *Messenger and Advocate*, November 6, 1834, reprinted in Francis W. Kirkham, *A New Witness for Christ in America: The Book of Mormon*, 3rd ed. (Independence, MO: Press of Zion's Printing and Publishing, 1951), i, 78–79.

3. See the accounts in the Jessee article cited in note 1.

4. William Smith's account is as suspect as Oliver's. William was only nine when Joseph had the First Vision and would have had to rely on others to supplement his own memory. Furthermore, the interview with William took place in 1893 when he was eighty-two. As Mr. Walters notes, William, like Oliver, was foggy about the date of the revival.

5. Kirkham, *A New Witness*, i, 84.

6. Kirkham, *A New Witness*, i, 78.

7. Kirkham, *A New Witness*, i, 78.

8. It may be that Joseph corrected Oliver only after the letters appeared. One reading of the letters, a conjectural one like Mr. Walters's reconstruction at the end of his essay, would hold that Joseph stopped Oliver after he read in print the December letter telling of the revival in Joseph's fifteenth year. It sounded like Oliver was going on to relate the story of the vision which Joseph still held back for fear of misunderstandings. Joseph may also have seen other flaws in the account. At any rate, in the next letter Oliver changed the time of the story from Joseph's fifteenth to his seventeenth year and hurried on to the visit of Moroni.

9. "Awakenings in the Burned-Over District: New Light on the Historical Setting of the First Vision," *BYU Studies* 9, no. 3 (Spring 1969): 301–20.

10. *Palmyra Register*, June 28, July 5, 1820. Cited in Backman, "Awakenings," 319n19.

11. M. P. Blakeslee, "Notes for a History of Methodism in Phelps, 1886," 7–8, copy located in the Brigham Young University Library. Cited in Backman, "Awakenings," 308n16.

12. Minutes of the Several Annual Conferences of the Methodist Episcopal Church, New York, 1820, 27 (hereafter cited as Methodist Minutes); Methodist Minutes, 1821, 27, cited in Backman, "Awakenings," 314n26.

13. Wesley P. Walters, "New Light on Mormon Origins from the Palmyra Revival," *Dialogue: A Journal of Mormon Thought* 4, no. 1 (Spring 1969): 77n43.

14. For the full story on Turner, see Richard Lloyd Anderson, "Circumstantial Confirmation of the First Vision through Reminiscences," in the special issue of *Brigham Young University Studies*, vol. 9, no. 3 (Spring 1969): 373–404.

15. Walters, "New Light," 77n40.

16. *Minutes of the Ontario Baptist Association* (Canandaigua, NY, 1818), 3; *Minutes of the Ontario Baptist Association* (New York, 1819), 2; cited in Backman, "Awakenings," 314n27.

17. Marilla Marks, ed., *Memoirs of the Life of David Marks* (Dover, NH, 1846), 26, cited in Backman, "Awakenings," 314n28.

18. Walters, "New Light," 77n40.

19. "Records of the Church of Christ in Geneva, State of New York," 146–56, 158–59, 136–38, First Presbyterian Church, Geneva, New York; "Minutes of the Session, 1819–1826," 260–86, located in the First Presbyterian Church, Geneva, New York, cited in Backman, "Awakenings," 310n22.

20. "Session Book of the First Presbyterian Church in Phelps," Book II, 11–19, Presbyterian Church, Oaks Corners, New York. *Extracts from the Minutes of the General Assembly of the Presbyterian Church, in the United States of America* (Philadelphia, 1821), 22; "Records of the Synod of Geneva (1812–1835)," 220–21, Harold B. Lee Library, Brigham Young University, Provo, UT; "Records of the Presbytery of Geneva," Book C, 37, Harold B. Lee Library, Brigham Young University; J. Jermain Porter, *History of the Presbytery of Geneva, 1805–1889* (Geneva, 1889), 25, cited in Backman, "Awakenings," 311n23–24.

21. "Records of the Presbytery of Geneva," Book C, 37–38, cited in Backman, "Awakenings," 311n25.

22. *Methodist Minutes* (1821), 27–28, cited in Backman, "Awakenings," 317n38.

23. *Extracts from the Minutes of the General Assembly* (1820), 321–22, cited in Backman, "Awakenings," 316n35.

24. Proceedings of the Baptist General Convention in the United States, at their Second Triennial Meeting, and the Sixth Annual Report of the Board of Managers (Philadelphia, 1820), 308–9. The figure of 1,500 was the total from only five associations. There were others which failed to report.

25. *Palmyra Register*, June 7, September 3, 1820, cited in Backman, "Awakenings," 316n33.

The First Vision, according to the Mormon prophet, came as a result of his prayerful inquiry concerning which church to join. He was forbidden to join any of them, for all were wrong. (Harold T. Kilbourn, Joseph Smith Seeks Wisdom From the Bible, *© 1975 Intellectual Reserve, Inc.)*

The Significance of Joseph Smith's First Vision in Mormon Thought

James B. Allen

This essay was originally published in Dialogue: A Journal of Mormon Thought *1, no. 3 (Autumn 1966): 29–45.*

In the year 1838, Joseph Smith began writing his formal *History of the Church*. The history commenced with the now famous account of what has been termed the "First Vision," in which he told of the appearance to him, in 1820, of two heavenly personages. The vision, according to the Mormon prophet, came as a result of his prayerful inquiry concerning which church to join, and in it he was forbidden to join any of them, for all were wrong. While not specifically named in the story, the two personages have been identified by Latter-day Saints as God the Father and his Son, Jesus Christ; Joseph Smith indicated that the one said of the other, "This is My Beloved Son. Hear Him!"

This singular story has achieved a position of unique importance in the traditions and official doctrines of the

Mormon Church. Belief in the vision is one of the fundamentals to which faithful members give assent. Its importance is second only to belief in the divinity of Jesus of Nazareth. The story is an essential part of the first lesson given by Mormon missionaries to prospective converts, and its acceptance is necessary before baptism. The nature and importance of the vision is the subject of frequent sermons by Church members in all meetings and by General Authorities of the Church in semiannual conferences.

Not only is belief in the First Vision of primary importance to Mormonism, but the story of the vision has what might be termed a number of secondary, although highly important, utilitarian functions. Joseph Smith's original purpose in writing the story was apparently to help demonstrate his reasons for not joining any church. In our time, however, it is used by Church leaders and teachers to demonstrate for believers many other aspects of the Mormon faith: the idea that God actually hears and answers prayers; the concept that there is a personal devil who tries to stop the progress of truth; and, perhaps most fundamental of all, the Mormon doctrine that the divine Godhead are actually separate, distinct, physical personages, as opposed to the Trinitarian concept within traditional Christianity.

The person who would understand the history of any institution must be concerned not only with chronology but also with an understanding of what the people in that institution were thinking, what they were being taught, and how these ideas compare with present-day thought. In connection with the story of the vision, then, it is important to ask certain questions: When was it first told? When was it first published? Did it have the significant place in early Mormon thought that it has today? If not, when did it begin to take on its present significance in the writings and teachings of the Church? Some thoughts on these questions might open the door to a better understanding of Mormon history and also demonstrate by example the gradually changing pattern of thought which one would expect to find in any church.

Public Knowledge of the Story

According to Joseph Smith, he told the story of the vision immediately after it happened in the early spring of 1820. As a result, he said, he received immediate criticism in the community. There is little, if any, evidence, however, that by the early 1830s Joseph Smith was telling the story in public. At least, if he was telling it, no one seemed to consider it important enough to record it *at the time,* and no one was criticizing him for it. Not even in his own history did Joseph Smith mention being criticized in this period for telling the story of the First Vision. The interest, rather, was in the Book of Mormon and the various angelic visitations connected with its origin.

The fact that none of the available contemporary writings about Joseph Smith in the 1830s, none of the publications of the Church in that decade, and no contemporary journal or correspondence yet discovered mentions the story of the First Vision is convincing evidence that at best it received only limited circulation in those early days. In February 1830, for example, a farmer who lived about fifty miles from Palmyra, New York, wrote a letter describing the religious fervor in western New York and particularly the coming forth of the Book of Mormon. No mention was made, however, of the idea that Joseph Smith had beheld Deity.[1] The earliest anti-Mormon literature attacked the Book of Mormon and the character of Joseph Smith but never mentioned the First Vision. Alexander Campbell, who had some reason to be especially bitter against the Mormons because of the conversion of Sidney Rigdon in 1830, published one of the first scathing denunciations of Joseph Smith in 1832. It was entitled *Delusions: An Analysis of the Book of Mormon*. It contained no mention of the First Vision. In 1834, E. D. Howe published *Mormonism Unvailed* [sic], which contained considerable damaging material against Joseph Smith, including letters of the Mormon apostate Ezra Booth, but again no mention of the First Vision. In 1839, John Corrill, another Mormon apostate, published a history of the Mormons, but he made no reference at all to Joseph Smith's claim to having conversed with the members of the Godhead. In 1842, J. B. Turner published *Mormonism in All Ages*, which included one of the bitterest denunciations of the Mormon prophet yet printed, but even at this late date, no mention was made of the First Vision.[2] Apparently not until 1843, when the *New York Spectator* printed a reporter's account of an interview with Joseph Smith, did a non-Mormon source publish any reference to the story of the First Vision.[3] In 1844, I. Daniel Rupp published *An Original History of the Religious Denominations at Present Existing in the United States*, and this work contained an account of the vision provided by Joseph Smith himself. After this time, non-Mormon sources began to refer to the story. It seems probable, however, that as far as non-Mormons were concerned, there was little, if any, awareness of it in the 1830s. The popular image of Mormon belief centered on such things as the Book of Mormon, the missionary zeal, and the concept of Zion in Missouri.

As far as Mormon literature is concerned, there was apparently no reference to Joseph Smith's First Vision in any published material in the 1830s. Joseph Smith's history, which began in 1838, was not published until it ran serially in the *Times and Seasons* in 1842. The famous "Wentworth Letter," which contained a much less detailed account of the vision, appeared March 1, 1842, in the same periodical. Introductory material to the Book of Mormon, as well as publicity about it, told of Joseph Smith's obtaining the gold plates and of angelic visitations, but nothing was printed that remotely suggested earlier visitations. In 1833 the Church published the *Book of Commandments*, forerunner to the present Doctrine and Covenants, and again no reference was made to Joseph's First Vision, although several references were made to the Book of Mormon and the circumstances of its origin. The first regular periodical to be published by the Church was the *Evening and Morning Star*, but its pages reveal no effort to tell the story of the First Vision to its readers. Nor do the pages of the *Latter Day Saints' Messenger and Advocate*, printed in Kirtland, Ohio, from October 1834 to September 1836. In this newspaper, Oliver Cowdery, who was second only to Joseph Smith in the early organization of the Church, published a series of letters dealing with the origin of the Church. These letters were written with the approval of Joseph Smith, but they contained no mention of any vision prior to those connected with the Book of Mormon. In 1835 the Doctrine and Covenants was printed at Kirtland, Ohio, and its preface declared that it contained "the leading items of religion which we have professed to believe." Included in the book were the "Lectures on Faith," a series of seven lectures which had been prepared for the School of the Prophets in Kirtland in 1834–35. It is interesting to note that, in demonstrating the doctrine that the Godhead consists of two separate personages, no mention was made of Joseph Smith having seen them, nor was any reference made to the First Vision in any part of the publication.[4] The *Times and Seasons* began publication in 1839, but, as indicated above, the story of the vision was not told in its pages until 1842. From all this, it would appear that the general Church membership did not receive information about the First Vision until the 1840s and that the story certainly did not hold the prominent place in Mormon thought that it does today.

Importance in Early Missionary Work

As far as missionary work is concerned, it is evident that here too the story of the First Vision had little, if any, importance in the 1830s. The best missionary tool in that day was apparently the Book of Mormon, and most early converts came into the Church as a result either of reading the book or of hearing the "testimony" of others who declared their personal knowledge of its authenticity. Such important early converts as Parley P. Pratt, Sidney Rigdon, Brigham Young, and Heber C. Kimball all joined because of their conversion through the Book of Mormon, and none of their early records or writings seem to indicate that an understanding or knowledge of the First Vision was in any way a part of their conversion. John Corrill tells of his first contact with the Mormons through Parley P. Pratt, Oliver Cowdery, Peter Whitmer, and Ziba Peterson. These were the famous missionaries to the "Lamanites" of 1830. Their message concerned the Book of Mormon, but Corrill reported nothing of having heard of a prior vision.[5] When Parley P. Pratt converted John Taylor in 1836, the story he told him was of the angelic visitations connected with the Book of Mormon, of the priesthood restoration, and of the organization of the Church. There is no evidence that anything was said of the First Vision. Rather, Taylor was converted on the basis of the Book of Mormon and the fact that Mormonism taught certain principles which he had already concluded were essential and which he had been waiting to hear someone preach.[6] The first important missionary pamphlet of the Church was the *Voice of Warning*, published in 1837 by Parley P. Pratt. The book contains long sections on items important to missionaries of the 1830s, such as fulfillment of prophecy, the Book of Mormon, external evidence of the book's authenticity, the Resurrection, and the nature of revelation, but nothing, again, on the First Vision. It seems evident that, at least in the 1830s, it was not considered necessary for prospective converts to Mormonism to know the story. It is assumed, of course, that if they believed in the authenticity of the Book of Mormon, as well as the other claims of Joseph Smith to divine authority and revelation, the story of the First Vision would not have been difficult for them to believe once they heard it.

To summarize what has been said so far, it is apparent that the story of Joseph Smith's First Vision was not given general circulation in the 1830s. Neither Mormon nor non-Mormon publications made reference to it, and it is evident that the general membership of the Church knew little, if anything, about it. Belief in the story certainly was not a prerequisite for conversion, and it is obvious that the story was not being used for the purpose of illustrating other points of doctrine. In this respect, at least, Mormon thought of the 1830s was different from Mormon thought of later years.

A possible explanation for the fact that the story of the vision was not generally known in the 1830s is sometimes seen in Joseph Smith's conviction that experiences such as these should be kept from the general public because of their extremely sacred nature. It is noted by some that in 1838 he declared that his basic reason for telling it even then, eighteen years after it happened, was in response to "reports which have been put in circulation by evil-disposed and designing persons" who had distorted the facts.[7] Furthermore, the young prophet said that he had been severely rebuffed the first time he told the story in 1820; and since it represented one of his most profound spiritual experiences, he could well have decided to circulate it only privately until he could feel certain that in relating it he would not again receive the general ridicule of friends.

Perhaps the closest one may come to seeing a contemporary diarist's account of the story is in the journal of Alexander Neibaur, which is located in the LDS Church Historian's Office. Hugh Nibley, grandson of Neibaur, makes the following commentary:

> The writer's great-grandfather, a Jew, one day after he had given Joseph Smith a lesson in German and Hebrew asked him about certain particulars of the first vision. In reply he was told some remarkable things, which he wrote down in his journal that very day. But in the ensuing forty years of his life... Brother Neibaur seems never once to have referred to the wonderful things the Prophet told him—it was quite by accident that the writer discovered them in his journal. Why was the talkative old man so close-lipped on the one thing that could have made him famous? Because it was a sacred and privileged communication; it was never published to the world and never should be.[8]

Nibley takes the point of view that the story of the vision was not told in those early years because of its sacred nature. With reference to Neibaur's journal, however, it must be observed that Neibaur did not become associated with Joseph Smith until the Nauvoo period, in the 1840s, and that the experience referred to did not take place until well after other accounts of the vision, including Joseph Smith's, had been written and published.

New Evidence of Limited Circulation in the 1830s

In spite of the foregoing discussion, there is some interesting evidence to suggest the possibility that the story of Joseph Smith's First Vision was known, probably on a limited basis, during the formative decade of Church history. One of the most significant documents of that period yet discovered was brought to light in 1965 by Paul R. Cheesman, a graduate student at Brigham Young University. This discovery is a handwritten manuscript apparently composed about 1833 and either written or dictated by Joseph Smith. It contains an account of the early experiences of the Mormon prophet and includes the story of the First Vision. While the story varies in some details from the version presently accepted, enough is intact to indicate that at least as early as 1833 Joseph Smith contemplated writing and perhaps publishing it. The manuscript has apparently lain in the LDS Church Historian's Office for many years, yet few, if any, who saw it realized its profound historical significance. The mere existence of the manuscript, of course, does nothing to either prove or disprove the authenticity of the story, but it demonstrates the historical fact that in the early 1830s the story of the vision was beginning to find place in the formulation of Mormon thought.[9] It might be noted that Fawn Brodie suggests that the story of Joseph Smith's First Vision was something which he invented sometime after 1834.[10] If Cheesman's discovery is authentic, Brodie's argument will have to be revised.

Another document of almost equal importance has recently been brought to light by a member of the staff at the Church Historian's Office.[11] It is located in the back of Book A-1 of the handwritten manuscript of the *History of the Church* (commonly referred to as the "Manuscript History"). The writing of the "Manuscript History" was personally supervised by Joseph Smith, beginning in 1838, although it is not known who actually transcribed each part of the work. Under the date of November 9, 1835, the story is told of a man visiting Joseph Smith calling himself Joshua, the Jewish minister. The conversation naturally turned to religion, and it is recorded that the Mormon prophet told his guest "the circumstances connected with the coming forth of the Book of Mormon, as recorded in the former part of this history."[12] From reading the

"Manuscript History," therefore, as well as the printed *History of the Church*, one would get the impression that at this time Joseph Smith related only the Book of Mormon story. In the back of the book, however, is a most curious and revealing document. It is curious in several ways. First, it was apparently written in 1835 by someone other than Joseph Smith, for it records the day-to-day events in the Prophet's life in the *third person*, as if it were a scribe recording them as he observed them. Next, it is not written in the finished style that characterizes the "Manuscript History," indicating that it was not intended for publication without some revision. Finally, in order to read the document, one must turn the book upside down, which suggests that the manuscript certainly was not intended to be part of the finished history. In short, it is almost certain that the document in the back of the book comprises the original notes from which the "Manuscript History" was later compiled and that it is actually a daily account of Joseph Smith's activities in 1835, as recorded by a scribe. The importance of the manuscript here lies in the fact that the scribe wrote down what Joseph Smith said to his visitor, and he began not by telling the story of the discovery of the Book of Mormon but with an account of the First Vision. Again, the details of the story vary somewhat from the accepted version, but the manuscript, if authentic, at least demonstrates that by 1835 the story had been told to someone.

The only additional evidence that Joseph Smith's story was being circulated in the 1830s is found in reminiscences of a few people who were close to Joseph Smith in that decade. While reminiscences are obviously open to question—for it is easy for anyone, after many years, to read back into his own history things which he accepts at the time of the telling—some of them at least sound convincing enough to suggest that the story might have been circulating on a limited basis. In 1893,

Edward Stevenson published his reminiscences. He first saw Joseph Smith in 1834, and, according to Stevenson,

> In that same year, 1834, in the midst of many large congregations the Prophet testified with great power concerning the visit of the Father and the Son, and the conversation he had with them. Never before did I feel such power as was manifested on these occasions....
>
> Although a mere widow's son, I felt proud and blessed of God, when he honored us by coming under our roof and partaking of our hospitality.... We were proud, indeed, to entertain one who had conversed with the Father and the Son, and been under the tuition of an angel from heaven.[13]

Lorenzo Snow heard Joseph Smith for the first time when he was seventeen years old. Years later, he recalled the experience in these words:

> As I looked upon him and listened, I thought to myself that a man bearing such a wonderful testimony as he did, and having such a countenance as he possessed, could hardly be a false prophet. He certainly could not have been deceived, it seemed to me, and if he was a deceiver, he was deceiving the people knowingly; for when he testified that he had had a conversation with Jesus the Son of God, and talked with Him personally, as Moses talked with God upon Mount Sinai, and that he also heard the voice of the Father, he was telling something that he either knew to be false or to be positively true.[14]

If this statement is accurate, it means that Joseph Smith was telling the important story in 1831. When reading the statement in context, however, it will be immediately noted that Snow did not say that he heard Joseph tell the actual story—only that he heard him testify that he had conversed with the Son and heard the voice of the Father. Other reminiscences may be found which would indicate that the story was being told in the 1830s, but at this point the extent of the telling is not clear, and the weight of evidence would suggest that it was not a matter of common knowledge, even among Church members, in the earliest years of Mormon history.

The Story Becomes Scripture

The question for historical consideration, then, is when and how the story of Joseph Smith assumed its present importance, not only as a test of faith for the Mormons but also as a tool for illustrating and supporting other Church doctrines.

It seems apparent that after Joseph Smith decided to write the story in 1838, the way was clear for its use as a missionary tool. It is not known, of course, how generally the membership of the Church knew of the story by the end of the decade, but in the year 1840, Orson Pratt published in England a missionary tract entitled *Interesting Account of Several Remarkable Visions and of the Late Discovery of Ancient American Records*. This early pamphlet contained a detailed account of the First Vision which elaborated upon several details that Joseph Smith touched on only briefly. Joseph Smith's account was published in 1842. In the same year, Orson Hyde published in Germany a pamphlet entitled *A Cry from the Wilderness, a Voice from the Dust of the Earth*. This also contained an elaborate account of the vision. It is evident then that in the early 1840s the story of Joseph Smith's First Vision took its place alongside the story of the Book of Mormon as a missionary message, and it is possible that Joseph Smith's decision to write it in 1838 was a sort of go-ahead for this action.

By the 1850s, the story of the vision had become an important part of Church literature. In 1851 it appeared in the first edition of the Pearl of Great Price, published in England by Franklin D. Richards. This volume was accepted as one of the standard works of the Mormon Church in 1880.[15] By this time, obviously, the story had become well known both to members and non-members alike and was being used as a basic missionary tool.

Utilitarian Functions

A more difficult question to answer concerns the various utilitarian functions of the story. Present-day Mormons use it to demonstrate such things as the factual existence of Satan, the doctrine that God can hear and answer prayers, and especially the concept of God and Christ as distinct and separate physical beings. It is clear, of course, that Joseph Smith taught these doctrines, but it is of special interest to note that, as far as any recorded material reveals, he never used the story of his vision specifically to illustrate them.

When did Church members begin to make such use of the story? Apparently, the early teachers of the Church relied upon scriptural evidence alone to demonstrate the Mormon doctrine of God, and not until well into the Utah period did they begin to use Joseph Smith's story to illustrate it. One of the earliest recorded sermons to make this use of the story was given by George Q. Cannon on October 7, 1883. Said President Cannon,

> Joseph Smith, inspired of God, came forth and declared that God lived. Ages had passed and no one had beheld Him. The fact that he existed was like a dim tradition in the minds of the people. The fact that Jesus lived was only supposed to be the case because eighteen hundred years before men had seen him.... The character of God—whether He was a personal being, whether His center was nowhere, and His circumference everywhere, were matters of speculation. No one had seen him. No one had seen any one who had seen an angel.... Is it a wonder that men were confused? that there was such a variety of opinion respecting the character and being

of God? . . . Brother Joseph, as I said, startled the world. It stood aghast at the statement which he made, and the testimony which he bore. He declared that he had seen God. He declared that he had seen Jesus Christ.

After that revelation faith began to grow up in men's minds and hearts. Speculation concerning the being of God ceased among those who received the testimony of Joseph Smith. He testified that God was a being of body, that He had a body, that man was in his likeness, that Jesus was the exact counterpart of the Father, and that the Father and Jesus were two distinct personages, as distinct as an earthly father and an earthly son.[16]

There were probably earlier sermons or writings that used the story of the First Vision to demonstrate the Mormon doctrine of God. Evidence indicates, however, that they were rare in these early days and that only gradually did this use of the story find place in the traditions of the Church. Suffice it to say that by the turn of the century, the device was regularly used. James E. Talmage, for example, in his *Articles of Faith*, used the story to illustrate the Godhead doctrine, and Joseph Fielding Smith, in his *Essentials in Church History*, makes a major point of this doctrinal contribution. In 1961 the official missionary plan of the Church required all missionaries to use the story in their first lesson as part of the dialogue designed to prove that the Father and the Son are distinct personages and that they have tangible bodies.

Comparison of the Accounts

As the story of Joseph Smith's vision was told and retold, both by him and other persons, there were naturally some variations in detail. The account written about 1833 told of his youthful anxiety over the "welfare of my immortal soul" and over his sins as well as the sins of the world. Therefore, he declared,

> I cried unto the Lord for mercy for there was none else to whom I could go and to obtain mercy and the Lord heard my cry in the wilderness and while in the attitude of calling upon the Lord in the 16th [see footnote] year of my age a piller of light above the brightness of the sun at noon day came down from above and rested upon me and I was filled with the Spirit of God and the Lord opened the heavens upon me and I saw the Lord and he spake unto me saying Joseph my son Thy Sins are forgiven thee, go thy way walk in my Statutes and keep my commandments behold I am the Lord of glory I was crucifyed for the world.[17]

In this story, only one personage was mentioned, and this was obviously the Son, for he spoke of having been crucified. If Edward Stevenson's account is correct, however, he heard Joseph Smith say in 1834 that he had seen both the Father and the Son.

In 1835, Joseph Smith's scribe heard him tell the story to a visitor. As recalled and recorded by the scribe, the Mormon leader's words were "nearly as follows":

> Being wrought up in my mind respecting the subject of Religion, and looking at the different systems taught the children of men, I knew not who was right or who was wrong but considered it of the first importance to me that I should be right in matters of so much moment, matter involving eternal consequences. Being thus perplexed in mind I retired to the silent grove and there bowed down before the Lord, under a realising sense (if the Bible be true) ask and you shall receive, knock and it shall be opened, seek and you shall find, and again, if any man lack wisdom, let of God [sic], who giveth to all men liberally & upbraideth not. Information was what I most desired, at this time and with a fixed determination to obtain it. I called on the Lord for the first time in the place above stated, or in other words, I made a fruitless attempt to pray My tongue seemed to be swollen in my mouth, so that I could not utter, I heard a noise behind me like some one walking towards me,

> I strove again to pray, but could not; the noise of walking seemed to draw nearer; I sprang upon my feet and looked around. but I saw no person, or thing that was calculated to produce the noise of walking. I kneeled again, my mouth was opened and my tongue loosed; I called on the Lord in mighty prayer. A pillar of fire appeared above my head; which presently rested down upon me, and filled me with unspeakable joy. A personage appeared in the midst of this pillar of flame, which was spread all around and yet nothing consumed. Another personage soon appeared like unto the first: he said unto me thy sins are forgiven thee. He testified also unto me that Jesus Christ is the son of God. I saw many angels in this vision.[18]

In this account, Joseph emphasized the difficulty he had in uttering his first prayer, and the "noise of walking" seems to suggest the evil opposition which became an essential element in the official version of the story. Furthermore, he told of having seen two persons, although one preceded the other. The two persons looked alike, and the second assured him that his sins had been forgiven. The most unusual statement, however, is Joseph's declaration that he saw many angels in this vision.

When Joseph Smith finally wrote, or dictated, the "Manuscript History" in 1838, he told of his great uneasiness in the midst of the religious confusion of 1820 and his quest to determine which of the churches was right. After reading James 1:5, he retired to the woods and began to pray. In this account he told of a force of darkness which tried to stop him from proceeding, then the appearance in a pillar of light of two personages. When the light appeared, the force of darkness left. One of the personages said to Joseph, "This is My Beloved Son. Hear Him!" The crux of the message from the Son was that he should join none of the churches of the time, for all of them were wrong. "When I came to myself," he said, "I found myself lying on my back looking up into Heaven."[19]

The story as told in Joseph Smith's published history of 1842 and in the Pearl of Great Price does not differ appreciably from his manuscript history.

The account published by Orson Pratt in 1840 greatly amplifies upon the story as told by Joseph Smith.[20] He describes in more detail, for example, the problems running through young Joseph's mind when he was "somewhere about fourteen or fifteen years old." The appearance of the light is described in more vivid detail, and the whole account takes on a more dramatic air than any recorded story told by Joseph himself. Describing the light, for example, Pratt wrote,

> As it drew nearer, it increased in brightness, and magnitude, so that, by the time that it reached the tops of the trees, the whole wilderness, for some distance around, was illuminated in a most glorious and brilliant manner. He expected to have seen the leaves and boughs of the trees consumed, as soon as the light came in contact with them; but, perceiving that it did not produce that effect, he was encouraged with the hopes of being able to endure its presence. It continued descending, slowly, until it rested upon the earth, and he was enveloped in the midst of it. When it first came upon him, it produced a peculiar sensation throughout his whole system; and, immediately, his mind was caught away, from the natural objects with which he was surrounded; and he was enwrapped in a heavenly vision and saw two glorious personages.[21]

According to this account, the young man was informed that his sins were forgiven and that the "fullness of the gospel" would be made known to him in the future. Neither of these statements is contained in the Pearl of Great Price account, but the first one is included in both the 1833 and 1835 manuscripts.

The Wentworth Letter, published in 1842, and Rupp's history, published in 1844, contained identical but very short accounts of the vision. The force of opposition was not mentioned, and the description of the visitation was shorter than in Joseph's earlier account. He told, however, of seeing two personages while he was "enwrapped in a heavenly vision" and said that "they" told him that all religious denominations believed incorrect doctrines. The idea that the "fullness of the gospel" should be given to him in the future was recorded here, in agreement with Orson Pratt's account.

Orson Hyde's account, published in 1842, is similar to the stories told by Joseph Smith and Orson Pratt. The two personages were not defined nor quoted directly, but they were said to exactly resemble each other in their features, and the promise to reveal the fullness of the gospel was mentioned.

The several variations in these and other accounts would seem to suggest that, in relating his story to various individuals at various times, Joseph Smith emphasized different aspects of it and that his listeners were each impressed with different things. This, of course, is to be expected, for the same thing happens in the retelling of any story. The only way to keep it from changing is to write it only once and then insist that it be read exactly that way each time it is to be repeated. Such an effort at censorship would obviously be unrealistic. Joseph apparently told his story several times before he released it for publication. People who heard it were obviously impressed with different details and perhaps even embellished it a little with their own literary devices as they retold or recorded it. Joseph himself wrote at least two different accounts for publication. These were printed the same year in the same periodical yet differed somewhat in their emphasis.

In this connection, four accounts are especially interesting, for they each suggest that, although two personages appeared in the vision, one preceded the other. The 1835 story is apparently the earliest that makes this distinction. In 1843 Joseph Smith told the story to a non-Mormon editor, who later quoted him in an article in the *New York Spectator*. As quoted by the editor, Joseph Smith said,

> While thinking of this matter, I opened the New Testament promiscuously on these words, in James, "Ask of the Lord who giveth to all men liberally and upbraideth not." I just determined I'd ask Him. I immediately went out into the woods where my father had a clearing, and I kneeled down, and prayed, saying, "O Lord, what church shall I join?" Directly I saw a light, and then a glorious personage in the light, and then another personage, and the first person said to the second, "Behold my Beloved Son, hear Him." I then addressed this second person, saying, "O Lord, what church shall I join?" He replied, "Do not join any of them, they are all corrupt." The vision then vanished.[22]

The third contemporary account to repeat the idea that one personage preceded the other is the diary of Alexander Neibaur. Writing on May 24, 1844, Neibaur said that Joseph Smith had told him that day of his early quest for religion. In Neibaur's words, Joseph Smith "went into the woods to pray, kneels himself down ... saw a fire toward heaven come nearer and nearer; saw a personage in the fire; light complexion, blue eyes, a piece of white cloth drawn over his shoulders, his right arm bear [sic]; after a while another person came to the side of the first."[23] A fourth reference to this idea is seen in the diary of Charles L. Walker on February 2, 1893. Walker wrote of hearing John Alger declare in "Fast meeting" that he had heard Joseph Smith relate the story of the vision, saying "that God touched his eyes with his finger and said, 'Joseph this is my beloved Son, hear him.' As soon as the Lord had touched his eyes with his finger he immediately saw the Saviour."[24] The latter, of course, is only reminiscence, but together with the earlier narratives it demonstrates at least that a few people had this concept of the vision as it gradually took its place among the fundamental teachings of the Church. Other variations may be noted in all the foregoing documents.

Additional accounts by people close to the Mormon prophet would undoubtedly reveal similar variations and amplifications. Through it all, however, there seems to be no deviation from Joseph Smith's apparent intent in telling the story in the first place: to demonstrate that he had had a visitation from Deity and that he was told that the religions of his day were wrong. The account published in the Pearl of Great Price in 1851 has become the standard account and is accepted by the Mormons as scripture.

Summary

This paper has been an attempt to trace the significance of the story of Joseph Smith's First Vision in the development of Mormon thought. It seems apparent that if Joseph Smith told the story to friends and neighbors in 1820, he stopped telling it widely by 1830. At the least, it can be demonstrated that the public image of Joseph Smith and his spiritual experiences did not include the story of the First Vision. Throughout most of the 1830s, the story was not circulated in either Church periodicals or missionary literature. In about 1833, however, Joseph Smith apparently made a preliminary attempt to write the story, but this account was never published. In 1835 he was willing to tell the story to a visitor. There is further evidence, based on reminiscences, to suggest that the story was known on a limited basis in the 1830s, but it is clear that it was not widely circulated. Non-Mormon accounts of the rise of the Church written in the 1830s made no mention of the story of the vision. It is apparent, furthermore, that belief in the vision was not essential for conversion to the Church, for there is no evidence that the story was told to prospective converts of the early 1830s.

In 1838, however, Joseph Smith decided to write the story for publication, and within a few years it had begun to achieve wide circulation within the Church. It was published first in 1840 by Orson Pratt as a missionary tool, and two of Joseph Smith's own versions were published in 1842. Since then, both Mormon and non-Mormon writers have made reference to it when dealing with the history of the Church. The story was accepted as scripture by the Mormons in 1880.

When it was first told, the story of the vision was used primarily to demonstrate the concept that Joseph Smith had been visited by Deity and that he had been told that all contemporary churches were wrong. After Joseph's death, however, members of the Church gradually began to appreciate its usefulness for other purposes. By the 1880s, if not earlier, it was being used in sermons as support for the Mormon doctrine of God, although Joseph Smith himself never used the story for that purpose.

In conclusion, this essay perhaps demonstrates the need for new approaches to Mormon history by sympathetic Mormon historians. Can we fully understand our heritage without understanding the gradual development of ideas, and the use of those ideas, in our history? It has been demonstrated that an understanding of the story of Joseph Smith's vision dawned only gradually upon the membership of the Church during his lifetime, and that new and important uses were made of the story after his death. In what other respects has the Mormon mind been modified since the 1830s? What forces and events have led Church leaders to place special emphasis on special ideas in given periods of time? What new ideas have become part of the Mormon tradition since the exodus from Nauvoo, or even in the twentieth century; what old ideas have been submerged, if not forgotten; and what ideas have remained constant through the years? In short, the writing of Mormon history has only begun. As in the case of other institutions and movements, there is still room in Mormonism for fresh historical scholarship—not necessarily for the apologist, although he will always be necessary and will always make an important contribution, and certainly not for the debunker. What is needed, simply, is the sympathetic historian who can approach his tradition with scholarship as well as faith and who will make fresh appraisal of the development of the Mormon mind.

Notes

1. The letter was reproduced in William Mulder and A. Russell Mortensen, eds., *Among the Mormons* (New York: Knopf, 1958), 28.

2. It is probable that Professor Turner had not seen Joseph Smith's written account of the vision when he was preparing his book, for both were published the same year. Turner shows familiarity with the earlier publications of Church history and would certainly have included the history published in the *Times and Seasons* if he had seen it. Orson Pratt's account, published in 1840, may also have escaped him as he prepared his manuscript, for Pratt's work was published in England for circulation there.

3. A quotation from the article appears later in this study.

4. See N. B. Lundwall, comp., *A Compilation Containing the Lectures on Faith* (Salt Lake City: Bookcraft, n.d.). It is interesting to observe—in connection with the general question of how certain precise teachings of the Church in the 1830s differed from those of today—that in the *Lectures on Faith*, the Father is defined as a "personage of glory and power," the Son is defined as a "personage of tabernacle," and the Holy Spirit is defined as the mind of the Father and the Son (see Lecture Fifth). As far as the vision is concerned, the only possible allusion to it is in section 1 of the Doctrine and Covenants, which reads, "Wherefore I the Lord, knowing the calamity which should come upon the inhabitants of the earth, called upon my servant Joseph Smith, Jr. and spake unto him from heaven, and gave him commandments; and also gave commandments to others, that they should proclaim these things unto the world." The same

statement is in the 1833 *Book of Commandments*, but most would agree that it hardly constitutes a direct reference to the First Vision.

5. John Corrill, *A Brief History of the Church of Christ of Latter Day Saints* (St. Louis: printed by author, 1839), 1.

6. *Autobiography of Parley P. Pratt* (Salt Lake City: Deseret Book, 1961), 136–51.

7. *History of the Church of Jesus Christ of Latter-day Saints*, ed. B. H. Roberts, 2nd ed. rev. (Salt Lake City: Deseret Book, 1946), 1:1; Paul R. Cheesman, "An Analysis of the Accounts Relating Joseph Smith's Early Visions" (master's thesis, Brigham Young University, 1965), 4–7.

8. Hugh Nibley, "Censoring Joseph Smith's Story," *Improvement Era*, July 1961, 522.

9. For a transcription of the entire document, see Cheesman, "An Analysis of the Accounts," appendix D.

10. Fawn M. Brodie, *No Man Knows My History* (New York: Knopf, 1946), 25.

11. The document was brought to the attention of this writer in June 1966, and he had the opportunity to examine it. Since the document is bound with the "Manuscript History," it is unusual that someone had not found it earlier and recognized its significance. It seems apparent, however, that, as in the case of Cheesman's document, few, if any, people had been aware of it. The fact that the use of the "Manuscript History" is highly restricted, due to its extremely high value, and that any research done in it is done through a microfilm copy could help account for the fact that researchers generally had not discovered what was in the back of the book.

12. Compare with Roberts's edition, *History of the Church*, 2:304.

13. Edward Stevenson, *Reminiscences of Joseph, the Prophet* (Salt Lake City, 1893), 4–5.

14. Quoted in LeRoi C. Snow, "How Lorenzo Snow Found God," *Improvement Era*, February 1937, 83.

15. T. Edgar Lyon, *Introduction to the Doctrine and Covenants and the Pearl of Great Price* (Salt Lake City: LDS Department of Education, 1955), 209; James R. Clark, *The Story of the Pearl of Great Price* (Salt Lake City: Bookcraft, 1955), 186–221.

16. George Q. Cannon, in *Journal of Discourses*, (London: Latter-day Saints' Book Depot, 1854–56), 24:340–41.

17. As transcribed in Cheesman, "An Analysis of the Accounts," 129. Note that Mr. Cheesman interpreted the handwriting in the original manuscript as saying that this event took place in the sixteenth year of Joseph's age. In private conversation, Mr. Cheesman indicated that the original document was actually not clear—the number could have been either sixteen or fourteen, but sixteen appeared to be more likely. In Joseph Smith's 1838 account, he said it happened in the fifteenth year of his age. Orson Pratt and Orson Hyde both said that it happened when Joseph was "somewhere about fourteen or fifteen years old." The Wentworth letter said "when about fourteen years of age." Joseph's brother, William Smith, wrote that the Smith family's concern with the prevailing religions of the day came when Joseph was about seventeen. See William Smith, *William Smith on Mormonism* (Lamoni, IA: Herald Steam Book, 1883). William, however, did not record the story of the First Vision. He related the religious revival which he ascribed to the discovery of the Book of Mormon. Joseph Smith's 1838 account is the only contemporary account to date the vision in a definite manner as occurring in the spring of 1820.

18. "Documentary History of the Church" (MS), located in LDS Church Historian's Office. From a separate section in the back of Book A-1, 120–21.

19. For a transcribed copy of the handwritten manuscript, see Cheesman, "An Analysis of the Accounts," appendix A.

20. For a copy of the Pratt story, see Cheesman, "An Analysis of the Accounts," appendix C.

21. Orson Pratt, *An Interesting Account of Several Remarkable Visions, and of the Late Discovery of Ancient American Records* (Edinburgh: Ballantyne and Hughes, 1840), 5.

22. *New York Spectator*, September 23, 1843, as quoted in Preston Nibley, *Joseph Smith the Prophet* (Salt Lake City: Deseret News, 1946), 31.

23. As quoted in Cheesman, "An Analysis of the Accounts," 29.

24. Diary of Charles L. Walker, as quoted in Cheesman, "An Analysis of the Accounts," 30.

Evaluating Three Arguments Against Joseph Smith's First Vision

Steven C. Harper

There are numerous books and many more websites that work to undermine faith in Joseph Smith's First Vision, but historically there have been just three main arguments against it that are repeated by others in print or on the web. The minister to whom Joseph reported the event announced that there were no such things these days. More than a century later, Fawn Brodie wrote, with literary grace to mask her historical deficiencies, that Joseph concocted the vision years after he said it happened. Then, a generation later, Wesley Walters charged Joseph with inventing revivalism when a lack of historical evidence proved that there was none, and therefore there must have been no subsequent vision. So by now it has become a foregone conclusion for some that there are no such things as visions and that Joseph failed to mention his experience for years and then gave conflicting accounts that didn't match historical facts.[1]

Each of the three arguments begins with the premise that the vision simply could not have happened as Joseph described it. Philosophers describe that kind of premise as *a priori*, a Latin term that describes knowledge that is, essentially, assumed. In other words, *a priori* knowledge does not rely on experience for verification. It is based on definitions, widely shared beliefs, and reason. Knowledge derived from experience is *a posteriori*. Joseph testified that he experienced a divine revelation and therefore knows that visions can and do happen. The epistemology in Joseph's First Vision accounts is *a posteriori*. The epistemology of Joseph's vision critics is *a priori*. They know that what Joseph said happened could not have happened because all reasonable people know that such things do not happen.

The Methodist Minister

"Some few days after I had this vision," Joseph reported, "I happened to be in company with one of the Methodist preachers" that had contributed to the religious fervor. "I took occasion to give him an account of the vision," Joseph said, continuing, "I was greatly surprised at his behavior; he treated my communication not only lightly, but with great contempt, saying it was all of the devil, that there were no such things as visions or revelations in these days; that all such things had ceased with the apostles, and that there would never be any more of them" (Joseph Smith—History 1:21). The preacher's premises, all *a priori*, were the following:

- Joseph's story was of the devil.
- There were no such things as revelations in what Dickens called "the age of railways."
- Visions or revelations ceased with the Apostles.

- There would never be any more visions or revelations.

No doubt this good fellow was sincere in each of these beliefs and was striving as best he knew to prevent Joseph from becoming prey to fanaticism. But he did not know from experience the validity of any of the four premises he set forth as positive facts. All he knew *a posteriori* is that he had not had a vision or a revelation. On what basis, then, could this minister evaluate Joseph's claims and make such sweeping statements?

An answer to that question lies in understanding the pressures on a Methodist minister in Joseph's area in 1820. Joseph did not name the minister to whom he reported the vision. It's not clear whether it was the Reverend George Lane, whom Joseph's brother William and Oliver Cowdery credited with awakening Joseph spiritually. Joseph "could have had contact with Reverend Lane at a number of points" during his ministry in Joseph's district between 1819 and the early 1820s, but he was always visiting the area from his home in Pennsylvania.[2] There were also local Methodist ministers to whom Joseph may have reported his experience. All of them were conscious that Methodism was tending away from the kind of spiritual experiences Joseph described and toward what they viewed as a more respectable, reasonable religion. John Wesley, the founder of Methodism, had worried that Methodists would multiply exponentially in number only to become "a dead sect, having the form of religion without the power."[3] And Methodism indeed grew abundantly because it took the claims of people like Joseph so seriously. Its preachers encouraged personal conversions that included intimate experiences with God, including visions and revelations. But then, as Wesley had worried, Methodism became less welcoming to such manifestations.[4] Just as Joseph was coming of age, Methodism was becoming embarrassed by what respectable people regarded as its excesses. Methodism had risen to meet the needs of the many people who could not find a church that took their spiritual experiences seriously. But with its phenomenal growth came a shift from the margin to the mainstream.

Joseph was likely naive about that shift, which is easier to see historically than it was at the time. Probably all Joseph knew is that he had caught a spark of Methodism and wanted to feel the same spiritual power as the folks he saw and heard at the meetings. He finally experienced that power in the woods, as so many Methodist converts, encouraged by their preachers, appeared to have done before him. So it was shocking to him when the minister reacted against what Joseph assumed would be welcome news.

As for the minister, he may have heard messages in Joseph's story in ways that led him to respond negatively, especially if Joseph told him the part about learning that religious professors spoke well of God but denied his power. No Methodist minister wanted to hear that their founder's fear had been realized. Yet by 1820, many of them were concerned about what had for nearly two hundred years been termed *enthusiasm*, "derived from Greek *en theos*, meaning to be filled with or inspired by a deity."[5] To be accused of enthusiasm in Joseph Smith's world was not a compliment. It meant that one was perceived as mentally unstable and irrational. Methodists had for several generations tried to walk a fine line that valued authentic spiritual experience yet stopped well short of enthusiasm. It seems likely that young Joseph was not attuned to the sophisticated difference that had been worked out by Methodist theologians. He reported to the minister what he thought would be a highly valued experience that seemed to resemble the experiences of other sincere Christians. But his experience was received as an embarrassing example of enthusiasm and was thus condemned.

Fawn Brodie

Fawn Brodie largely shaped the skeptical interpretations of Joseph's First Vision. She first articulated major criticisms that others have since adopted and published and that circulate widely today. In the first edition of her biography of Joseph, published in 1945, Brodie cited his 1838 history, the one excerpted in the Pearl of Great Price. She reported that her efforts to research at the Church Archives were thwarted.[6] She tried but could not access Joseph's 1832 diary. She did not draw on Joseph's 1835 journal or the undiscovered 1832 account in Joseph's Letterbook. She therefore concluded that no one had spoken of the vision between 1820 and about 1840. She interpreted that limited evidence to mean that Joseph concocted the vision in the wake of an 1837 banking crisis "when the need arose for a magnificent tradition."[7]

Fawn Brodie did not change her assumptions when she revised her biography of Joseph after the 1832 and 1835 accounts were discovered and published. She did not reconsider her interpretation in the light of evidence that showed Joseph had written and spoken openly of the vision on more than one occasion earlier than 1838. Rather, with characteristic insinuation, she simply substituted *1830* for *1834* in this sentence about the vision: "It may have been sheer invention, created some time after 1830 when the need arose for a magnificent tradition."[8] She also noted in her second edition the differences in details between the accounts, suggesting that their inconsistencies evidenced Joseph's invention and embellishment of the story.

Fawn Brodie persuaded her publisher by emphasizing her "attitude of complete objectivity," but privately she and her closest adviser knew of her psychological need to understand Joseph's life and escape his influence. She reflected that writing the book enabled her to assert her independence. She called it a

Fawn Brodie largely shaped the skeptical interpretations of Joseph's First Vision when she wrote No Man Knows My History: The Life of Joseph Smith, *first published in 1945 by Alfred A. Knopf.*

"compulsion to liberate myself wholly from Mormonism." She decided in the process of preparing the biography to see in the historical facts evidence that Joseph consciously concocted the vision with intent to deceive. Having read an early draft of her biography, a close confidant wrote that he was "particularly struck with the assumption your MS makes that Joseph was a self-conscious imposter." Though sympathetic to her work, this adviser worried about what he called her "bold judgments on the basis of assumptions." A later reviewer noted similarly that she regularly stated "as indisputable facts what can only be regarded as conjectures supported by doubtful evidence."[9]

It is not hard to empathize with Fawn Brodie. Having been raised as a Latter-day Saint, she chose to leave the faith and underwent a painful reorientation process that required her to reinterpret Joseph Smith's First Vision. None of us are so very different from her. Our identities and psychologies are bound up in our various commitments. We cannot escape Joseph Smith's First Vision any more than she could, and we work to make sense of the evidence for ourselves in ways that are satisfying to our intellects and to our souls. But whatever her motives and our efforts to empathize, it is Brodie's method that concerns us here. Critical interpretations of Joseph's vision like hers share a common hermeneutic or explanatory method. They *assume* how a person in Joseph's position, or persons in his neighborhood, must have acted if his story was true and then show that his accounts vary from the assumed scenarios. They usually postulate a hypothetical alternative to Joseph's own explanation.[10]

Rev. Wesley Walters

That approach is also what the Reverend Wesley Walters used. He originated the enduring argument that Joseph's canonized First Vision account is anachronistic, or out of historical order. He was pastor of the United Presbyterian Church in Marissa, Illinois, when he published in the fall of 1967 an innovative article that asserted that there was no evidence of religious revival in Palmyra, New York, in the spring of 1820, and therefore Joseph's claim to have been influenced by such religious fervor must be false.[11] Richard Bushman said that Walters "performed a very positive service to the cause of Mormon History because he was a delver. He went deep into the heart of the archives. And Mormons had accepted a lot of things as simple facts—for example, that there was a revival in Joseph Smith's neighborhood around the 1820 period."[12] Walters noted accurately that prior to his work, Mormon scholars had "*assumed* that Joseph Smith's account must be correct."[13] According to Bushman, Reverend Walters "made us realize that we can't assume anything. Everything had to be demonstrated and proved."[14]

That realization led Truman Madsen and the Institute of Mormon Studies at BYU to sponsor a team of talented, well-educated young Mormon historians to research all the evidence they could find.[15] As a result of their research, it is clear that there are two main weaknesses in the Walters argument, namely, the fallacies of negative proof and of irrelevant proof. Historian David Hackett Fischer defined the fallacy of negative proof as "an attempt to sustain a factual proposition merely by negative evidence. It occurs whenever a historian declares that there is no evidence that X is the case and then proceeds to affirm or assume that not-X is the case."[16] Walters argued creatively that "a vision, by its inward, personal nature, does not lend itself to historical investigation," but "a revival is a different matter." He posited, therefore, that he could disprove Joseph's claim to a vision by showing "that in 1820 there was no revival in any of the churches in Palmyra and its vicinity."[17] He erred against the historical method by arguing, in other words, that a lack of evidence for a Palmyra revival was proof that the vision did not occur.

Reverend Walters also erred in arguing an irrelevant proof. Joseph's accounts do not claim that the revivalism centered in Palmyra itself, as Walters argues, or that the revivalism occurred in 1820. Rather, Joseph said that the excitement began in the second year after his family moved to Manchester, New York, meaning in 1819, and he located the "unusual excitement on the subject of religion" around Manchester, not Palmyra. Joseph used a Methodist term to describe a wider geographical scope than Walters's emphasis on the village of Palmyra. Joseph said "the whole *district* of country seemed affected" by the revivalism (Joseph Smith—History 1:5; emphasis added). To nineteenth-century Methodists, a district was somewhat akin to today's Latter-day Saint stake or a Catholic diocese. Joseph claimed only that there was unusual religious excitement in the region or district around Manchester that began sometime in 1819, during the second year after his family's move there (v. 5).

There is evidence that an intense revival stirred Palmyra in 1816–17, when Joseph moved there with his family. It may have catalyzed Joseph's 1832 description of his mind becoming seriously concerned for the welfare of his soul "at about the age of twelve years."[18] Then about 1818, Joseph's family purchased a farm in Manchester, a few miles south of Palmyra. The next summer, Methodists of the Genesee Conference assembled at Vienna (now Phelps), New York, within walking distance of the Smith farm. The Reverend George Lane and dozens of other exhorters were present. One participant remembered the result as a "religious cyclone which swept over the whole region."[19] Joseph's contemporary and acquaintance Orsamus Turner remembered that Joseph caught a "spark of Methodist fire" at a meeting along the road to Vienna.[20] A Palmyra newspaper and the diary of a Methodist minister confirm a weekend camp meeting in Palmyra in June 1820 at which "about twenty people were baptized and forty became Methodists."[21] If he had known about this evidence, given the way he consistently interpreted evidence in support of his conclusion, Reverend Walters may have objected that a June 1820 camp meeting would have been too late to catalyze Joseph's early spring vision. And if so, he might be quite right—but not necessarily. It snowed heavily on May 28 that year, and given his realities in that environment, what Joseph may have thought early spring meant might be different from our assumptions of what it must mean. But Joseph's descriptions are not dependent on external events in Palmyra or in 1820. The diaries of Methodist itinerant Benajah Williams evidence that Methodists and others were hard at work in Joseph's district all the while. They combed the countryside and convened camp meetings to help unchurched souls like Joseph get religion. The response was phenomenal, especially in western New York, the home of nearly one-fourth of the six thousand Presbyterian converts in 1820. Baptist churches expanded similarly.[22] Methodism expanded most impressively as traveling preachers like Williams gathered anxious converts.[23]

Reverend Walters focused on the word *reformation* used by Oliver Cowdery to describe the scope of the religious excitement, and on the Reverend George Lane, whom both Cowdery and William Smith, Joseph's brother, credited with being "the key figure in the Methodist awakening." Walters wrote that "there is no evidence" for these claims, which was an unwise thing to do.[24] Undiscovered evidence is not the same as nonexistent evidence, and when Walters made the bold claim that no evidence existed, researchers quickly set out to see for themselves. Among the several evidences discovered since are the Williams journals. They document much religious excitement in Joseph's district and region of the country in 1819 and 1820. They report that Rev. George Lane was indeed in that area in both of those years and that while there in July 1820, he "spoke on Gods method in bringing about Reffermations."[25] Indeed, the Williams diaries attest that not only Lane but many Methodist preachers in Joseph's time and place catalyzed unusual religious excitement, as Joseph described. Writers who have not studied this evidence continue to parrot Walters and claim that "there was no significant revival in or around Palmyra in 1820," but the evidence fits Joseph's description nicely.[26]

Though Walters interpreted them otherwise, Joseph's accounts are consistent with the mounting evidence. He said that the unusual religious excitement in his district or region "commenced with the Methodists" and that he became "somewhat partial" to Methodism (vv. 5, 8). The Walters thesis, though heartfelt and tenaciously defended by him and uncritically accepted and perpetuated by others, no longer seems tenable or defensible.[27] Walters succeeded in establishing "the fact that his [Joseph's] immediate neighborhood shows no evidence of an 1820 revival" without showing that anything Joseph said was false.²⁸ Thin evidence for revivalism in Palmyra Village in 1820 is not evidence that there was not a vision in the woods near Manchester in the wake of well-documented religious excitement "in that region of country" (v. 5).

Latter-day Saints historians of the First Vision have credited Walters with awakening them to investigate the context of Joseph's accounts, but they fault him for forcing his thesis.²⁹ We can easily understand, however, his determined efforts and unwillingness to give up his point. Joseph's most definitive account of his vision relates how he told his mother, "I have learned for myself that Presbyterianism is not true." He also quoted the Savior as saying that the Christian creeds "were an abomination" (vv. 19, 20). Latter-day Saints who feel defensive about the reverend's efforts to discredit the vision should be able to empathize with his response to Joseph's testimony. In one sense, his determined and enduring devotion to his cause is admirable. Even so, his arguments are not as airtight as they may seem, and his evidence, or lack thereof, does not prove what he claims it does.

Similarly, the critics' *a priori* certainty that the vision never happened as Joseph said it did is not a proven historical fact based on the testimony of witnesses or on hard data. Rather, those determined beliefs reflect each critic's heartfelt, reasoned belief about what was possible. Their commitment to skepticism about the kind of supernatural events Joseph described prevented them from believing in the possibilities that the historical accounts of the First Vision offer. In other words, all of the unbelieving explanations share a common hermeneutic or interpretive method, sometimes called the hermeneutic of suspicion, which in this case simply means interpreting Joseph Smith's statements skeptically, unwilling to trust that he might be telling the truth. One historian who doesn't believe Joseph Smith said that he couldn't trust the accounts of the vision because they were subjective, and that it was his job to figure out what really happened. But how will this skeptical scholar discover what actually happened when he is unwilling to trust the only eyewitness or the process of personal revelation? Such historians assume godlike abilities to know, yet they don't trust God's ability to reveal truth or theirs to receive it. They don't seem to grasp the profound irony that they are replacing the subjectivity of historical witnesses with their own. I call their method "subjectivity squared." They dismiss the historical documents and severely limit possible interpretations by predetermining that Joseph's story is not credible. When Joseph's 1832 account was discovered in the 1960s, opening to Fawn Brodie new interpretive possibilities after her original thesis, she did not respond with willingness to consider that Joseph might be telling the truth but simply fit the new evidence into her previous conclusion. And because the evidence is now more abundant than ever, parts of Fawn Brodie's thesis are not as compelling as they once were. The evidence she analyzed in her second edition suggested to her that Joseph embellished each telling of the vision until it matured into the canonized 1838–39 account. But even later accounts do not continue to become longer, more detailed, or more elaborate. Rather, these accounts return to sounding like Joseph's earlier, less-developed accounts. This evidence can be interpreted as Joseph's intention to make his 1838 account definitive and developed for publication, whereas he left some accounts less developed, including ones later than 1838, because they were created for other purposes. Some were delivered on the spur of the moment and captured by someone later remembering them and writing them down.

The discovery of considerable evidence of revivalism in both 1819 and 1820 in and around Palmyra, and especially in the broader region Joseph described, did not alter the argument

Wesley Walters continued to make. No matter what evidence came to light, he interpreted it according to his original conclusion. He chose not to see the possibilities available to those who approach Joseph's accounts on a quest to discover if he could possibly be telling the truth.

For those who choose to read Joseph's accounts with the hermeneutic of suspicion, the interpretation of choice is likely to remain that Joseph elaborated "some half-remembered dream" or concocted the vision as "sheer invention."[30] Those are not historical facts. They are skeptical interpretations of the fact that Joseph reported that he saw a vision. There are other ways to interpret that fact. Indeed, the several scholars who have studied the accounts of the vision for decades and written the seminal articles and the only scholarly book on the vision share what one of them described as a hermeneutic of trust.[31]

One will arrive at the same conclusions as the skeptics if one shares their assumptions about what the facts mean. But if one is open-minded, other meanings for the same facts are possible. The danger of closed-mindedness is as real for believers as for skeptics. Many believers seem just as likely to begin with preconceived notions rather than a willingness to go where Joseph's accounts lead them. The reasoning process of many believers is no different from Fawn Brodie's. Some *assume*, for instance, that Joseph would obviously have told his family of the vision or written it immediately, that he always understood all of its implications perfectly or consistently through the years, that he would always remember or tell exactly the same story, or that it would always be recorded and transmitted the same. But none of those assumptions is supported by the evidence. Some believers become skeptics in short order when they learn of the accounts and find that their assumptions of what would happen if Joseph told the truth are not supported by the historical record.

Richard Bushman had just won the historians' prestigious Bancroft Prize when he responded with civility and grace to Reverend Walters. When I asked him why he chose to be so courteous, Bushman replied, "Simply as a tactical matter in any kind of controversy, it never serves you well to show scorn towards your opponent. That may make the people who are on your side rejoice and say, 'Kick them again.' But for those who are in the middle who are trying to decide which truth is right, you just alienate them—you just drive them into the hands of your opponent."[32] Sometimes, in an effort to defend the faith, Latter-day Saints have responded with hostility to the critics of Joseph's vision. If there ever was an appropriate time for such a spirit, it is now past.

We are removed enough from the battlefront that we can respond less defensively and try instead to meet the needs of "those who are in the middle who are trying to decide which truth is right." I disagree with the *a priori* assumptions and historical interpretations of Fawn Brodie, Reverend Walters, and the Methodist minister who reproved Joseph, but I empathize with them. I may well have responded as they did if I were in different circumstances. Indeed, the minister's response and the reverend's are not so different from many Latter-day Saint defenses of our faith. Each of these critics is a child of God who is inherently valuable and interesting. They are vulnerable personalities, like the rest of us. They worked hard to figure out how to relate to Joseph Smith's First Vision. I wish to treat them as I would like to be treated by them and as Joseph taught the Relief Society sisters in Nauvoo. To them he said that "the nearer we get to our heavenly Father, the more are we dispos'd to look with compassion on perishing souls—to take them upon our shoulders and cast their sins behind our back. . . . If you would have God have mercy on you, have mercy on one another."[33]

Notes

1. Dan Vogel, *Joseph Smith: The Making of a Prophet* (Salt Lake City: Signature Books, 2004), xv.

2. *The Latter Day Saints' Messenger and Advocate* (Kirtland, OH), December 1834, 42. William Smith, *William Smith on Mormonism* (Lamoni, IA: 1883), 6. *Deseret Evening News*, January 20, 1894, 11. Larry C. Porter, "Reverend George Lane—Good 'Gifts,' Much 'Grace,' Marked 'Usefulness,'" 199–226 of the present volume.

3. John Wesley, "Thoughts upon Methodism," in *The Methodist Societies: History, Nature, and Design*, ed. Rupert E. Davies, vol. 9 of *The Bicentennial Edition of the Works of John Wesley*, ed. W. Reginald Ward and Richard P. Heitzenrater (Nashville: Abingdon, 1976–), 527.

4. Christopher C. Jones, "The Power and Form of Godliness: Methodist Conversion Narratives and Joseph Smith's First Vision," *Journal of Mormon History* 37, no. 2 (Spring 2011): 88–114. Jon Butler, *Awash in a Sea of Faith: Christianizing the American People* (Cambridge: Harvard University Press, 1990), 241. See John H. Wigger's chapter, "Methodism Transformed," in his book *Taking Heaven by Storm: Methodism and the Rise of Popular Christianity in America* (Urbana and Chicago: University of Illinois Press, 1998).

5. Ann Taves, *Fits, Trances & Visions: Experiencing Religion and Explaining Experience from Wesley to James* (Princeton, NJ: Princeton University Press, 1999), 17.

6. Newell G. Bringhurst, *Fawn McKay Brodie: A Biographer's Life* (Norman: University of Oklahoma Press, 1999), 84–85.

7. Fawn M. Brodie, *No Man Knows My History: The Life of Joseph Smith the Mormon Prophet* (New York: Knopf, 1945), 25.

8. Fawn M. Brodie, *No Man Knows My History: The Life of Joseph Smith the Mormon Prophet*, 2nd ed. (New York: Vintage, 1995), 25.

9. Bringhurst, *Fawn McKay Brodie*, 80, 87, 95, 105, 115.

10. Bringhurst, *Fawn McKay Brodie*, 106.

11. See, for example, Wesley P. Walters, "New Light on Mormon Origins From the Palmyra Revival," reprinted in *Dialogue* 4, no. 1 (Spring 1969): 60–67.

12. Richard L. Bushman, interview by Samuel Alonzo Dodge, July 31, 2009, Provo, UT, transcription in possession of the author.

13. Walters, "New Light on Mormon Origins," 61.

14. Richard L. Bushman, interview by Samuel Alonzo Dodge, July 31, 2009, Provo, UT, transcription in possession of the author.

15. Truman G. Madsen, "Guest Editor's Prologue," *BYU Studies* 9, no. 3 (Spring 1969): 235–40.

16. David Hackett Fischer, *Historians' Fallacies: Toward a Logic of Historical Thought* (New York: Harper, 1970), 47.

17. Walters, "New Light on Mormon Origins," 61.

18. Quoted in John Welch, ed., *Opening the Heavens: Accounts of Divine Manifestations, 1820–1844* (Provo, UT: Brigham Young University Press, 2005), 4.

19. Quoted in Milton V. Backman Jr., "Awakenings in the Burned-Over District: New Light on the Historical Setting of the First Vision," 171–98 of the present volume.

20. Orsamus Turner, *History of the Pioneer Settlement of Phelps and Gorham's Purchase, and Morris' Reserve* (Rochester, NY: William Alling, 1852), 213. Richard Lloyd Anderson evaluates Turner's credibility as a witness in "Joseph Smith's Accuracy on the First Vision Setting: The Pivotal 1818 Palmyra Camp Meeting," 91–170 of the present volume.

21. Aurora Seager records this in a diary about "a camp-meeting at Palmyra" he attended in June 1818. See E. Latimer, *The Three Brothers: Sketches of the Lives of Rev. Aurora Seager, Rev. Micah Seager, Rev. Schuyler Seager, D.C.* (New York: Phillips & Hunt, 1880), 12, quoted on pages 2–3 of D. Michael Quinn, "Joseph Smith's Experience of a Methodist 'Camp Meeting' in 1820," *Dialogue* Paperless E-Paper 3, December 20, 2006.

22. Jon Butler, *Awash in a Sea of Faith*, 268–69. Backman, "Awakenings in the Burned-Over District."

23. John H. Wigger, *Taking Heaven by Storm* (Oxford: Oxford University Press, 1998), 3–6.

24. Walters, "New Light on Mormon Origins," 62, 76.

25. Benajah Williams, diaries, in possession of Michael Brown, Philadelphia.

26. Robert D. Anderson, *Inside the Mind of Joseph Smith: Psychobiography and the Book of Mormon* (Salt Lake City: Signature Books, 1999).

27. Backman, "Awakenings in the Burned-Over District," 309. Richard L. Bushman "The First Vision Story Revived," *Dialogue* 4, no. 1 (Spring 1969): 85.

28. Walters, "New Light on Mormon Origins," 69.

29. Dean C. Jessee, James B. Allen (July 27, 2009), Richard Lloyd Anderson (July 29, 2009), Larry C. Porter (July 30, 2009), Richard L. Bushman (July 31, 2009), Milton V. Backman Jr. (August 12, 2009), interviews by Samuel Alonzo Dodge, transcriptions in possession of author.

30. Brodie, *No Man Knows My History*, 2nd ed., 25.

31. Richard L. Bushman, interview by Samuel Alonzo Dodge, July 31, 2009, Provo, UT, transcription in possession of the author.

32. Richard L. Bushman, interview by Samuel Alonzo Dodge, July 31, 2009, Provo, UT, transcription in possession of the author.

33. Discourse, June 9, 1842, Nauvoo, IL, "A Record of the Organization and Proceedings of the Female Relief Society of Nauvoo," 61–64, Church History Library, The Church of Jesus Christ of Latter-day Saints, Salt Lake City. Also in *History of the Church of Jesus Christ of Latter-day Saints*, ed. B. H. Roberts, 2nd ed. rev. (Salt Lake City: Deseret Book, 1957), 5:23–25; and *The Words of Joseph Smith*, ed. Andrew F. Ehat and Lyndon W. Cook (Provo, UT: Religious Studies Center, Brigham Young University, 1980), 122–24.

Once the First Vision assumed its predominant place in Mormon writing and preaching, it became much more than Joseph Smith's personal experience—it became a shared community experience. (Del Parson, The First Vision, © 1987 Intellectual Reserve, Inc.)

Contributors

Samuel Alonzo Dodge graduated in April 2010 from Brigham Young University with a BA in history. His essay "Enclosures and Open Land" was published in the BYU student journal *Americana* (2009). He was a recipient of BYU's Office of Research and Creative Activities project grant, which led to writing and presenting his essay "The History of the History: Rediscovering Joseph's First Vision" at the Mormon History Association meeting in 2010. He also coproduced a historical documentary *Joseph Smith's First Vision: Seeking the Accounts* (2010) and served a full-time LDS mission to the Dominican Republic. He is currently a graduate student of early United States history at the University of Massachusetts–Amherst.

STEVEN C. HARPER is a historian for The Church of Jesus Christ of Latter-day Saints and an editor of *The Joseph Smith Papers*. He served from 2002 to 2012 as a professor of Church history and doctrine at Brigham Young University. He earned a PhD in early American history from Lehigh University. He has been a Gest Fellow at Haverford College and the Lawrence Henry Gipson Dissertation Fellow at Lehigh University, and he received the T. Edgar Lyon and Juanita Brooks Awards from the Mormon History Association and a Brigham Young University Young Scholar Award. He authored *Promised Land* (2006), *Making Sense of the Doctrine and Covenants* (2008), *Joseph Smith's First Vision: A Guide to the Historical Accounts* (2012), and numerous articles on Mormonism and the early American republic.

DEAN C. JESSEE is a general editor of *The Joseph Smith Papers*. He earned an MA in LDS Church history from Brigham Young University. He worked for the Archives and the History Division of the Historical Department of The Church of Jesus Christ of Latter-day Saints from 1964 to 1981, followed by nineteen years of service at the Joseph Fielding Smith Institute for Latter-day Saint History at Brigham Young University. His gathering and publishing of Joseph Smith's papers led to the current *Joseph Smith Papers*. His publications include *Personal Writings of Joseph Smith* (1984, 2001 rev. ed.); *Papers of Joseph Smith*, vols. 1 and 2 (1989, 1991); *Brigham Young's Letters to His Sons* (1974); and numerous articles regarding early LDS history. He is a past president of the Mormon History Association.

JAMES B. ALLEN received his PhD in history from the University of Southern California in 1963 and was a professor of history at Brigham Young University until 1992. He served in the LDS Church as assistant Church historian (1972–79), was chair of the History Department at BYU (1981–87), and was Lemuel Hardison Redd Jr. Chair in Western American History at BYU (1987–92). He has authored, coauthored, or coedited fourteen books and around ninety articles on western American and LDS history. He was awarded the Evans Biography Award for *Trials of Discipleship: The Story of William Clayton, A Mormon* (1987), was named Distinguished Faculty Lecturer at BYU (1984), was made a Fellow of the Utah State Historical Society (1988), and received the Leonard J. Arrington Award for a Distinctive Contribution to the Cause of Mormon History (2008).

MILTON V. BACKMAN JR. served as an LDS missionary to South Africa and later in the US Air Force during the Korean War. Upon completing his military service, Backman graduated with a degree in history from the University of Utah and went on to receive his PhD from the University of Pennsylvania in 1959. Backman briefly taught American history at West Texas State University before being hired by Brigham Young University in 1960. He has written several important articles and books concerning Mormon history, including *American Religions and the Rise of Mormonism* (1970), *Joseph Smith's First Vision* (1971), and *The Heavens Resound: A History of the Latter-day Saints in Ohio, 1830–1838* (1983). Backman served as president of the Mormon History Association from 1978 to 1979.

RICHARD LLOYD ANDERSON is a research historian and volume editor for *The Joseph Smith Papers*. He earned a JD from Harvard Law School and a PhD in classics at the University of California, Berkeley. He authored *Understanding Paul* (1983, 2007 rev. ed.), *Joseph Smith's New England Heritage* (1971, 2003 rev. ed.), *Investigating the Witnesses of the Book of Mormon* (1981), and many articles on early Christian history and early Mormonism. He is coeditor of the *Documentary History of Oliver Cowdery*. He served in World War II in the US Navy as an aviation radioman. He retired as professor emeritus from BYU after nearly forty years of teaching history and religion. Awards include Honors Professor of the Year and Phi Kappa Phi Award for Scholarship and Citizenship.

LARRY C. PORTER is a research and review editor of the *The Joseph Smith Papers* and professor emeritus of Church history and doctrine at Brigham Young University. He received a PhD in history of religion from BYU, where he taught for thirty-one years. His service included chair of the Department of Church History and Doctrine and director of the Church history area of the BYU Religious Studies Center. He also held the Richard L. Evans Chair of Religious Understanding. He received the Richard Lloyd Anderson Research Award from Religious Education at BYU and the Leonard J. Arrington Award for a Distinctive Contribution to the Cause of Mormon History from the Mormon History Association. He coauthored or edited several important books, including *Truth Will Prevail: The Rise of*

the Church of Jesus Christ of Latter-day Saints in the British Isles, 1837–1987 (1987), *The Prophet Joseph Smith: Essays on the Life and Mission of Joseph Smith* (1988), and *Lion of the Lord: Essays on the Life & Service of Brigham Young* (1996).

RICHARD LYMAN BUSHMAN is a general editor of *The Joseph Smith Papers*, former Howard W. Hunter Visiting Chair of Mormon Studies at Claremont Graduate University, and Gouverneur Morris Professor of History Emeritus at Columbia University. He earned a PhD in history from Harvard University. He taught at Brigham Young University, Boston University, and the University of Delaware before joining the Columbia faculty. He won the Bancroft Prize for *From Puritan to Yankee: Character and the Social Order in Connecticut, 1690–1765* (1967) and also published *Joseph Smith and the Beginnings of Mormonism* (1984), *King and People in Provincial Massachusetts* (1985), and *The Refinement of America: Persons, Houses, Cities* (1992), *Believing History* (2004), and *Joseph Smith: Rough Stone Rolling* (2005).

JOHN W. WELCH is the Robert K. Thomas Professor of Law at the J. Reuben Clark Law School at BYU, where he teaches courses on tax-exempt organizations, ancient laws in the Bible and Book of Mormon, and Joseph Smith and the law. He was educated at Brigham Young University with a BA in history and an MA in classical languages. He studied Greek philosophy at Oxford University as a Woodrow Wilson Fellow, earned his law degree at Duke University, and practiced law in the Los Angeles firm of O'Melveny and Myers. He is well known as the founder of FARMS (the Foundation for Ancient Research and Mormon Studies), and since 1991 he has served as the editor in chief of BYU Studies. He was also a director of special projects for the BYU Religious Studies Center, the general editor of the Collected Works of Hugh Nibley, and a member of the board of editors for Macmillan's *Encyclopedia of Mormonism*. He has authored a number of publications presenting striking discoveries concerning Joseph Smith and the law, the Sermon on the Mount, the parable of the Good Samaritan, the trial of Jesus, King Benjamin's speech, the Book of Mormon as a handbook of Church administration, and the nature and roles of evidence in law, science, and the nurturing of faith.

Index

A

abomination, 75, 88–89nn32–33
accounts of First Vision
  audiences of, 46–60
  changes in, 86n18
  circulated in 1830s, 290–94
  comparison of, 296–302
  consolidation of, 60–78, 79–83
  contemporaneous, 21–31
  differences in, 44–46, 263–64, 275–77
  historical interest in, 43–44
  impediments to, 1–2
  importance of studying all, 55
  of Joseph Smith, 150–51n3
  of Oliver Cowdery, 122–31, 136–37, 236–38
  of Pomeroy Tucker, 143–45
  produced by Joseph Smith, 4–21
  publicity of, 92
  record keeping and, 2–4, 33

accounts of First Vision *(cont.)*
  research concerning, xvii–xviii
  of Smith family, 118–21
  subsequent recollections of, 31–33
  of William Smith, 138–41
age of Joseph Smith at time of First Vision, 63–65, 306n17
  See also date of First Vision
Alger, John, 33
Allen, James B.
  Improvement Era article of, 42
  research of, xviii
  testimony of, 44
Anderson, Richard L., xvi–xvii
apostasy, 74–76, 260n65
a posteriori knowledge, 308
a priori knowledge, 308
argument(s) against First Vision
  of Fawn Brodie, 311–13, 318
  of Methodist minister, 308–10
  responding to, 319–20

argument(s) against First Vision (*cont.*)
   of Wesley Walters, 313–19
art, 241
Articles and Covenants of the Church, 85–86n13
audiences
   of initial First Vision account, 46–49
   of surviving First Vision accounts, 49–58

B

Backman, Milton V., xv–xvi, 269
Baptist Church, growth in, 185, 190–91, 273–75
Barstow, George, 19–20
Bennett, James Gordon, 166–67n135
Bible, Joseph Smith's knowledge of, 146, 167n141
Book of Mormon
   in missionary work, 288–89
   public knowledge of, 285–87
   Restoration of gospel and, 239
   Trinitarianism and, 233–34
Brodie, Fawn
   arguments of, against First Vision, 311–13, 318
   First Vision accounts and, xviii
   First Vision scholarship and, xii, xix–xx
   research challenging claims of, xix, 291
   research of, xvi, 145
Bunting, Lydia, 221

C

Campbell, Alexander, 285–86
camp meetings. *See* Palmyra camp meeting (1818); religious revivals

Cannon, George Q., 241–43
canonization of First Vision, 294–95
Cheesman, Paul R., 43, 291, 306n17
Chenango District, 103
Christensen, C. C. A., 241
Christianity at time of First Vision, 74–76, 87–88n28
Church of Jesus Christ of Latter-day Saints, The, record keeping in, 2–3, 33. *See also* Mormon doctrine and thought
Cole, Abner, 145
community experience, First Vision as, 247–51
concerns of Joseph Smith at time of First Vision, 65–67, 87–88nn27–28, 93–98, 101
conflict. *See* contention
contention
   around Palmyra, 95
   influence of, on Joseph Smith, 75–76
   in Smith family, 101
conversions
   to Baptist Church, 185
   competition for, 160n72
   from 1820 religious revivals, 189–92
   of George Lane, 201–2
   to Methodism, 153n17, 193n3
   in Palmyra, 94–98
   at Palmyra camp meeting, 108–9, 111–12
   to Presbyterianism, 181–85, 192–93n3, 196n39
   at quarterly conferences, 103
   from religious revivals, 186–89, 271–75
   of Smith family to Presbyterianism, 131–33
Corrill, John, 286, 288

corruption at time of First Vision, 74–75
Couser, James, 95, 107, 180
Cowdery, Oliver, account of
  correction of, 280n8
  gaps in, 122–31
  George Lane in, 217–20
  Joseph Smith's History and, 9, 136–37, 237
  Wesley Walters's account and, 265–68
  William Smith's account and, 140–41, 162n83
Cowdery, Warren, 10
creeds, 230–31
Cry from the Wilderness, a Voice from the Dust of the Earth, A (Hyde), 25–27, 58–60, 294
Curtis, Joseph, 32

D

Darwin, Charles, 243
date of First Vision, 63–65, 126–31, 306n17
doctrine, false, 75. *See also* Mormon doctrine and thought
dogma, 230–31

E

Eastern Christians, 185–86
education of Joseph Smith, 1–2
"Eight Contemporary Accounts of Joseph Smith's First Vision—What Do We Learn from Them?" (Allen), 42
Ein Ruf aus der Wüste, Eine Stimme aus dem Schoose der Erde (Hyde), 25–27, 58, 59–60, 294
employment of Smith family, 142–43, 270
enthusiasm, 264, 310

evolution hypothesis, 145–46

F

faith, 278–79
false doctrine, 75
Finney, Charles G., 255n15
First Vision
  description of event, 68–76
  events following, 77–78, 122
  as shared community experience, 247–51
Foote, David, 220
Foote, Irene Lane, 220
Free Masonry, 213–14
Freewill Baptists, 185, 273

G

Genesee Conference
  description of, 178–79
  George Lane and, 129–31, 206, 209–10, 213–14, 216–17
  Joseph Smith's attendance at, 116–18
  research on, 203–4
Genesee District, 98–102, 138, 153n17
Geneva, New York, 274
Giles, Charles, 102, 109, 112, 153n17
God
  appearance of to Joseph Smith, 70–73
  nature of, 231–36, 241–44, 248, 255n15, 257n37, 296, 304n4
gospel
  fulness of, 76
  Restoration of, 239, 244, 247
Great Apostasy, 74–76

H

Hale, Elizabeth, 211
Hale, Emma, 211

Hale, Isaac, 211–12
Harvey, Benjamin, 207–8
Harvey, Sarah, 207, 220–21
hermeneutics of suspicion, 277, 317–18
hermeneutics of trust, 277
History of the Church, 2–3, 291–92
Holland Purchase Mission, 202–5
Holmes, Erastus, 11, 53
Holy Ghost, 304n4
home(s) of Smith family, 114–15, 139, 155–56n43, 157–60nn64–66
Horne, Mary Isabella Hales, 31–32
Howe, E. D., 286
Hyde, Orson, account of, 25–27, 58–60, 70–71, 300

I

importance of First Vision, 244–45, 283–84
Improvement Era, 42
Interesting Account of Several Remarkable Visions, and of the Late Discovery of Ancient American Records, A[n] (Pratt), 21–25, 58–59, 294
irrelevant proof, fallacy of, 314

J

Jennings, Samuel, 158–59n65
Jessee, Dean C., xviii
Jesus Christ
  appearance to Joseph Smith of, 70–73
  nature of, 232–35, 248, 255n15, 257n37, 296, 304n4
  reality of, 73–74
Joseph Smith History (1832)
  content of, 4–7

Joseph Smith History (1832) *(cont.)*
  context of, 49–51
  dating of, 36–39
  Joseph Smith's religious search in, 150–51n3
  Oliver Cowdery's account and, 123–25, 136–37
Joseph Smith History (1838)
  content of, 12–19, 298
  context of, 54–56
  dating of, 37–38n19
  Joseph Smith's religious search in, 150–51n3
  Lucy Mack Smith's account and, 118
  publication of, 240
  religious revivals in, 137–38, 268–69
  scribes for, 35n7
Joseph Smith journal account (1835), 7–12, 51–54
"Joseph Smith's First Prayer," 241
Joseph Smith's History (1834–36), 9, 11–12
Joshua. *See* Matthias, Robert

K

knowledge, *a priori* and *a posteriori*, 308

L

Lane, Charles, 207
Lane, George
  business career of, 207–9
  early years of, 200–202
  final years of, 220–22
  influence of, on Joseph Smith, 214–20, 265–67, 316
  ministry of, 202–7, 209–14
  in Oliver Cowdery's account, 128–30
  in William Smith's account, 137

Lane, Irene, 220
Lane, Lydia Bunting, 221
Lane, Nathan, 200
Lane, Sarah Harvey, 207, 220–21
Lanesboro, Pennsylvania, 211–12
Latter Day Saints' Messenger and Advocate, 122, 125, 217–18, 265–68, 286
"Lectures on Faith," 231, 234–35, 287, 304n4
lessons learned from First Vision, 73–76, 247–50, 295–96
Lewis, Nathaniel, 212

M

Madsen Truman G., research efforts of, xiv–xv, xvii–xix, 313–14
"Manuscript History," 291–92, 298, 305n11. *See also* Joseph Smith History (1838)
Manwaring, George, 241
Matthias, Robert, 8, 10, 51–53, 291
message given at First Vision, 73–76
Messenger and Advocate, 122, 125, 217–18, 265–68, 286
Methodism
  Free Masonry and, 213–14
  growth of, 98–102, 153n17, 174–75, 190, 193n3, 272
  Joseph Smith's involvement in, 98–102, 144, 149, 153n17
  as mainstream religion, 309–10
  in Palmyra, 175–80
  religious revivals and, 104, 111–12, 114, 209–10
  Turner's knowledge concerning, 169n153
Methodist minister, 161n75, 308–10.
  See also Lane, George

missionary work, 288–90, 294
money digging, 276
Mormon doctrine and thought
  authority and calling of Joseph Smith in, 240–42
  comparison of First Vision accounts and, 296–302
  creeds and, 230–31
  from 1880s to present day, 244–51
  between 1840 and 1880, 238–40
  in 1830s, 228–30
  First Vision in, 283–85
  Joseph Smith's use of First Vision and, 236–38
  nature of God and, 231–36, 241–44
  public knowledge of First Vision and, 285–87, 290–94
  use of First Vision in, 295–96
Moroni
  appearances of, 122, 125
  Lucy and William Smith's accounts of, 139–40
  in Oliver Cowdery's account, 127
  Restoration of gospel and, 239
  William Smith's account of, 120
Mulholland, James, 38n19, 54
music, 241

N

negative proof, fallacy of, 314, 316
Neibaur, Alexander, account of, 29–30, 58, 114, 136, 290, 301
New Light on Mormon Origins from the Palmyra Revival (Walters), xii–xiv
No Man Knows My History (Brodie), xii, xix

O

"Oh, How Lovely Was the Morning," 241

Ontario Baptist Association, 273
Ontario Circuit, 98–99, 104, 116–17, 272
Ontario District, 216–17
opposition preceding First Vision, 69–70

P

Palmyra, New York
  churches and meetinghouses in, 180–81
  conversions in, 94–98, 189
  Methodism in, 169n153, 175–80
  religious revivals in, 269–70, 315–17
  Smith family residences in, 114–15, 139, 155–56n43, 157–60nn64–66
  See also Palmyra Village
Palmyra camp meeting (1818)
  attendance and conversions at, 108–13
  Joseph Smith's attendance at, 113–18, 135–36
  Seager journal documenting, 104–8
Palmyra Register, 95, 188
Palmyra Village, 106–8, 139
  See also Palmyra, New York
Parrish, Warren, 51–52
Pearl of Great Price, 294–95
Peck, Andrew, 176
Peck, George, 102, 109–12, 117
persecution
  effect of, on record keeping, 33–34
  1838–39 account and, 54–55
  following First Vision, 47–48, 77–78, 118–19, 161n76, 230, 253nn5–6, 264, 289
Phelps, William W., 9
Phelps Village, New York. *See* Vienna Village, New York

Pierce, Marmaduke, 212–13
Pratt, Orson, account of
  audiences of, 58–59
  content of, 21–25, 299
  William Smith account and, 121
Pratt, Parley P., 31
prayer preceding First Vision, 68–70
Presbyterianism
  growth in, 99, 181–85, 188–90, 192–93n3, 196n39, 274–75
  in Palmyra, 180–81
  Smith family and, 131–34, 164–65n113
priesthood, 248
Primary sesquicentennial program, 251
publicity on First Vision, xvi–xvii
public knowledge of First Vision, 285–87, 290–94

Q

quarterly conferences, 102–4

R

record keeping
  in early Church, 2–3, 33
  Joseph Smith on, 35n8
  persecution's effect on, 33–34
religion(s)
  false doctrine and contentions of, 74–76, 87–88n28
  increased interest in, 171–72
  Joseph Smith's study of, 93–98, 115, 150–51n3, 172–75
  records concerning Palmyra, 180–86, 272–75
religious revivals
  attendance and conversions at, 272–75
  conversions from, 186–89
  dating of, 126–31
  defined, 95

religious revivals *(cont.)*
   in 1838 Joseph Smith history, 137–38
   1820 conversions from, 189–92
   events and attendance of, 176–80
   in First Vision accounts, 61–63
   George Lane and, 203–6, 208–16
   influence of, on 1832 account, 49
   influence of, on Joseph Smith, 65–67, 135–36, 172–75
   locations of, 268–70, 314–15
   Methodism and, 98–102
   in New York, 171–72
   Orsamus Turner on, 149–50
   quarterly conferences and, 102–4
   research concerning, xiii, xv–xvi, 93–98
   Smith family attendance at, 142–43
   and Smith family conversions, 131–34
   as Walters's evidence, 264–75, 315–17
   See also Palmyra camp meeting (1818)
Restoration, beginning of, 239, 244, 247
revivals, religious. *See* religious revivals
Richards, Levi, account of, 27–28, 57
Roberts, Brigham H., 244, 257n37
Roberts, Robert, 108
Rupp, Israel Daniel, 20–21, 56–57, 286, 299–300

S

Sacred Grove, 184, 245
sacredness of First Vision, 230, 289–90
Satan, 69–70
scholarship, First Vision
   developments in, xi–xx, 261–63
   importance of, ix–x
   new approaches in, 303–4
Scipio circuit, 202
Seager, Aurora, 104–8, 111–12, 114, 155n38
Seymour, Zachariah, 159n65
shared community experience, First Vision as, 247–51
Smith, Alvin, 132–33, 159n65
Smith, Emma Hale, 211
Smith, Hyrum, 132–34, 164–65n113
Smith, Joseph
   age of, at First Vision, 63–65, 306n17
   authority and calling of, 240–42
   education of, 1–2
   evolution of, 145–46
   on record keeping, 3–4
Smith, Lucy Mack
   on appearance of Moroni, 139–40
   church activity of, 133–34, 164–65n113
   conversion of, 132–33
   account of, 118, 159n65
   First Vision related to, 46
Smith, Samuel, 132–34, 164–65n113
Smith, Sophronia, 132–34, 164–65n113
Smith, William, account of
   content and reliability of, 119–21, 138–41, 279n4
   George Lane in, 130–31, 137, 219–20
   Oliver Pratt account and, 162n83
Smith family
   church activity of, 133–34, 164–65n113

Smith family *(cont.)*
  conversion of, to Presbyterianism, 131–33
  employment of, 142–43, 270
  First Vision accounts of, 118–21
  homes of, 114–15, 139, 157–60nn64–66
  James Gordon Bennett on, 166–67n135
  Orsamus Turner on, 148–49
  reverence of, for scripture, 167n141
  Tucker's knowledge of, 142–43, 155–56n43
Snow, Lorenzo, 293
Snow, William, 176
spiritual manifestations at revivals, 177–78
Stevenson, Edward, 32, 252–53n2, 293
suspicion, hermeneutics of, 277, 317–18
Susquehanna District, 129, 210

T

Taylor, John, 288
testimony, 278–79
Times and Seasons, 56, 287
timing of First Vision, 63–65, 126–31, 306n17
Trinitarianism, 232–34
trust, hermeneutics of, 277
truth, hermeneutics of trust and, 277
Tucker, Pomeroy, xvii, 114–15, 119, 141–46, 155–56n43
Turner, J. B., 286
Turner, Orsamus
  biographical sketch of, 146–50, 168n148
  on Joseph Smith, 107, 113, 135–36, 179–80

Turner, Orsamus *(cont.)*
  knowledge of, xvii, 169n153, 304n2

U

use of First Vision, 288–90, 294, 295–96

V

Vienna Road, 149
Vienna Village, New York, 107, 111, 117–18, 178–80
Vogel, Dan, 116
Voice of Warning, 288–89

W

Walker, Charles, account of, 32–33, 301
Walters, Wesley
  arguments of, against First Vision, 313–19
  First Vision accounts and, xviii
  First Vision scholarship and, xix–xx, 261–63
  religious revivals and, 264–75
  research challenging claims of, xiv–xvi, xix
  research of, xii–xiv, 91, 93–97
  variations in First Vision accounts and, 275–77
Wentworth Letter (1842), 19–20, 56–57, 299–300
Wesley, John, 309
White, David Nye, account of, 28–29, 57–58
Williams, Benajah, 164n103, 316
Williams, Frederick G., 5, 36–39
writing skills of Joseph Smith, 1–2
Wyoming circuit, 205–7, 212–13